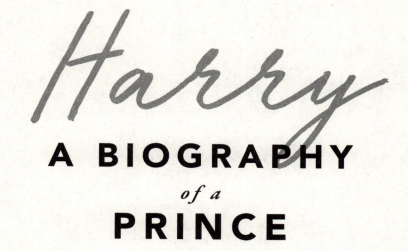

Harry
A BIOGRAPHY
of a
PRINCE

ANGELA LEVIN

PEGASUS BOOKS
NEW YORK LONDON

HARRY: A BIOGRAPHY OF A PRINCE

Pegasus Books, Ltd.
148 West 37th Street, 13th Floor
New York, NY 10018

Design by www.envydesign.co.uk

First Pegasus Books hardcover edition May 2018

ISBN: 978-1-68177-910-2

10 9 8 7 6 5 4 3 2 1

Printed in the United States of America
Distributed by W. W. Norton & Company, Inc.

CONTENTS

To my family

Introduction

The first thing Prince Harry said to me was: 'I know you have been following me around for quite some time, Angela, and wondered whether you would like to come over and ask me some questions?'

'By the way,' he continued as he shook my hand, 'are you watching *The Crown*? [the Netflix drama that follows the life of Queen Elizabeth II from 1940 to today] I am, but I wish they'd stopped at the end of the first series. They absolutely must not move on to the younger generation.' A firm handshake followed by a jokey one-liner was, I knew by then, Harry's default way of breaking the ice.

It was spring 2017 and we were talking in the visitors' drawing room in Kensington Palace. He indicated that I should sit down on the pale khaki sofa, while he chose a peach-coloured corduroy armchair. Talking to a senior royal who doesn't like the press makes it difficult to know where to start. I was unsure how much time I would have with him and didn't want to waste it with small talk. I wanted an insightful conversation and decided to go for the Big Question, aware that if he felt it was too intrusive I could be asked to leave, but if it got through to him we could get on well.

I began: 'When you go on your royal visits do you also try to work through your own issues with the people you meet? I mean, is it a kind of therapy?'

He was silent for more than a few seconds. 'Wow!' he said. 'That's a monster question to ask.' There was a long pause, then he smiled. 'You are right, of course.' We were on our way.

The prince held my eyes as he spoke, and he put a lot of energy into the conversation. He talked quickly and somewhat impatiently, as if he couldn't get the words out fast enough. He was polite and approachable, but firm when he didn't want to go further into a subject. If I voiced something he agreed with he would sometimes reply, 'Exactly.' Then he would move on rather than expand on the topic. He is in a rush to make his mark and seems to treat life as a race, too. He explained: 'I want to make something of my life. I now feel there is just a smallish window when people are interested in me before [Prince] George and [Princess] Charlotte [his brother William's children] take over and I've got to make the most of it.'

Our conversation was wide-ranging and, not surprisingly,

soon turned to his late mother, Diana, Princess of Wales. He told me that the most important thing she did for him was to 'keep me safe'.

It was one of many poignant moments during our conversation. This one goes straight to the heart of every child, rich or poor. Children need parents who make them feel safe and give them the right environment in which to grow and flourish. They also need to feel they are accepted and loved for who they are.

Without his mother, who died when he was twelve years old, Harry has had a really tough time. Her death changed him from being an adorable, mischievous boy who was beginning to comprehend what it meant to be third in line to the throne and forever one large step behind his big brother, into a wilful, impulsive pre-teen who, as he grew, behaved badly, rarely handed in his school work on time, drank and smoked too much, and connected with too many unsuitable girls. At times he seemed to be on a mission to self-destruct and a catastrophe waiting to happen, one that risked bringing shame on the whole royal family, even affect its future.

I believe that his ongoing longing to please his mother and remain a good boy in her eyes is the primary reason he has come back from his personal abyss. She is freeze-framed in his mind as a young woman of thirty-six, the same age incidentally as Meghan Markle when she and Harry got engaged. It comforts him to believe that Diana is still somehow in touch and aware of what he does, especially when it involves causes she cared about. 'I instinctively know what my mother would like me to do,' he said. He has since stated that she was 'jumping up and down' at the news of his engagement and 'looking forward to being a grandmother again'.

Harry understands the pain of loss and being abandoned both professionally and personally, and uses this to inspire others to move on. He is perceptive and quick at cutting through to the essence of things and what is and isn't important. But he can get irritable and impatient if others aren't up to speed.

I had the good fortune to follow Prince Harry on his various royal duties on and off for more than a year in 2016 and 2017 for *Newsweek* magazine. I watched how he behaved in a wide variety of situations and eventually I was given the chance to talk personally to him at Kensington Palace on more than one occasion.

At the time Harry had the reputation of being still something of a party boy, but as a committed royal watcher I had noticed a more serious side of him beginning to emerge. I told members of his support team, who grilled me several times before agreeing the project could go ahead, that I believed he was going through a transformation, finding a role for himself within the royal family, and that he at last wanted the public to take him more seriously. Luckily they thought I was 'spot on' and told me they would put my request to Harry. It was important, they said, that they picked their timing carefully as he wasn't always in the right mood.

It took months of waiting and occasional polite emails reminding them I was still around before a trip to Nottingham to watch him in action was suggested. I turned up well in advance of Harry's arrival. He didn't say anything but looked straight at me for a couple of seconds and gave me the tiniest nod. So far so good, I thought.

Eventually I was offered a date and time to talk with him. One of the key things he wanted to get across was how much he 'longed to be something other than Prince Harry', which is perhaps why he can sometimes seem uncomfortable in his own skin. He also wants 'to be ordinary'. In practice his 'ordinariness' can only be a gesture while he has access to several palaces, is ferried around in limousines with blackened windows accompanied by outriders, and uses his incredible contacts to get what he wants. The top people he knows cover a wide cross-section and many do somersaults to ensure his wishes come true. Even his grandmother, the Queen, stretches boundaries to make him happy.

Nor do the public want him to be ordinary. Nearly everyone he met during the time I followed him on his royal duties, especially if they were under thirty, were in awe that 'an actual prince' had come to see them. It was also why they listened so intently to what he said.

His ability to connect with people is far from ordinary too. Very few individuals could ask someone they had just met intimate questions about their state of mind without seeming intrusive, but Harry can and does.

I asked if he ever worried that too much 'ordinary' might water down the royal brand and take away its mystery. 'It's a tricky balancing act,' he agreed. 'We don't want to dilute the magic.'

His journey from rebellious outsider to one of the world's most popular royals has required much soul-searching. The toxic atmosphere of his home life during his childhood and the sudden death of his mother have left deep scars. Prince William has tried to work through his own problems and has seen the value of a warm home life through his wife Kate and her middle-class family. Harry has tried to do so through the charities he supports, which is much harder. He is also more emotional than his brother.

There is still some way to go, but now he has Meghan Markle by his side. The divorced American actress and glamorous feminist doesn't conform at all to the stereotype of a royal consort, but she knows what she wants and what Harry needs, which among other things is a bit of mothering. Like the best couples, he can also define himself through and with her and is fiercely protective of her needs, too. Dr David Starkey, the historian and constitutional expert, who I spent time with while writing the book, thinks they are a good match: 'The role of philanthropy is entrenched in both of them which will give wonderful opportunities to display the touchy-feely aspect of his mother.'

The second thing Harry said his mother did for him 'was protect me from the media and escape from them'. Based on how the Princess of Wales was treated after her separation from Prince Charles and the circumstances of her death, neither Harry nor William have an easy relationship with journalists, but they know the media gives their causes the oxygen of publicity. The Duchess of Cornwall, whom I previously followed for some months, regularly chats to journalists and photographers when she is on the road, and knows many by name. By contrast, Harry concentrates entirely on the work in hand while the following press corps is largely kept out of his way. The froideur has recently warmed slightly. '[William and Harry] realise that not all the press are the same,' a Palace source told me.

For a while, the prince told me, press intrusion was one of the factors which led him to think he might cut himself off from the royal family altogether and seek a different role elsewhere. He is particularly drawn to Africa. The idea 'began when I was in my mid-twenties,' he said. 'I needed to fix the mistakes I was making and what was going on with me. I thought I might make my own life somewhere else.' But after some hard soul-searching he chose instead to try to both 'make a difference' plus have 'an element of a private life' within the royal family.

It was about then that Harry suddenly stopped talking, looked very solemn and told me how appalled he is in retrospect that he and William had to walk behind his mother's coffin and that he didn't think any child should have to do that 'under any circumstances'. It was a poignant revelation that went round the world and highlighted how what seemed appropriate to expect of two grief-ridden children twenty years ago at the Princess's funeral today seems almost callous.

It is perhaps one of the reasons why until a few years ago it looked as if Harry would become the worst possible young royal role model. He ran with a wealthy fast set and partied with too many scantily clad young women. Although some of his bad behaviour was typical of a teenager, behaving like an adolescent in his late twenties became a cause for concern. Harry admitted to me: 'For too many years I just didn't want to grow up.'

He has since faced up to his demons and worked hard to overcome them. As a result he exudes an extraordinary combination of royal stardust, accessibility, confidence and mischief, a mixture that enables him to connect instantly with people of all ages and types, and reminds you of the best side of his mother. Sometimes his extraordinary natural gifts are not enough for him: 'It is very important for me that what I do is authentic.'

He has also longed to find his life's partner and someone who would love him for himself. That too seems to have been settled, as he and Meghan knew very early on they had something very special together. David Starkey told me he approves: 'He has found someone who can stand up to all the strain of being in the public eye and because of her confidence protect him. She mothers him a bit but he needs it and some women love to do it. She is still childless, while he is still a boy/man.'

At the time of writing Harry had three key objectives. The first was to honour and extend his mother's legacy. It was one reason why he had chosen to focus on HIV. The second was to support the Queen, who is now in her nineties and was passing on an increasing number of her duties to her grandchildren. The third was to take the stigma out of mental health issues, something previous generations of royals would never had dreamt of. In the future, he and Meghan may well develop a whole new agenda, as he hinted in the TV interview in November 2017 that marked their engagement. He said there was a 'hell of a lot of stuff and work that needs doing' and 'with lots of young people running around the Commonwealth that's where we're going to spend most of our time, hopefully.'

Harry talked to me most about the Queen – 'she is so remarkable' – and his late mother – 'she had the most wonderful sense of humour and always wanted to make things fun for us as well as protect us.' He said less about William and Kate and almost nothing about his father or his stepmother Camilla, Duchess of Cornwall, which may or may not have been significant.

He also implied that being royal is not all that it is cracked up to be. 'Is there any one of the royal family who wants to be king or queen?' he asked. 'I don't think so but we will carry out our duties at the right time.' It's very important to him to support his brother on his path to be a future king. Together they are 'involved in modernising the British monarchy', he said, which could be an incentive not to loosen ties with the royal family.

He also explained about the responsibility of being royal as compared to being famous. 'If you're born into it as we were I think it's normal to feel as though you don't really want it.' He feels it is quite different when someone becomes famous because they have a natural talent. He insisted: 'We don't want to be just a bunch of celebrities but instead use our role for good.'

David Starkey says he doesn't stand a chance: 'Harry may

not want to be a celebrity but he is and can't possibly avoid being one. While Meghan is TV royalty. There has always been an affinity between royalty and actors going back to Shakespeare and Thomas More. In the Tudor period it was completely understood that the royal household lent out their actual royal robes for actors to wear on stage. And in the 1920s it was said that the royals were our best film stars. It remains true. In this respect Harry is a bit like his mother in that he wants all the advantages of being a celebrity without the scrutiny.'

Harry is aware that I have been writing his biography. It has been an enormous privilege. What has surprised me most is that despite telling me he felt he had no proper role and is still searching to 'make a difference', the truth is he has already made his mark. He could have chosen to be one of the idle rich. Instead he has created a respected charity that has saved the lives of countless children in Africa. He has also given innumerable wounded ex-servicemen and women, who gave their all to fight for their country, a will to live and hope for the future. To cap it all, he's found Meghan. They will no doubt be a formidable double act keen to put the world to rights and not the least afraid of showing their feelings in public. Not bad for a thirty-three-year-old. His is also the compelling story of a sensitive, mischievous little boy who grew up assuming he had no real role in life. There has been tragedy, rebellion, disappointment and, at last, redemption.

CHAPTER 1

Welcoming Meghan

A mere four days after announcing their engagement, Meghan Markle joined Harry, her new fiancé, for their first public engagement as a couple. Harry chose Nottingham, where he has forged strong links, to show off his bride-to-be to the nation. It was also the city he chose to invite me to in October 2016 as part of my year following him on his royal duties.

His trip in December 2017 with Meghan was to mark World Aids Day – something close to the heart of his mother, Diana, Princess of Wales, who in the late 1980s changed people's perception of Aids by shaking the hand of a patient suffering from the illness. It also enabled him to stay in touch with the Full Effect programme, which through early intervention, mentorship and training supports children at risk from becoming involved in youth violence and crime.

Full Effect is an offshoot of the Duke and Duchess of Cambridge and Prince Harry's Royal Foundation, set up to take forward their charitable ambitions, which Meghan is set to be a part of after the wedding.

The couple travelled by train before being picked up by a royal limousine and taken to the National Justice Museum based at the Shire Hall and County Gaol in the city's historic Lace Market area. Crowds had gathered in their thousands behind the street barriers and massively outnumbered those who had turned out to see Harry on his own the previous year. Meghan was wrapped up against the cold in a £585 maxi navy coat by Canadian brand Mackage, and wore £229 knee-high boots by Kurt Geiger. Harry had a long navy coat, too, with a cream scarf round his neck.

It was a royal official event like no other. Their overt lovey-dovey behaviour had never been seen at a royal engagement before and it felt more like watching a scene from a Hollywood feel-good love story than a reserved inner city walkabout. The couple held gloveless hands, perhaps so that her diamond engagement ring was on view, fingers entwined. They put their arms round each other. Meghan also clung on to Harry's arm and stroked his back. Did she need the physical contact to help ease her nerves and reassure Harry that she was coping, or was she just being motherly as she had been during the BBC TV interview on the day their engagement was officially announced?

Dr David Starkey believes their overt physical contact is a rather good thing. 'Touchy-feely is the new way and I believe Meghan will be the one to set the royal rules,' he says.

'Meghan is a kind of Madam Macron [the much older wife of French President Emmanuel Macron], only better-looking.'

The crowds loved it, too. Chants of 'Harry, Harry' and 'Meghan, Meghan' filled the air as they held out their hands, waved flowers, cards and UK and US flags. There were countless thick coats, fleeces and woolly hats to protect them against the bitter cold as they waited for hours to congratulate their prince on his engagement. Harry's charisma and easy charm has made him popular, even adored, by people of all ages and types around the world. People feel he is one of them, recognise he has had a bad time and want him to be happy.

The couple beamed at the cheering crowds and exchanged countless loving glances between each other. If they were breaking royal protocol by their physical contact, they didn't seem to care. They wanted the world to know they were in love. Their behaviour was very different to that of the Duchess of Cambridge, who is less demonstrative and has yet to put a royal foot wrong. She will laugh when she and Prince William are on public duty but the most physical they usually get in public is for Kate to rest her hand on William's thigh for a couple of seconds or the Prince to fleetingly touch her back; twice when they have walked to church on Christmas morning they have held hands. Meghan, who was born in Los Angeles, is more emotionally open, and at this early stage in her royal story, couldn't be expected to have absorbed the minutiae of what is and is not considered appropriate.

The loved-up couple initially began their walkabout

together making slow progress down a line of excited royal watchers on their way to the Nottingham Contemporary gallery. As a TV star Meghan is used to the limelight, but royal demands are far more complex. Walkabouts are carefully timed and there is a need to manage the unexpected. Meghan behaved as if she was born to it. She even broke away from Harry and, with the clacking of her heels nearly drowned by the noise of the crowds, walked over to meet well-wishers on the other side of the street, a big step for a novice. She and Harry then neatly synched, joining and separating from each other along the way. Unlike the Prince of Wales, who felt jealous when the crowds clamoured for Diana rather than him, Harry looked incredibly proud. Harry is a master at walkabouts: he scans the crowd looking for someone who is, for example, wheelchair-bound, elderly or holding a charity mascot that he can talk about.

Meghan was happy to wholeheartedly embrace the occasion. She shook hands with men, women and children and introduced herself by saying: 'Hi, I'm Meghan', telling them it was a 'thrill to be here' and how happy she was. She talked about the weather, thanked them for 'braving the cold' and even managed to find a hand-warmer in her handbag to give to a young woman whose hands were icy. She admired lots of babies and even smiled when people told her repeatedly that 'Diana would have loved you'. She did, however, politely decline to do selfies. 'We're not allowed,' she smiled.

Meghan had arrived carrying a £495 burgundy tote bag by Scots label Strathberry (which sold out within 11 minutes of its appearance). Kate rarely has a large handbag on walkabouts and Meghan soon discovered why. With her handbag in one hand and several bunches of flowers in the other she soon found she couldn't shake any more hands. She looked around anxiously, found an aide and handed the lot over so both hands were free. Her long shining hair got in her way, too, and she kept brushing it back from her eyes, but one spectator thought it could have been a sign of nerves: 'She seemed natural and warm. I bet she was terribly nervous but she didn't show it,' she said.

Irene Hardman, eighty-one and a passionate royal fan, was greeted by both Harry and Meghan. Over the past several decades she has given the Prince, Prince William and Prince Charles a pack of Haribo sweets every time one of them visits Nottingham. She said: 'Meghan was told I had a goody bag for her and Harry. She walked over with Harry, so I gave her the bag. She put her arms around me and kissed me. How incredible.'

Comments like: 'They're so genuine' were heard repeatedly. Meghan proved herself adept at extricating herself from conversations. She also picked up a dropped glove and handed it back over the security barrier, which is not usual royal behaviour. One journalist described her way of doing things as the 'Markle Sparkle', while another affectionately called her 'dainty and petite'.

The thirty-minute walkabout stopped at Nottingham Contemporary, which was holding the World Aids Day charity fair hosted by the Terrence Higgins Trust. It was warmer inside and their coats came off. Harry was wearing a white shirt and blue blazer. Meghan was casually but immaculately dressed in a black polo neck top, tucked into a belted £595 camel midi skirt by Joseph. They met Ale Araphate, twenty-one, captain of a football team for Champions For Change – a project that uses sport to reach African communities in the Midlands and to talk about HIV/Aids. He said of Meghan: 'She is beautiful. Only a prince can have a lady like that!' Chris O'Hanlon of Positively UK, a charity that helps people newly diagnosed with HIV, talked to them about his own diagnosis and the importance of fitness in dealing with it. He said: 'I spoke to Meghan about my passion for yoga. She said, "Absolutely, I love incorporating it into my life, it's something I've always done."'

Although Meghan quickly proved her social skills, any hawk-eyed royalist would notice that she broke royal consort protocol on several occasions. When visiting the Nottingham Academy to meet head teachers taking part in the Full Effect programme, she walked through a door ahead of Harry and led the way down the line talking to various dignitaries. The protocol is always that the royal goes first. It was too early to say whether this was to do with her well-known championing of female equality, she was just swept along in the moment or no one had told her the rules. Harry, who has always been a rebellious, unconventional and non-conformist royal, didn't seem the least bothered about following in her footsteps. David Starkey commented: 'Meghan walked in before Harry precisely because today that happens with a normal couple and the man defers to the woman.'

Just a couple of times when she tried to hold his hand or

grab his arm, he put his hand behind his back. It seemed his subtle way of saying it's fine to be touchy-feely with the crowds outside, but isn't quite appropriate once we have arrived to talk about Aids. Meghan got the message. Although she made more of an impact before her marriage than other royal newly-weds, including the Princess of Wales, the Duchess of Cambridge, the Duchess of York and the Countess of Wessex, Meghan has a lot to learn about the minutiae of royal dos and don'ts, both in the UK and on a royal visit abroad.

A highlight of the day was watching rappers involved in the Full Effect programme perform in a short play. Prince Harry has a longstanding and close relationship with Trevor Rose, who has worked with tough, disaffected youth for decades. I was also invited to meet Trevor during Prince Harry's trip to Nottingham in 2016. Trevor, an extraordinary character, runs aspects of Full Effect from the Community Recording Studio in St Ann's, a rundown area of Nottingham with high crime levels. He was bowled over that Prince Harry chose to introduce his bride-to-be to him on her first royal visit. 'What an absolutely amazing honour,' he told me. 'When I heard a few days before that they were coming I couldn't believe it. I am not usually a speechless person but I was then.' He beamed. 'It also meant I only had a couple of days to put a performance together.'

Part improvised and part scripted, it told the story of a young couple who decide to go public about their secret relationship – hints of Harry and Meghan – and ended with a character in a top hat getting an invitation to a royal wedding. 'Meeting Harry and getting to know him has made us all feel in St Ann's like we have a big brother,' Trevor laughed. 'And now we have a big sister-in-law. Harry coming today is a perfect example of his commitment and support of the young people. All the kids recognise that he is really interested in hearing what they have been doing and I believe he genuinely cares. Today they have been really buzzing and can't believe it.'

Prince Harry and his fiancée chuckled as they watched the performance and when it was over Meghan delighted the young cast by complimenting them on their acting skills. 'The kids were so pleased Meghan came on stage,' said Trevor, 'and talked to them about acting and improvisation. She seemed so natural and Harry looked incredibly happy. Definitely. The really beautiful thing was that Harry couldn't take his eyes off her.

'Meghan was having a right laugh. I hope it won't be a long time before he has little ones. He is such a good guy, I want to see him happy and bring a little one to see us.'

A few decades ago it would not have been acceptable for a mixed-race American divorcée actress to marry a senior royal. In Nottingham that day the general feeling was she would be a realistic and refreshing addition to the royal family, leading the way in modernising royalty and making an excellent ambassador to any of the causes she puts her heart and mind to.

Harry will no doubt encourage her. Together they might tear up the royal rulebook and ditch much of the protocol that would follow in the footsteps of Princess of Wales, who was the most maverick of rebellious royals. She had also disliked many of the traditions of royal family life, including not being able to go to bed at family occasions before the Queen. But it was only after Harry's birth that Diana found the courage to show her determination not to toe the royal line.

CHAPTER 2

Diana's Second Boy

Saturday 15 September 1984 dawned warm and misty as Diana, Princess of Wales, was woken by the early pangs of labour. Shortly afterwards she, Prince Charles and an ever-present bodyguard left Windsor Castle for London and the private Lindo Wing of St Mary's Hospital, Paddington. The couple arrived at 7.30am, and were taken to the same spartan 12ft square, £140 per night room where she had given birth to Prince William, their first son and the royal heir, two years previously. It had a bleak view over Paddington Station.

The Princess of Wales had refused to do what generations of royal mothers had acquiesced to: give birth in a palace. For centuries it had been the custom that the Home Secretary, as a senior member of the Cabinet, would attend royal births to ensure the new arrival was a genuine descendant of the monarch and not an imposter smuggled in. When Prince Charles was born at Buckingham Palace in 1948, the practice was discontinued. Instead, Diana followed the advice of Mr George Pinker, at the time the Queen's gynaecologist and a senior consultant at St Mary's. He believed no chances should be taken with childbirth and that giving birth in hospital was the best place for both mothers and newborn babies.

Once in their private room, Charles was asked to put on a hospital gown. He stayed with his wife throughout her nine-hour labour, occasionally feeding her ice cubes. His decision to be at William's birth had also been a significant break with royal protocol and made William the first offspring of an heir to the throne to have his father present at the birth. It was in sharp contrast to Charles's own birth, when his father, Prince Philip, had played an energetic game of squash with a friend while the Queen went through the birthing process, and only left the squash court when he was told his baby son had arrived. A Palace aide said at the time: 'It has been a tradition that royal fathers normally join their men friends and sip port while waiting to hear the good news.' Prince Charles felt differently. He told a friend: 'I am, after all, the father ... and I suppose I started this whole business so I intend to be there when everything happens.'

Diana had been very sick while pregnant with William, which was only partly due to her pregnancy. She suffered from bulimia, an eating disorder that involves binge-eating followed by self-induced vomiting. Although she was still bulimic, her morning sickness was less intense the second time round.

Harry arrived in the world at 4.20pm weighing 6lb 14 oz, a little less than William who'd been 7lb 1½ oz. It was believed he was a week early, something that Buckingham Palace refused to confirm or deny. It can be assumed, however, that if the birth had been imminent, Charles and Diana would have stayed close by at Kensington Palace rather than at Windsor Castle.

His mother decided on his name. 'I chose the names William and Harry because the alternatives were Arthur and Albert,' she explained. 'No thank you. There weren't fights over it. It was just a fait accompli.'

Immediately after the royal baby's safe arrival Prince Charles called the Queen on a specially installed phone in their private room. Her Majesty was with the Queen Mother at Balmoral, the Scottish home of the royal family where she traditionally goes for her summer break. Charles then rang Diana's father, Lord Spencer, at Althorp Estate, his home in Northamptonshire. He was naturally delighted, and as soon as he heard the news ordered the Union Jack to be lowered from the roof and the Spencer personal standard in red, yellow and black run up in its place. He then stepped excitedly through the front door and told any visitors he saw: 'We have had a boy. Diana has had her second boy. She is very well and so is the baby. I'm so pleased, particularly for Prince William. He will be thrilled. It will be lovely for him to have a companion, a playmate, and someone to fight with. It's lovely to have two boys. I hope one day he will play cricket for Gloucestershire. He is a lucky little boy because he has such wonderful parents. He will have a very good start in life.' He then sighed. 'It's such a relief everything went off well, without complications.'

Diana, however, felt anxious because she knew Charles had wanted a daughter rather than another son. She revealed to the author Andrew Morton, researching his international bestseller *Diana: Her True Story,* published in 1992, that she had seen from ultrasound pregnancy scans that she was carrying a boy but had kept the news from her husband, fearing he would feel she had let him down. The stress of keeping such a special fact secret for months speaks volumes about their crumbling, dysfunctional relationship. Several tapes, known as the 'Diana tapes', in which Diana recorded some of her innermost feelings during that period, were published in June 2017, to mark the twenty-fifth anniversary of Morton's original book. 'Charles always wanted a girl,' she claimed on one tape, adding that he exclaimed when he first saw the baby, 'Oh God, it's a boy … and he's even got red hair.'

It's an allegation that is open to doubt. Two months after Harry's birth Prince Charles gave a rare interview on American television in which he described Harry as being 'absolutely adorable' adding: 'It's interesting with a second child, very often – a lot of people have told me this – that with the second one you're more relaxed as parents, I think, and therefore able to communicate an atmosphere of greater relaxation to the child.' As proof of his theory he said Harry was 'extraordinarily good, sleeps marvellously and eats very well.' Nonetheless, his alleged reaction wounded the vulnerable young mother to the core. 'Something inside me closed off,' Diana told Morton. 'By then, I knew Charles had gone back to his lady [Camilla Parker Bowles], but somehow we'd managed to have Harry.'

Diana also revealed in the tapes that the period between the two boys' birth was 'total darkness. I can't remember much. I've blotted it out. It was such pain. However, Harry appeared by a miracle. Charles and I were very, very close to each other the six weeks before Harry was born, the closest we've ever, ever been and ever will be. Then, suddenly, as Harry was born, it just went bang, our marriage. The whole thing went down the drain.' She claimed Charles made her feel inadequate in 'every way'. She was delighted to have Harry as it gave her a second chance to be loved unconditionally.

Outside the hospital about 300 patient and devoted royal watchers from all walks of life had gathered, along with the world's press, and cheered when they heard the good news. The birth was also marked by two coordinated forty-one-gun salutes that erupted simultaneously from Hyde Park and the Tower of London. The following day a celebratory three-hour peal of bells was rung at St Mary's parish church in Tetbury, Gloucestershire, close to Highgrove House, the country home of Charles and Diana, which Prince Charles had bought in 1980. Bells were also rung at the parish church on the royal estate at Sandringham, Norfolk, where Princess Diana was born. Prime Minister Margaret Thatcher, who was spending the weekend at Chequers, sent a message of congratulations to the royal couple.

Baby Harry was third in line to the throne and the Queen's

fourth grandchild but it was not enough to make her change her plans. She was not due to be in London until the following Friday, just before she left for an official tour of Canada. The following day, however, she, Prince Philip, the Queen Mother and Prince Edward drove to the village church at Crathie, near Balmoral, where the service contained prayers for the new baby. Due to other commitments in Japan and Switzerland, Prince Philip did not see his new grandson until he was almost four weeks old when he made a brief visit to Highgrove House, Charles and Diana's Country home. At the time there were rumours of a rift between him and Prince Charles over his apparent lack of interest in the newest addition to the Royal Family.

The official announcement of the birth of Prince Henry Charles Albert David was chained to the gates of Buckingham Palace at 5.55pm and prompted a round of applause. An official bulletin was also posted on the gates of Balmoral. A royal spokesman added that although the baby would be christened 'Henry', afterwards he would be known as 'Harry'. Prince Charles later said that, as a child, Harry was only called Henry when he had been 'very, very, naughty'.

Two hours after the birth Charles came through the hospital doors, smiling broadly. He shook hands with many of the rather crushed well-wishers who had mounted a vigil behind the metal barriers, and announced: 'My wife is very well. The delivery couldn't have been better. It was much quicker this time.' He added that the baby had 'pale blue eyes and hair of an intermediate colour' and that the birth had been 'a marvellous experience'. He then went home to Kensington Palace.

He was back at 9 o'clock the next morning with Prince William and his nanny Barbara Barnes. William was dressed in bright red shorts, white shirt with red embroidery and short white socks. Clutching his father's hand, he enthusiastically climbed the large steps into the hospital. The crowd of more than 1,000 cheering onlookers were left to wonder whether he was more excited at seeing his mother or meeting his baby brother. Diana was told William was on his way and as he walked down the hospital corridor she poked her head out of the doorway of her room and called his name. William ran into her arms. Diana then allowed him to hold his baby brother's hand. The newly extended family spent some intimate time together, before Nanny Barnes came into the room, which was by then full of flowers from family and friends. She had a good look at her new charge and at 10am left the hospital with William. She held his hand tightly while he managed the quite tricky combination for a two-year-old of both waving at the crowds and walking down the hospital steps, before he climbed into the waiting Daimler to return to Kensington Palace.

Diana and Charles had argued about how their children should be brought up. Charles wanted to employ his old nanny, Mabel Anderson, to whom he had been very attached. Diana refused because she said Mabel was too old and too traditional. Instead she chose Barbara Barnes, the daughter of a forester, despite being almost twice Diana's age, because her approach towards her charges was conciliatory and easy-going and included plenty of hugs. Barbara had had no formal training in childcare and refused to wear a uniform but had years of experience and glowing references. It wasn't long before the modern approach Diana initially thought was ideal began to annoy her.

Charles left the hospital at 12.35pm for lunch at Kensington Palace and returned at 2.27pm. Four minutes later he and Diana, who was cradling her newborn son in her arms, appeared at the top of the hospital steps. The crowd enthusiastically waved Union flags and cheered. They were not, however, rewarded with a glimpse of Harry's face, as he was well wrapped up in a lacy blanket to protect him from the chilly autumn air. Several smiling nurses also peered out from upper-floor windows trying to catch a glimpse of the royal party. Diana had chosen a wide-shouldered scarlet calf-length coat and low-heeled scarlet shoes to wear to take him home. Her hair was brushed into a bouffant style and she looked so fresh and glamorous that she could have been a star of *Dynasty*, the American prime-time soap opera that was then a huge hit on British TV screens.

As she stood on the steps she turned to face her husband, her expression a mixture of love, vulnerability and yearning. Charles, however, stood with his hands behind his back, a gesture typical of Prince Philip, and did not return his wife's gaze. It seemed even at this joyous thankful time the mismatched couple could not conceal their differences. Diana stepped into the back of a blue Daimler and with Harry cradled in her arms was driven to Kensington Palace. Times have changed. When the Duchess of Cambridge left St

Mary's with baby Prince George in 2013, he was tucked into an approved safety baby seat.

Anne Wallace, a nurse who had helped Diana with newborn William, was waiting at Kensington Palace. She had been engaged for the first five or so weeks of Harry's life to support Diana and monitor the baby's daily progress. Prince Charles did not stay long. Instead he was driven to Smith's Lawn at Windsor to play polo for the Windsor Park team. There he confided to the groundsman: 'William has taken to the new baby like a duck to water. It's worth a guinea a minute watching him enjoy himself with the baby. He's been climbing in and out of his cot.' An onlooker at the match was heard to disapprove of the prince choosing polo rather than staying at home. 'He should be with his wife,' she declared. 'What's he doing playing polo?' Her husband's reply was also overheard: 'He's done his bit.' A teenager asked Prince Charles a question on many spectators' minds: 'What does Princess Diana think of you playing polo today?' Charles laughed and replied: 'Oh, she doesn't mind.' The match was followed by an impromptu toast of champagne to celebrate Harry's birth served very un-royally in a plastic cup from the back of a Land Rover.

Early visitors to see the baby prince included Prince Andrew, Lady Sarah Armstrong-Jones and Diana's father, who came with his second wife Raine, formerly McCorquodale, the exuberant, flamboyant daughter of romantic novelist Barbara Cartland. They emerged after an hour, smiling broadly to declare: 'He's a lovely baby.'

When Harry was ten days old, the family decamped to Highgrove where they were inundated with hundreds of messages of congratulation, bouquets and presents. They also visited Althorp for the weekend a few weeks later.

Diana instantly adored Harry and breastfed him for eleven weeks, eight weeks more than she had with William. No longer a first-time mother, she felt more confident handling and showing her love for her new baby. From the start she was acutely aware that the paths of her two sons would be very different. William was born to be king and his life was mapped out with that firmly in view. Harry could experiment and choose his own way. She loved them equally and both she and Prince Charles agreed that Harry would never be made to feel second best.

The age gap between the two boys was twenty-seven months and William, a forthright, boisterous child, was, like many first siblings, mightily put out that a new arrival was encroaching on his territory. He initially showed his displeasure by shouting, stamping his feet and throwing food about in an effort to get attention. He didn't, however, take out his irritation on Harry. Instead he was instinctively protective and watchful of his baby brother, who was initially a quiet, gentle baby, characteristics that he would soon grow out of.

Diana was proud of how gentle William was towards his brother. On 20 September 1984, just five days after Harry's birth, she wrote to Cyril Dickman, a steward who had worked at Buckingham Palace for more than fifty years. The letter only surfaced in December 2016, and records how Prince William doted on Harry. She wrote: 'William adores his little brother and spends the entire time swamping Harry with an endless supply of hugs and kisses hardly letting the parents near!' She added that she and Prince Charles were 'totally overwhelmed by the reaction to Harry's birth' and that she 'could hardly breathe for the mass of flowers'. Diana even praised Charles's attitude to Harry. 'Charles loves the nursery life,' she continued, 'and couldn't wait to get back and do the bottle and everything.'

The reality was that Diana had now done her duty by efficiently and quickly reinforcing the future of the monarchy by providing both an heir to the throne and a standby, but she understandably hated the way Harry was insensitively often called 'the spare'. Diana's strong maternal instinct and innate sense of fairness made her determined that both princes would be treated equally and both would share the limelight. She said: 'Royal first-borns may get all the glory, but second-borns enjoy more freedom. Only when Harry is a lot older will he realise how lucky he is not to have been the eldest.' When the boys were young she tried to make sure they were photographed together as much as possible. It was one of the few things she and Prince Charles agreed on.

The truth is that a second child has to compete for his parents' attention, and the pressure on Harry to make his mark was strong, the more so as he gradually became aware that William was a future king. He was a hard act to follow. Michael Lewis, former chairman of Bowden House psychiatric clinic, wrote shortly after Harry's birth about what he believed he faced:

During the crucial five years of his life Prince William will always be there, older, bigger and stronger. He will be walking when the new prince can only crawl. He will be running rings around the new prince when he is just able to stumble about. In order to catch up with his older brother and break through his superior attitude, Prince Harry will sharpen his wits, develop considerable charm and improve his personality. Or opt out of the struggle and become gentler and somewhat reclusive. While the older son grows into an establishment figure and does what is expected of him, the younger son invariably wishes to be a non-conformist and more of a funster knowing that he can gain nothing by competing with his brother, which is a battle he can never win. Brothers are the greatest single influence on each other's lives, far more than parents because they spend more time with each other during the crucial nursery years.

Harry has always been more emotionally vulnerable and thin-skinned than William and in 2017 admitted that he had needed help with mental health issues. It's unfair to blame his troubles solely on being a royal second son with no particular goal, but added to his dysfunctional home life, warring parents and the tragic and traumatic loss of his mother, it wouldn't have helped make his life easier.

Harry's christening took place on 21 December 1984 in St George's Chapel, Windsor when he was three months old. He looked adorable in the 143-year-old royal lace christening gown as he lay contentedly in his mother's arms.

Diana looked the epitome of sophistication and elegance in a navy dress with wide shoulders and a broad-brimmed navy hat. There was almost no interaction between her and Prince Charles but at one point he brusquely told her, 'He's dribbling', and she quickly wiped Prince Harry's chin.

Prince William, a typical impish, energetic toddler, didn't like not being the centre of attention. He wriggled nonstop when he was told to sit down next to his father and looked equally cross that he wasn't allowed to hold his baby brother. His behaviour made it very difficult for Lord Snowdon, the former husband of Princess Margaret, who was trying to take the official photographs. His assistant commented afterwards: 'Every time he [William] did something naughty they all roared with laughter. No one admonished him and he was being a thorough pest.' At one point Charles tried to occupy him by telling him the history of the christening gown. William rolled his eyes, which must have been instinctive rather than deliberate. Diana didn't take his behaviour seriously and jokingly gave him the sobriquet of 'Your Royal Naughtiness'.

Harry, like William, was given six godparents. Diana had been annoyed that she couldn't choose William's godparents as both Prince Charles and the Queen had insisted that, with one exception, they had to be part of the royal establishment, relatives of the royal family or aristocrats. Diana had more leeway with Harry, but still had to submit her list to the Queen for approval. Two suggestions were initially turned down but the Queen approved the replacements. The final selection was: Lady Sarah Armstrong-Jones (later Chatto), daughter of Princess Margaret and Lord Snowdon; Prince Andrew, Duke of York; Diana's former flatmate Carolyn Bartholomew; Lady Celia Vestey, a friend of the Queen; Bryan Organ (royal artist) and Gerald Ward, both friends of Prince Charles. Princess Anne was not chosen, nor did she come to the christening.

Diana, who privately at home often felt depressed and alone, something that made her bulimia worse, could, however, hide her mood when her royal duties demanded. But she later revealed that even the joy of Harry's christening was spoilt by Charles's alleged tactlessness. Speaking to Andrew Morton in 1991 she said: 'Charles went to talk to my mother at Harry's christening and said: "We were so disappointed – we thought it would be a girl." Mummy snapped his head off, saying: "You should realise how lucky you are to have a child that's normal."'

'Ever since that day,' she added, 'the shutters have come down – and that's what he does when he gets somebody answering back at him.'

In addition she talked intimately to her voice coach Peter Settelen. He had been contacted to help her gain confidence as a public speaker and it is an indication of her desperation at the time that she confessed so much personal detail, which she let him record. Her conversations, earlier referred to as 'Diana tapes', which were recorded at Kensington Palace in 1992 and 1993, formed the basis of a Channel 4 documentary, *Diana In Her Own Words,* to mark the twentieth anniversary of her death in 2017. In them she described her wedding as 'the worst day of my life'. She discussed her sex life with the prince, saying there was 'never a requirement for it from him – once every three weeks about and I kept thinking it followed a pattern.' Diana also admitted that 1987 marked the last time 'we were close as man and wife'. From then on Prince Charles slept in his dressing room.

Whatever the rights and wrongs, the background and upbringing of both Charles and Diana significantly reduced the chance that they would have a positive and successful relationship together. Neither of them had been given enough love, stability or self-confidence in their formative years. It was a rotten blue print to pass down to their children. Charles had struggled all his life to win his parents' approval but always felt he had failed them, and particularly his father. He knew he was too soft to be the son his father expected or wanted. He had more than enough of the material things in life, but emotionally his needs were not satisfied. The Queen is not known to be emotionally demonstrative. The Duke, who was abandoned as a child, didn't know how to be. As a result, according to Dickie Arbiter, a former press secretary to the Queen, 'Charles was brought up not to show his emotions.'

His inability to relate to Diana made him feel even worse about himself, but it wasn't entirely his fault. The Princess of Wales also came from a damaged background. Her parents had an unhappy marriage. Her mother, Frances Roche, always seemed to be crying, and Diana saw her father, Johnnie, the eighth Earl Spencer, slap her across the face. A year before Diana was born, Frances had a son who died shortly after birth. Johnnie never forgave her, although she did finally manage to have a boy, Charles, the current Earl Spencer. Frances left the family home when Diana was six and soon afterwards went to live with Peter Shand Kydd in the far reaches of Scotland. Diana's older sisters, Jane and Sarah, and her younger brother Charles remained with their father. Like many aristocrats at the time he had not been involved in childcare and instead employed one au pair after another to tend to the children.

Diana was naïve and lacked confidence. No one else had divorced parents at school and at fourteen she said she wasn't good at anything. As a teenager she fed herself on romantic novels by Barbara Cartland (coincidentally, as mentioned previously, the mother of her stepmother), in which handsome men swept modest young ladies off their feet and they all lived happily ever after. She married Prince Charles when she was just twenty years old; he was nearly thirteen years older, a gap that was unbridgeable because of their very different characters. Diana was instinctive, spontaneous, insecure and needy, while Prince Charles by comparison seemed middle-aged. He had an established routine and, like his mother, put duty before family. Diana was bitterly disappointed that Charles didn't behave like one of her literary heroes. She also found that the existence of Camilla Parker Bowles, the love of Charles's life, hovered over her like a ghostly shadow. In addition, their friends were incompatible and they had no common interests. They should never have married.

William and Harry's childhood was steeped in this

troubled, toxic atmosphere and could have been one reason why William threw countless tantrums and Harry was rather withdrawn. The combination of living with parents who were unhappy together and increasingly at loggerheads inevitably affected them. It is common for parents to pass on their destructive behaviour to the next generation, and it was feared the brothers would stumble if not crash once they were older. Fighting the pitfalls they faced took a lot of hard work and soul-searching for both of them, but was particularly difficult for Harry. It is a huge credit to them that they seem to have saved themselves from a dysfunctional future.

The Queen used Harry's arrival and christening a few days later as the basis of her annual Christmas Message in 1984. She was aware of the poor state of her son's marriage and in retrospect she seems to be giving a subtle hint to him and Diana to bond for the sake of the family. In her address she said the birth of her fourth grandchild 'was a source of great family celebration'. She talked about children's 'unstinting trust', 'readiness to forgive' and how 'we should all learn from them as much as they learn from us', particularly 'their sturdy confidence and devastating honesty.' Sadly, her advice wasn't taken up.

There was an unwritten rule that royal child-rearing should be distant and uninvolved, something Diana totally rejected. Her own dysfunctional upbringing and experience as a nanny before she met Charles made her determined to adopt an entirely different approach. She wanted her boys never to doubt that they were loved, which in return helped to replace the love she had missed out on during part of her childhood and in her marriage.

William was such an energetic, noisy, unruly toddler that when he was six months old Olga Powell, then fifty-two, was brought on board to be deputy nanny to Barnes. She outlasted three further full-time nannies to eventually become the top nanny in her own right and was much loved by both boys.

Nanny Barnes, however, did not fare so well. It began to go wrong when it became obvious that William, who called her Baba, adored her. He also spent more time with her than he did with his mother and, in the way small children do, ran to the person who was with him the most. Diana, who already felt neglected by her husband and isolated from the world, was horrified. She didn't want a nanny to replace her in her child's life. Jealousy overwhelmed her. She wanted to be the one who brought her sons up and spent as much time with them as her royal duties allowed. She also arranged her schedule to fit in with her children whereas Charles did not cancel an engagement or alter its timing. He was also by now staying away from both their London and country homes on a regular basis.

Once a member of staff, friend or relation was out of favour with Diana, something that could happen from one day to the next, there was rarely any turning back. Nanny Barnes was an unwitting victim of Diana's fickleness. Diana undermined her by insisting she discussed any wrongdoing by the children with her first before telling them off. This put her in an impossible position. Ken Wharfe, who was William and Harry's personal protection officer for two years and subsequently Diana's, and who watched Harry's development from the age of two until he was nine, felt it was obvious that Barbara Barnes gave more attention to William than to Harry. He wrote scathingly in his book, *Diana: Closely Guarded Secret*: 'Barbara favoured William far more than Harry, which didn't appeal to Diana. I remember a few trips down to Highgrove with Barbara when Harry was very small, and he would be ignored almost to the point where it didn't really matter what happened to him. He was quite prone to car sickness and we used to have to stop several times on the M4 for him to – poor bloke – throw up on the hard shoulder. I used to say: "Maybe he should see someone about this" and she would say: "Oh, he's all right. He's fine."'

Nanny Barnes was not the only one who did not follow both Diana and Charles's wish that Harry should be treated in the same way as William. Even the Queen Mother would, perhaps insensitively, invite William on his own to see her at Clarence House, leaving Harry at home.

Nanny Barnes saw the writing on the wall and announced on 15 January 1987 that she was leaving. It was William's first day at Wetherby Pre-Preparatory School in west London. He was devastated, Harry less so. Diana failed to explain anything to the princes who had depended on their nanny for so many aspects of their life. To them she simply vanished. Small children often blame themselves when the people they rely on and love leave them. It was the first time they felt abandoned but not the last.

Ruth Wallace succeeded Nanny Barnes. She had been nanny to Prince and Princess Michael of Kent's children,

Lord Frederick and Lady Gabriella Windsor, who were both very polite. Charles had asked Princess Michael how she came to have such well-behaved children and she put it down to their 'wonderful' nanny, so Diana coaxed her to join them. Harry called her 'Roof'. She had a difficult job taming William who she felt had been far too spoilt. She stayed for three years but left because she found the toxic atmosphere between the royal couple too unpleasant. By the time she left, William had stopped throwing tantrums and Harry had started to come out of his shell. The Queen had voiced her concern about the fast turnover of nannies as she believed it disrupted nursery routine.

All the nannies Diana employed were old-fashioned in that they liked routine, order and politeness. The one consistent person for William and Harry was deputy nanny Olga Powell, who was shrewd enough to realise from the start that Diana would be jealous if she felt William and Harry were getting too close to her. A former courtier said: 'Diana just didn't trust them enough to let them do their work properly. It was very disruptive for the children.'

One of the few aspects of the princes' life that was normal was their diet. Favourite foods when they were toddlers were Rice Krispies for breakfast, shepherd's pie or fish fingers for lunch, and baked beans or egg on toast for supper. Chocolates and sweet drinks were kept for special occasions. Weekends were usually spent at Highgrove House, where another self-contained nursery awaited them. It had been decorated with pine, rather than mahogany like the rest of the house, and green netting was strung across the stairwell in case William decided to practise leaping down the stairs.

★ ★ ★

The royal summer break lasts between August and October when the family traditionally gathers for varying amounts of time at Balmoral. In 1985 it began just a month before Harry was one year old with a cruise on the royal yacht *Britannia* from Southampton around the Western Isles. Security was particularly tight at Southampton as the police had recently uncovered an IRA plan to make it one of their target towns. It was a wet and windy summer's day when they were due to set off. Harry, a sensitive child, was disturbed by the wind blowing his tufts of red hair and clung tightly onto his mother. He was also startled by the loud Royal Navy salute

Once the family returned to Kensington Palace in October, Alastair Burnet became the first journalist to be granted a TV interview by the Prince and Princess of Wales. Although there was almost no interaction between the couple their unhappiness wasn't glaringly obvious largely because the two young princes stole the show. William was dressed in red shorts with a red and white checked long-sleeved shirt, white socks and red sandals, while a bemused Harry, who was just one and a little wobbly on his feet, wore a white frilly romper suit. The most enchanting part of the documentary was the boys' attempts to play the piano. They obviously hugely enjoyed bashing away at the keys and William, who called it 'the pano', roared with laughter when Harry managed to stay upright long enough to reach some of the notes. At one point William was asked to give Harry a kiss. He obliged by kissing him on top of his head, then thoroughly wiped his mouth with his arm. Meanwhile, Prince Charles held a spotless white handkerchief over his face, which he lifted up and down playing peek-a-boo to try to get Harry to smile for the camera. The programme topped the television ratings and the resulting book and video sales raised £1 million for charity.

As an antidote to their rich and indulgent lives Diana, despite coming from a wealthy aristocratic background herself, decided she wanted her children to have as broad an experience of life as was possible. She made sure they saw how others less fortunate than themselves lived and met people who had very few chances in life. This represented a significant shift for royal children. Nor did she want them to miss out on what other children did, like going to pantomimes and the cinema. She couldn't have imagined what a strong and lasting influence she has had on both princes' lives. It will no doubt shape William's reign when he becomes King and has been a huge motivating factor for Harry.

One such trip occurred in July 1987, just before Harry was about to start at nursery. He and William went to play at a centre for children of working parents in Holborn, central London, run by Camden Council. Both brothers were dropped off unannounced with their nanny and two protection officers. They played with other children for about an hour and they might have remained incognito had five-year-old William not overheard his protection officer telling a curious ten-year-old that his name was Roger. William heard him and shouted out: 'No it's not. My name's William.'

At Christmas, the Princess twice took them to meet Father Christmas at renowned London stores, first Harrods then Selfridges. The specially arranged Harrods visit took place before the store opened to the public. The Princess of Wales was greeted personally by Mohamed Al-Fayed, who then owned the luxury store. First stop was the elves' grotto. Harry readily told them he wanted some Christmas cake as a present while William behaved rather grandly and told the elves: 'I am not telling you what I want for Christmas. I'm only talking to Father Christmas.'

Al-Fayed then took them to Toy Kingdom on the fourth floor where the princes made straight for two mini-motorbikes. Harry drove round and round, but, fearless even then, shouted at his mother: 'I want to drive something faster.' They stayed for 45 minutes and both left clutching a teddy bear. Three days later Diana took them to Selfridges. This time the staff were not told of the royal visit in advance. It meant they had to queue to see Santa like everyone else even though they were at the store at 9am. Harry left clutching another teddy, this one almost as big as himself.

Not surprisingly both princes had vast amounts of toys. When they were small they particularly loved teddies and squeaky animals. They also had a rocking horse each. William's was black and the larger of the two; Harry's was white. As they grew older they preferred toy helicopters, racing cars and tanks. William favoured games and puzzles, Harry played endlessly with a set of toy soldiers.

Aside from toys, they had a pet rabbit and a gerbil. They also loved watching the red Wessex helicopter taking off carrying one or both their parents to a royal engagement, and Harry was particularly fascinated by the regular military parades.

At Highgrove they enjoyed more outdoor activities in the estate's fifteen acres of grounds. Harry liked going round the garden holding hands with his father who pointed out various plants and flowers. 'Harry loves animals and plants,' Prince Charles observed. 'I tell him all about them and that they have feelings too and mustn't be hurt.'

The royal family traditionally spends Christmas at Sandringham in Norfolk. A highlight was a trip to see a pantomime. One year Diana took the princes as part of a fourteen-strong party to see a matinee of *Cinderella* at the Princess Theatre in Hunstanton, a local seaside town, where they were seen shouting and cheering from their private box.

For the Princess of Wales it was a couple of hours of light in an increasingly dark time. She was refusing to conform to royal protocol, not least to punish the senior royals for ignoring her and not being supportive. Her relationship with her husband had deteriorated too. As a result she was regularly self-harming, binge-eating and making herself sick. Sometimes they couldn't bear to be together in the same room.

CHAPTER 3

In His Brother's Footsteps

Prince Charles had initially wanted William and Harry to start their education at home with a governess, as both he and Diana had done. Diana balked at the very idea. Instead she wanted their schooldays to be as normal as possible so they would have an opportunity to mix with other children. Despite them both wanting the best for their sons, it became increasingly difficult for the two of them to even talk about their education rationally and calmly. Diana felt so rejected she kept weeping and hurling insults at her husband. Prince Charles, who had no idea how to cope with her histrionics or how to please her, also felt utter despair. In the end he left the choice to her. It made sense as he had not been happy in the schools his parents had chosen for him.

To convince Charles she was right, Diana researched every potentially appropriate school within a five-mile radius of Kensington Palace and gave Charles the prospectuses to read. Her method was effective and they both agreed to send William to Jane Mynors' £300-a-week kindergarten in Chepstow Villas, a leafy road in Notting Hill, West London. His natural exuberance and confidence helped him settle in easily. He was given the nickname 'Basher' and once threatened a classmate he obviously didn't particularly like with the words: 'I will send my knights to kill you when I am king.' Despite this, both parents approved of the way the school dealt with William's high spirits, and believed it was providing a good initial grounding for the future. It was an easy decision to let Harry follow in his big brother's footsteps. The school had put in extra security precautions when William joined two years previously. This included special locks on the door, so there was little more to be done for his brother.

Harry's first day was 16 September 1987, one day after his third birthday. Charles and Diana managed to put their personal woes behind them for a short time and decided to make it a family event. At 9.45am the couple turned up at the school gates in a royal limousine with William as well as Harry, while a bevy of photographers waited behind a barrier.

William got out first and smiled at the cameras. Harry followed looking tense and nervous and holding his small Thomas the Tank Engine sausage bag very tightly. He stayed close to his mother as she led him across the pavement to meet and shake hands with Mrs Mynors. Diana also told Harry to wave at the cameras, which he did with a smile. William, supremely confident that he knew the ropes, then grasped his brother's shoulder, spun him round to face the school stairs and frogmarched him down to the basement towards his classroom. Harry managed to get away from him and was close to tears until his mother caught up with them, hugged him tightly and then gently led him to join eleven other children in Cygnets, the youngest of the school's three classes.

He was given his own coat hook labelled 'Harry' and a blue painting smock labelled 'Prince Harry'. Two hours later he reappeared outside the school gate accompanied by his detective and peeking through his morning's work – a pair of binoculars made from two toilet roll tubes. It sparked a public outcry that holding toilet rolls to his eyes was unhygienic. Mrs Mynors refused to comment.

Once both princes were at school Diana ensured that their school holidays, sports days and nativity plays were meticulously entered into her diary. This enabled her team to plot her royal duties around her motherly ones. Whenever possible she also ensured that she drove her sons to and from school. Her presence at the start and end of his school day helped Harry, as he found the first few weeks at nursery quite traumatic. Unlike William he needed lots of reassurance and understanding. Even today he sometimes has an air of vulnerability and sadness. It's part of what has endeared him to so many people of all ages and types around the world and perhaps why Meghan Markle sometimes feels the need to be motherly towards him.

Also unlike William, it took Prince Harry a few years before he became the life and soul of the playground. When it was break time at the nursery he initially refused to join in the games and when another child approached him he'd run away, hide in a quiet corner of the playground or sit by himself on a bench, often close to tears. One mother remarked that he was 'as quiet as a mouse, poor little thing'. Occasionally he would stand alone for the entire ten-minute break and if another child came up to him and pulled at his clothes, often as a way of getting him to join in a game, he would start crying. It must have been difficult for his bodyguard, who was always close by, not to comfort him but with orders 'not to interfere', he didn't come to Harry's aid.

It was equally difficult to get Harry to speak to the other children and even to his teachers. He also rarely held up his hand in class to ask to go to the toilet. Instead the teachers had to look out for him wriggling and with a pained expression on his face before taking him to the bathroom. His vulnerability made him an easy target for bullies, especially as he didn't fight back. On the positive side, he concentrated hard when the teacher read stories to the class and he enjoyed painting and making paper models.

Sharp-eyed teachers also noted that whenever one of them praised William for being good at something like clay modelling, if Harry was doing the same thing he would throw his own work on the floor. It was perhaps an early sign that he was going to do things his way. He seemed happiest in his own little world, left alone to get on with what he wanted to do and how he wanted to do it, without interference.

A leading psychologist stated at the time that sending Harry to the same nursery as his extrovert brother was a big mistake; vulnerable children like him who were put under pressure to compete would certainly fail. This meant his childhood 'risked being a nightmare'. Time has proved that Harry can function well both on his own and with his brother, and by the time he reached his early thirties he was regularly stealing the royal spotlight away from William with his instinctive charm and gentle mischief-making.

As Harry got used to the nursery's routine and the other children he gradually came out of his shell, and once during his first term felt courageous enough tell another child: 'Mummy doesn't go to Sainsbury's – we have our own farm.' He was also given the part of a non-speaking goblin in the school nativity play. At one point he came out of character to wave at his mother sitting smiling in the front row.

Harry caught several of the normal childhood illnesses, including chickenpox and various virus infections, during the early days at nursery. When he was four he had a hernia operation. A congenital groin issue, said to be an undescended testicle, was corrected at the same time. Diana stayed all night with him at the hospital sleeping on a mattress on the floor in his room. Charles continued his Italian painting holiday but telephoned home every hour. By now their marriage had become a cold and empty shell. The operation went according to plan and Harry returned to nursery nine days later. This time he dashed inside enthusiastically. He emerged two hours later proudly holding two paintings, one of a brilliant orange sunset, which no doubt went straight up on the wall in his nursery.

Shortly after Harry's hernia operation his bodyguard

David Sharp left royal service. For weeks afterwards Harry kept bursting into tears that he was no longer around and years later still regularly asked Diana when he was coming back. It was an early example of how when Harry really cares for someone he finds it very hard when they leave him.

Sharp was not the only person around the little prince that he developed a strong attachment to. Another was James Hewitt, the redheaded Guards officer who became Diana's riding instructor and then her lover. She admitted she 'adored' him during the now famous 1995 interview on BBC's *Panorama* documentary. Decades later, one of the first things people ask about Prince Harry is whether his biological father is Hewitt rather than Prince Charles. Although the likeness between Hewitt and Harry is extraordinary, particularly when Harry was in his twenties and clean-shaven, it has been firmly stated by many, including Hewitt himself, that he wasn't Harry's father and that he and Diana didn't know each other until after Harry was born. Hewitt announced in 2002: 'Admittedly, the colour of [Harry's] hair is similar to mine and people say we look alike. I have never encouraged these comparisons and although I was with Diana for a long time I must state once and for all that I'm not Harry's father. When I met Diana he was already a toddler.'

The soldier-mad toddler was fascinated by everything to do with the army, so it's no surprise he took to Hewitt straight away. He wore a military uniform, rode horses and made his mummy happy. Harry was always incredibly close to his mother and when Diana showed strong feelings for Hewitt he followed her example. Harry initially called him 'mummy's friend' and subsequently the more intimate 'Uncle' James, a sobriquet Diana encouraged both boys to use for her subsequent lovers.

Harry was engrossed by Hewitt's military stories and thrilled when he arrived at Kensington Palace, and he and William were allowed to come downstairs after their bath and spend time with him. Hewitt encouraged Harry's affection and had a miniature Household Cavalry uniform made especially for him. Harry adored it and wore it nearly to threads. Hewitt also took him to visit Combermere Barracks in Windsor, home of the Household Cavalry, and let him climb on a life-sized tank. Harry was in his element and announced excitedly: 'I'm going to be a soldier when I grow up.'

At the time Harry was too young to notice Hewitt's flaws. When I met Hewitt in the late 1990s, I found him to be self-centred and not very bright. He also had a rather grand opinion of himself and felt sure that his devoted attention brought about Diana's metamorphosis from shy, gawky girl to the most beautiful woman in the world. He told me: 'I gave her confidence in every way and she relied on me a lot... She clearly adored me and I like to think I helped her. She was very vulnerable.'

Rumours about Charles and Diana's alleged affairs and the collapse of their marriage had been circulating in the media since their honeymoon and gathered momentum each year. In the mid-1980s an allegation was made that Diana had become too close to Sergeant Barry Mannakee, a police officer with the Royal Protection Squad who began working for her when Prince Harry was one. A year later he was suddenly assigned to other duties and died in a road traffic accident in 1987, giving rise to unsubstantiated claims that his death was not an accident. Mannakee was nearly fifteen years older than Diana, listened to her woes, saw how vulnerable she was and tried to support her. He must have been very important to her, as she talked about him to her speech coach Peter Settelen seven years later, on tapes which were broadcast in the earlier mentioned Channel 4 documentary. She confessed to him that she was desperate for friends, that he was 'the greatest friend I have ever had' and that she understood that she 'played with fire and got burnt'. She also said she was heartbroken when he died.

Her relationship with Hewitt continued for five years when, much to her displeasure, he was posted to Germany and then to Iraq at the start of the first Gulf War. Harry later confided in an army colleague that despite being just five years old he had noticed a distinct change in his mother's mood when Hewitt was posted to Germany. Diana had by then renewed her acquaintance with James Gilbey, whom she had known before she married Prince Charles. He belonged to the Gilbey's gin family and at the time worked as a Lotus car dealer. He was also renowned for his ability to make the women he came across feel special. He and Diana met at a party hosted by Julia Samuel, daughter of the Guinness brewing family. At the end of the evening Diana gave him her telephone number and urged him to call. He did and they met several times in the ensuing weeks. Harry did not like Gilbey, who referred to him and William as the 'lovebugs'.

As a result he wouldn't comply with his mother's wish to call him 'uncle'. At the same time as having a relationship with Gilbey, Diana wrote what is believed to have been more than a hundred passionate letters to Hewitt. But by the time he returned to the UK she refused to take his calls. In 1992 intimate phone calls between Diana and Gilbey that had taken place in 1989 were released to the press. They were dubbed 'Squidgygate' because during the calls Gilbey called Diana 'Squidgy' or 'Squidge' fifty-three times, but only called her 'darling' fourteen times.

By this time Prince Charles was living at Highgrove while Diana remained at Kensington Palace. Although Harry and William were young enough to be protected from the media's intense interest in their parents' shenanigans, small children quickly pick up on a hostile atmosphere between their parents even though they dare not talk about it. It can be very scary for them too as it undermines their stability and they can feel their parents' unhappiness is their fault.

A report by the Early Intervention Foundation (EIF) in 2016 found that 'ongoing conflict between parents can affect a child's mental health, the development of their social and emotional skills, academic attainment – and can impact their ability to form future relationships. It can also damage their physical health, lasting through their adult lives and into the next generation. And it starts ... as young as six months ... The reality is [children are] highly perceptive and attuned to how their parents relate to each other.' The EIF also found that the children of divorced parents are 'more damaged by the arguments that occurred during the marriage, than by the split itself'. Although they had so much of what money can buy, the early years were tough for both princes and undoubtedly affected their development.

Meanwhile, a despairing Prince Charles wrote to a friend: 'How awful incompatibility is. How dreadfully destructive it can be for the players in this extraordinary drama.' He turned to his former lover and close friend Camilla Parker Bowles, believing she was the only person who could comfort him and understand his woes – some friends thought he was on the verge of a nervous breakdown.

Charles and Camilla had originally met at a polo match in 1970 and subsequently became close. However in 1974 she married British army officer Andrew Parker Bowles. They had two children, Laura and Tom, but she divorced him in 1995. Camilla and Charles were always in touch, but it was denied their relationship was sexual during his marriage until after its collapse.

Perhaps partly because of the turmoil at home, the princes built up their own particularly strong bond. Like most small boys they fought a lot but William was very protective of Harry if anyone tried to hurt him. He watched out for his manners too. They had improved but Harry had developed a habit of sticking out his tongue. This is possibly not his fault. Press photographers in search of a better picture would stick their tongues out at Harry to try to goad him to do the same to them. For a while he automatically stuck his tongue out whenever he saw a cameraman. This stopped in August 1988 when William thoroughly told him off. Harry had gone with his mother and brother to the Portland Hospital in central

London to visit his new cousin Princess Beatrice, the first child of Sarah, Duchess of York and Prince Andrew. As the royal car drove away, Harry poked out his tongue and blew raspberries through the window at the gathered press. William, now a bossy six-year-old, said: 'Stop it Harry, that is very naughty.' He did.

A few months later, despite this behavioural slip-up, Harry was considered to be old enough to join the royal family on the balcony of Buckingham Palace for the first time to watch the Trooping the Colour ceremony. He stood in front of Diana who held him tight and kept tickling his cheeks during the display.

At the time the royals rarely if ever showed their emotions in public, not least because it was frowned on by the Queen, but Diana no longer wanted to conform. Although Prince Charles followed in the footsteps of his mother and put duty before family, Diana began to take increasing pleasure in rebelling against royal tradition. She felt all the royals had let her down. Perhaps too she initially felt it was the only way she could make an impact. She refused to dress William and Harry in the velvet-collared coats and short trousers that Charles had worn when he was a child. She enjoyed dressing glamorously and wanted her children to look smart and modern, too. Instead she chose matching outfits like double-breasted powder blue coats with a white trim, polo shirts and long shorts in blue and white. Many years later in an ITV documentary, Prince Harry took pleasure in mocking what he wore. 'I genuinely think she got satisfaction out of dressing myself and William up in the most bizarre outfits

– normally matching. I wore weird shorts and little shiny shoes... Looking back at the photos, it just makes me laugh and I think: "How could you do this to us?"'

He was also self-conscious about the page-boy outfit he had to wear when he was five for the wedding of Diana's brother Charles and his first wife, model Victoria Lockwood, at St Mary's Church, Great Brington, close to Althorp House. Harry described it as a 'bit girlish' and particularly resented wearing a dark green hat trimmed with burgundy taffeta. He obviously had ideas on style at a very young age.

Diana also enjoyed planning conspiracies with her boys, some of which verged on the reckless. In September 1988, when the family were as usual staying at Balmoral for the summer, she evaded her security minders and the police by creeping out with Harry very early one morning and driving nine miles to the Craigendarroch Hotel, which had a luxury leisure centre. She arrived at 7am and took Harry for a swim. A member of hotel staff said at the time: 'Princess Diana seemed a bit nervous on her own', and that usually the hotel manager was told in advance when a member of the royal family would turn up so the police could check the hotel and grounds. The hotel staff recognised her and told their manager, who rang the police, and within minutes two unmarked cars arrived at the hotel to ensure her and Harry's safety.

She also behaved irresponsibly in March 1993 a year after her official separation when she was on a skiing holiday in Lech, Austria, with William and Harry. Their bodyguard Ken Wharfe described how Diana and the boys were guarded 'all the time', but one night Diana jumped out of the window of her suite on the first floor, which had a 20ft drop into the snow – and stayed out all night. Her antics were only discovered at 5.30am the next day when she rang the doorbell to the exclusive Albert Hotel. Her excuse was: 'I needed some air.'

September 1989 marked the time Harry had to take a five-year-old's giant step and move from nursery to big school. He arrived at Wetherby's pre-prep school in Notting Hill four days before his fifth birthday and four days after the term began due to a viral infection. This time he had no misgivings and raced along the pavement to greet his new headmistress, Miss Frederika Blair. He shook her hand, then with a confident smile and, keeping his tongue firmly inside his mouth, turned and smiled at the cameramen who were eager to catch his reaction to his new school. He strode confidently up the steps of the boys-only school accompanied by the Princess of Wales and William before joining the other twelve boys and teacher Alexandra Barnes in Form One Green.

Harry initially attended mornings only and on his first day made a model of an elephant, an animal that remains a favourite of his. Harry, who is believed to be mildly dyslexic, found schoolwork difficult, but he enjoyed being in the school. Just before the end of term he sang a Christmas solo at the school's carol concert at St Matthew's Church, Bayswater. Several in the audience, including Princess Diana, brushed away a tear at his rendition of 'Rudolf the Red-Nosed Reindeer'. Not to be outdone, seven-year-old William, who had started at the school two years earlier, also sang a solo number – a chorus of 'Gloria in Excelsis Deo'. The princess took her mother, Frances Shand Kydd, to the show and said she was 'as pleased as punch' with their efforts and the fact that they were both in tune.

Diana's relationship with her mother was volatile and there were often blocks of time when she refused to speak to her. Diana was particularly affected by her parents' separation and in her child's mind interpreted her mother moving away as abandoning her because she didn't love her enough. It fuelled her lifelong insecurity. William and Harry enjoyed seeing their maternal grandmother and often called her 'Supergran'. Despite the distance from her home on the island of Seil, near Oban in Scotland, she'd occasionally travel down to Highgrove to try to break the long, icy silences between Diana and Charles and create a better atmosphere for William and Harry. When mother and daughter were going through a good patch, Diana would take her sons to her mother's whitewashed farmhouse on the remote island, where they spent time by the sea and played in the countryside.

Harry's increasing naughtiness began to cause trouble. When he was five he asked bodyguard Ken Wharfe if he could use his police radio. It seemed an innocent request but nearly turned into a major disaster. Wharfe recounts what happened in his book, *Diana: Closely Guarded Secret*: 'Because he was such an endearing character I handed it over. We invented a game. I told him to go to specific locations within the palace and check in over the radio.' Harry complied and radioed from a couple of safe locations.

All then went quiet until Wharf remembers: 'He radioed in to inform me he'd gone to the record shop on Kensington High Street ... what shoppers must have thought to see the Queen's grandson walking alone down the busy street clutching a police radio, I have no idea. I ordered him to come back and ran to meet him, but I knew we'd been on the verge of a security disaster. The Metropolitan Police would have taken a very dim view, but that's nothing compared to what the Princess would have said. Luckily she never found out.'

It was an early example of Harry's recklessness – one moment he would be behaving and the next going off the rails. As he grew older a combination of lack of self-control, poor judgment and too much alcohol resulted in him, for example, wearing a swastika at a fancy-dress party, taking off all his clothes during a game of strip billiards in Las Vegas, and jumping from the balcony of the Goring Hotel the night before his brother's marriage.

Prince Charles agreed that Diana could also choose the princes' next school. She picked Ludgrove School, a £2,350-a-term independent boarding school in Berkshire founded in 1892. It could accommodate around 180 boys aged 8–13. The then-headmaster Gerald Barber described the school ethos: 'We tried to turn out a fellow with good values, good friendships and enthusiasm and doing well.'

It made sense to remove William and Harry from the emotional turmoil and animosity at home. Boarding also meant they were kept away from the now daily maelstrom in the press of innuendo, gossip and jaw-dropping facts about both parents' behaviour. Before William could join the school the 130-acre grounds were re-fenced, every glass window was reinforced, and video cameras were installed at strategic positions. In addition, bodyguards sat in the classrooms and occasionally told the princes to behave.

William went off to Ludgrove in September 1990. Harry was to follow in 1992. It was around this time that the behaviour of both boys began to change. Now they were eight and six respectively their manners significantly improved. They were used to shaking hands, saying thank you and, as they got older, writing thank-you notes. Meanwhile, the difference between their personalities widened. William was becoming more independent but increasingly wary and withdrawn, while Harry was becoming more unpredictable and naughty, traits he told me he still relishes. Diana knew Harry could behave badly but often brushed off his misdemeanours with a laugh, merely saying Harry 'got into mischief'.

He also began to realise how good he was at making people laugh. One of his favourite songs at that time was a variation of a traditional nursery rhyme, which went as follows: 'Humpty Dumpty sat on a wall eating squashed bananas. Where do you think he put the skins? Down the king's pyjamas.'

They liked different things to eat too. William had a more sophisticated palate and loved home-grown vegetables, fruit and poached eggs from the hens at the Highgrove estate. Harry adored more traditional children's food like fish fingers, fry-ups, beans on toast, hamburgers, Coca-Cola and endless chocolate. During school holidays Diana regularly treated them to lunch in restaurants but kept sweet things to a minimum.

She desperately wanted her children to have the stability that she missed as a child and for them to feel truly loved and wanted. 'I want to bring them up securely,' she said. 'I love my children to death and get into bed with them at night,' adding: 'I am just demented about my own children. And it's mutual.' She grew closer to them as her relationship with Charles fell apart, but in practice she seemed to forget that she was an adult and they were the children. This role reversal resulted in her increasingly leaning on William, telling him her troubles, discussing her lovers and becoming emotionally dependent on him. It was a heavy burden to place on his young shoulders, as his perception and experience were limited to those of a young boy. Nonetheless he tried to be the man of the house and felt responsible for his mother's state of mind and happiness. In the 2017 ITV programme *Diana, Our Mother: Her Life and Legacy*, to commemorate the twentieth anniversary of her death, he expressed his long-lasting guilt that he 'let our mother down' because he 'couldn't protect her'. It was heartbreaking to hear.

Harry didn't have the unenviable role of man of the house, but when William went to boarding school Diana sought comfort in his presence. She took him with her whenever she could and particularly if there was a royal family event she had to attend. Once there she would often cling to him like a human comfort blanket. She showered him with love and kisses and the bond between them grew even stronger. Harry is much more emotional than his brother, but gave me the impression that he suffered slightly less than William from her sometimes desperate need for him, but perhaps even more than his brother from her loss.

Overall, however, contrary to expert opinion and statistics, time has shown that the intensity of Diana's love for her sons not only gave them the courage and strength they needed to work through their troubled and traumatic childhood, but also a humanitarian legacy on which to base their goals.

Despite feeling bereft without her boys, Diana accepted them going to boarding school with resilience and selflessness. She told a friend: 'I'm not going to be sad because it's best for Harry', adding: 'Too many people stared at us every morning when we went to his previous school. Tourists used to hang out of hotel windows watching us. He won't have to put up with that at Ludgrove.' She also took comfort from feeling that Harry would cope easily with leaving home. 'He is a real little joker, full of fun and loves meeting new people.'

Both boys were encouraged to develop extracurricular activities. William was keen on football (he ended up in the Ludgrove First XI), tennis and the high jump. Harry was better than his brother at riding, mountain-biking and skiing. The first time he rode Smokey, his Shetland pony, he was so at ease his groom Marion Cox, who regularly accompanied him down the lanes around Highgrove, found it difficult to believe he had never ridden before. He seemed to have the same special way with horses as he was beginning to show with people. Although he could be reckless and loud he knew when to be gentle with a horse and those he rode seemed to recognise this.

William and Harry's first skiing trip took place in April 1991, when Diana took them to the Austrian skiing resort of Lech, without Charles. Paul Harris, then a *Daily Mail* reporter, was sent to report on their trip. He told me:

Soon after I got to the nursery slopes, William, then eight, and Harry, six, arrived with their police protection officers and instructor. I think it was only their second day of tuition but it soon became obvious they had learned quickly, despite the fact that much of the snow was turning to slush at that time.

What was instantly apparent was the difference between the pair in the way they approached this new sport. At the top of the slope, on his first long run, Harry crouched down, tucked his arms into his side and launched himself with melodramatic gusto. He sped downhill in a straight line at maximum speed and let out a Geronimo-style exclamation. His face was contorted with excitement and he laughed out loud when he reached the end of the run.

'William, meanwhile, stayed where he was, motionless. If I had to guess I would say he was crying. After a few moments with his instructor he skied gingerly to about halfway down the slope and came to a gentle halt, while Harry was already tramping uphill again for a second go. I think I had witnessed an intriguing dissimilarity in the character of the young princes – one that would repeatedly show itself in their adult lives.'

Harry was equally fearless in water. When he was eight, he, his mother and William went away on a friend's yacht in the Aegean. One day he dived more than 30ft from the stern of the boat into the water below, then roared with laughter as he surfaced.

Both boys loved to go shooting with their father when they went to stay at Balmoral, but initially stood around with toy guns and imitated him. Diana disliked hunting intensely and particularly didn't want Charles to take them fox hunting, but he didn't listen, perhaps because he could see his sons enjoyed it so much. He did, however, make a small compromise by taking Harry hare coursing rather than to a fox hunt. Diana felt it was just as bad as animals were still going to be killed during the chase.

The year 1992 was a tough year for the royal family. The Queen referred to it as her 'annus horribilis' in a speech in November to mark the fortieth anniversary of her Accession. On 19 March it was announced that the Duke and Duchess of York had separated and would be seeking a divorce. This was soon followed by news that Diana's father, Earl Spencer, had been admitted to hospital with pneumonia. Although the Earl had been suffering from a heart condition, it was not thought to be dangerous enough to stop the princess taking another break skiing in Lech. She went to see her father in hospital on Wednesday 25 March the day before the planned holiday to reassure herself that it was safe to leave him. The Prince of Wales was to join Diana and their sons as an attempt at family togetherness in their increasingly cold marriage. The Princess had also invited some of the princes' friends to join them – eight-year-old Harry Soames, seven-year-old George Grumbar and the princes' cousin eleven-year-old Laura Fellowes, daughter of Diana's sister Jane.

Viscount Linley, Charles's cousin, was also coming. The holiday began as a great success and the princes thoroughly enjoyed skiing and tobogganing in the snow. Diana contacted the hospital every day: she was told her father was doing well and happily monitoring England's progress in the cricket World Cup. Three days into the holiday Diana was in an excellent mood, even laughingly offering reporters piggyback rides down the mountain. She, Charles, William and Harry had lunch together in a mountain chalet undeterred by flurries of snow whipped up by the biting wind. The princess then retired to her room at the Hotel Arlberg and soon afterwards appeared on the balcony with wet hair, dressed in a white towelling bathrobe. She was watching William and Harry enjoying a snowball fight with their father and friends when the telephone rang. She answered it, went back to the window and told the photographers to go away. A Palace spokesman informed the press that Diana had just received the news of her father's death. Earl Spencer had suffered a heart attack at 2pm. He died almost immediately and, the hospital said, peacefully. He also died alone. Charles broke the news to his sons who were both extremely fond of their grandfather. After some minutes of silence, Harry asked: 'Does this mean we can't go skiing today?'

Diana remained behind the closed shutters with Charles for hours, although how much comfort he was able to give her at this point in their marriage is questionable. She wanted to return home immediately but no plane was available and they had to wait until the following morning. They agreed to spare the young princes the trauma of the funeral and left them on holiday with their then nanny, Jessie Webb.

In August 1992, Andrew Morton's explosive biography *Diana: Her True Story* was published. It wasn't known at the time that Morton had Diana's agreement and had used her own words. It contained allegations of adultery, self-harming and eating disorders and became an instant bestseller, one that destroyed any illusions about her and Charles's marriage. Coming as it did in the middle of the school holidays, it must have left William mortified that his classmates and teachers would know so much personal information about him. No wonder the ten-year-old became very withdrawn.

Although Harry coped better on the surface, if he had been looking forward to going to his new prep school, the book must have also filled him with dread at the thought of meeting fellow pupils. As well as shattering Charles and Diana's public façade, the book also highlighted Diana's lack of judgment and perhaps mental ill-health, as surely it cannot by any stretch of the imagination be the willing action of a mother who loved her children beyond anything else.

★ ★ ★

Harry's first term at Ludgrove began on 7 September 1992. He arrived with his trunks, tuckbox and two personal detectives. He was shown his dormitory: it slept four other boys and was smaller than a footman's bedroom at Buckingham Palace. There were iron bedsteads and a linoleum floor, but boys were allowed to decorate the walls with posters of pop stars, cars and planes. Royal titles were ignored by the school, but Harry's royal status meant he would be called by his first name rather than his surname like the other boys. New boys were also given the nickname 'squits'. His school uniform was blue or grey corduroy trousers, blue shirt and blue V-neck sweater.

The school matron woke the boys up at 7.15am. The routine was that they then went to the communal bathroom to wash and brush their teeth. Prayers followed in the oak-panelled dining room decorated with the names of old boys. Lessons started immediately after breakfast for the fourteen boys in Harry's class. A brand-new 130-acre, £500,000 sports complex had just been completed and there was fencing, swimming, riding, table tennis, soccer, clay-pigeon shooting and even a nine-hole golf course for Harry to choose from. The lunch bell rang at 12:20pm and the 180 or so boys would make their way to the dining room. They had to eat a portion of fresh fruit every day. Sweets were only allowed three times a week. Harry was, however, allowed to ask his mother to send cake for a treat. Dinner was served at 5.20pm. The boys were allowed to watch selected TV progammes early each evening and at weekends. *Neighbours*, the Australian soap opera starring Kylie Minogue was allowed, while the grittier *EastEnders* was not. Bedtime for junior boys was 6.30pm with a compulsory quiet period in which to read before lights were switched off at 8pm.

Harry was allowed one phone call a week to his mother and he would get three weekends at home each 12-week term. Pocket money was restricted to £5 a term. The school was known for its discipline but there was no corporal punishment. Bad behaviour or wrongdoing was punished with weekend detention, going to bed early or losing the sweet allowance. Diana found it difficult that she couldn't speak to Harry every day, give him huge hugs and especially not be able to tuck him up in bed at night.

Harry had only been at school for a few weeks when a member of staff mentioned that his mother was coming to see him. It seemed rather strange, particularly when he and William were taken by a teacher into a private room to wait for Diana to arrive. In a voice barely above a whisper and looking down at the floor to avoid seeing their faces, she told them that the following day the Prime Minister, John Major, was going to announce in Parliament that she and their father were separating and wouldn't be living together any more. William burst into tears but Harry's instant comment – 'I hope you will both be happier now' – revealed how perceptive he was. He also asked if there was anything he could do to make Mummy and Daddy happy again.

Harry's seeming ability to cope, his ease with people and general gusto led Diana to believe that he would handle being king more easily than William. She even called him Good King Harry. According to Chris Hutchins's book *Harry: The People's Prince*, a passenger on a flight sitting close to Diana and Harry overheard her ask him what would he do if he had to take William's place and be the next king. Apparently

Harry thought for a few seconds and replied: 'I shall be King Harry. I shall do all the work.' Diana felt less confident in William. '[William] doesn't want to be king and I worry about that. He doesn't want his every move watched.' In fact both boys were damaged but handled the break-up in different ways.

It was bad timing that the princes' nanny Jessie Webb had just left. She had started working for the royals five years previously. She managed the children confidently, believing that they should be treated as ordinary boys rather than spoilt princes, and they both became very fond of her. (William later asked her to come out of retirement to help part time when Prince George was a baby). She also took responsibility for removing them when the animosity between their parents created a strained atmosphere. She would try to distract their attention, especially when their mother was weeping. Almost inevitably, she too became the object of Diana's jealousy by growing close to her boys. Diana stopped speaking to her and it was agreed that she would leave once Harry started at Ludgrove. Coinciding as it did with the announcement that Diana and Charles were separating, the timing was terrible and both boys must have felt totally abandoned. The feeling of abandonment is difficult for a child to manage and can make it difficult for them when they are older to trust a partner.

Once Jessie left, her deputy Olga Powell finally took over the top job. Later, on the day that Harry heard about his parents separating, he reached out to her by letter to tell her the news. Mrs Powell, who Harry called Granny Nanny, was not easily given to tears, but she said she cried throughout the day she received his letter.

On 9 December 1992, the day after Diana went to the school to warn her sons, both boys joined Gerald Barber, their headmaster, in his study to hear John Major announce the official separation of their parents to a packed House of Commons: 'It is announced from Buckingham Palace that, with regret, the Prince and Princess of Wales have decided to separate. Their Royal Highnesses have no plans to divorce and their constitutional positions are unaffected. This decision has been reached amicably and they will both continue to participate fully in the upbringing of their children.' To hear such news without a parent to give reassurance and a hug must have been an unimaginable strain, particularly as they had to maintain a stiff upper lip in the presence of the headmaster.

Harry phoned his mother three days later and asked her to come to the school for tea. While she was there she talked to teachers about how the boys were getting on and found out that although Harry had made a good start he had subsequently regressed and was showing little or no interest in most subjects, a sign no doubt that his damaged background had begun to take its toll.

CHAPTER 4

A Broken Home

Harry's brave and mature comment when his parents separated – 'I hope you both will be happier now' – not only showed how aware he was of his parents' misery, but that he was also trying to put their needs above his own. Unfortunately the acrimony between them became worse rather than better after they separated. They both tried to score points against each other, often speaking through friends who would blame the one they weren't supporting for the irreparable collapse of the marriage.

In the early 1990s, divorce was less common and carried more of a stigma than it does today. So although William and Harry were unlikely to have been the only children at school who had a broken home, divorce only affected a small minority. None of them, however, would have had the excruciating experience of having their parent's mutual antagonism played out in front of the whole world. Being at boarding school did mean the princes were protected from some of the more lurid details that appeared in the media but they were no doubt the source of much whispering among their peers.

Christmas is always a difficult time for children from a broken home and William and Harry, like other children of warring parents, were pulled in different directions as Charles and Diana fought to spend it with them but not each other. The festival, coming just a few weeks after the break-up, was the start of future exeats, and holidays spent toing and froing between the parents.

It was made clear to Diana that William and Harry would unquestionably spend Christmas 1992 with their father and the rest of the royal family at Sandringham. The Queen, however, issued a personal invitation, that was both a royal command and a peace gesture, for Diana to join them; she initially accepted and then cancelled. The festivities would have been very awkward for Diana but her presence would have undoubtedly helped William and Harry to enjoy themselves. It may not be coincidental that Harry took his first defiant puff of a cigarette that same year when he was only eight.

It wasn't until the summer of 2017 in a TV interview that Harry openly and neatly summarised his and William's plight: 'The two of us were bouncing between the two of them and we never saw our mother enough or we never saw our father enough ... there was a lot of travelling and a lot of fights on the back seat with my brother... which I would win.' He also confessed: 'As a kid I never enjoyed speaking to my parents on the phone. We spent far too much time speaking on the phone rather than speaking to each of them because of [the divorce] ... So there was all of that to contend with. And I don't pretend that we're the only people to have to deal with that. But it was an interesting way of growing up.'

Adapting to parents who had very different attitudes to life was not easy, especially as Diana's way of dealing with her children could be contradictory and inconsistent.

On the plus side, Diana wanted her boys to feel positive about their life, despite the separation. She gave them a broader horizon than most royals, encouraged them to appreciate that they had far more than most people and that they should work hard. To underline her point she took them both to a shelter in Westminster where they met a number of homeless men who owned little more than the clothes they were wearing. Harry told me how grateful he is: 'My mother took a huge part in showing me an ordinary life, including taking me and my brother to see homeless people. Thank goodness I'm not completely cut off from reality.'

Despite her own privileged background Diana was instinctively driven to help people who had very few chances in life. She could have had no idea at the time what a lasting and powerful effect this would have on their lives. Both sons wanted to follow in her footsteps. Helping those in need or shunned by society has become the bedrock of their royal beings.

Their 'more normal' existence also contained lots of fun.

Harry described his mother as 'a total kid through and through', whose motto was 'you can be as naughty as you want, just don't get caught'.

Unusually for a royal she was also very demonstrative in public and showed how much she loved her sons with uninhibited hugs and kisses. She enjoyed taking them on roller coaster rides, even to the extent of getting soaked whizzing down a water slide in fits of laughter. They also went to shows and pop concerts, although instead of queuing like ordinary people they were usually reverently ushered inside to their seats and would often meet the stars backstage afterwards. They would play tennis with her at the Harbour Club in Chelsea, ride BMX bikes, go go-karting and be regulars at McDonald's. The boys enjoyed special treats too. When Harry was nine Diana took him with her when she went to review her regiment, the Light Dragoons, in Germany, where he was thrilled to be allowed to ride on a tank and observe a mock battle.

Although she did her best to keep them happy and safe, she didn't or couldn't protect them from her mood swings and in the later part of her life seemed to lose sight of what was best for them. Nor was she discreet over the men she had relationships with. Instead she encouraged them to bond with her men friends who came to the palace, and she leant on both children, but especially William, far too heavily for emotional support. Nor did she seem to try to hide her changes of mood or her tears. Instead she expected them to help her cope with her feelings of isolation, rejection and depression, a need they didn't have the maturity or experience to manage.

Young children need to be looked after by their parent, not the other way round. She would no doubt have been horrified to know that turning her children into surrogate parents was profoundly damaging and using them both to protect her was nothing less than exploitative. Equally, that emotional mistreatment can have the same damaging affect as physical neglect. A psychologist explained: 'It is the type of behaviour that, when a child grows into an adult, leads him to believe that other people's needs are always more important than his own, that he always has to be mature or "grown-up" and most significantly that he cannot rely on people to be there for him. A child is also likely to feel a failure and ashamed when they cannot make their parent feel better.'

When one of Diana's relationships broke up she soon found a new man to love. She quickly fell for British Pakistani heart surgeon Dr Hasnat Khan, then thirty-six, who she called 'the one'. Wise, unselfish mothers protect their children from meeting possibly transient men in their lives, but Diana introduced Dr Khan to the boys early on in the relationship and he stayed regularly at Kensington Palace. She even began investigating mixed-faith marriages and asked how they would feel if she married Khan, who was a practising Muslim.

Her action highlights the huge gap in her understanding of the difference between confiding in a close friend who could tell her the truth, and young boys who must have been frightened that she might overreact if they said something she didn't wanted to hear. In fact the boys got on well with Dr Khan, but the bond didn't last. He disliked the intrusive personal publicity, nor did he want to offend his Muslim relatives, and broke off the relationship. Yet again the princes lost another adult they were beginning to trust, just as they had lost their nannies. Diana also introduced them to Will Carling, former captain of England's rugby team, which was particularly awkward as he was married. The sad truth was that after her marriage failed she seemed to seek out other unsuitable men in her search for love.

★ ★ ★

Based at Highgrove, Charles was consumed with guilt that he had made Diana so unhappy and in doing so had also let down the Queen, the Queen Mother, Prince Philip, his sons and the British people. He found a rare moment of solace in a letter he received from his normally critical father, who wrote that he felt Charles had displayed the 'fortitude of a saint' by putting up with Diana.

He was also keen to rebuild his image as a caring father. His sons would now be coming regularly to Highgrove so he asked twenty-eight-year-old Alexandra Legge-Bourke, known as Tiggy – a name that stuck because of the Beatrix Potter stories she loved as a child – to help. She was ready and very willing. Her mother and aunt had been ladies-in-waiting to Princess Anne. She had run her own nursery, called Tiggywinkles, and had also worked as an assistant to Charles's private secretary Richard Aylard. Tiggy was an adventurous, uncomplicated enthusiast who particularly enjoyed skiing, riding, fishing and shooting. She also readily took the princes to pony clubs, gymkhanas, polo lessons and tea with their friends. And she could get them to do as they were told without being overtly strict. Tiggy was such a success that she was soon joining Charles and the boys when they went on holiday or stayed at Sandringham or Balmoral.

When William and Harry came to Highgrove Charles tried to arrange for them to have children of around their age to play with. Their cousins Peter and Zara Phillips and Princesses Beatrice and Eugenie, who were also the offspring of divorced parents, regularly came to stay. Tiggy adored both boys and behaved more like an uninhabited big sister than an employee. She did however make the mistake of calling them 'my babies', which made Diana boil with jealousy. The princess felt so threatened by the burgeoning relationship between the three of them that she began to criticise Tiggy constantly, so much so that Camilla Parker Bowles dropped to second place on her bête noir list. She was within her rights to voice her disapproval of Tiggy smoking in front of William and Harry, of course, but became so hostile that she reportedly made a list of dos and don't rules for her to observe. This included that she must leave the room when Diana talked to her sons on the telephone, that she didn't spend 'unnecessary time in the children's rooms ... read to them at night, nor supervise their bathtime nor bedtime. She is to carry out a secretarial role in the arrangement of their time with their father [and] that is all.' She was not to be seen in the same car as William or Harry or be photographed close to them. Diana even accused Charles of having an affair with her. Tiggy gave a teasing response: 'I give them what they [William and Harry] need at this stage, fresh air, a rifle and a horse and she [Diana] gives them a tennis racket and a bucket of popcorn at the movies.'

Harry got on with Tiggy particularly well and they regularly had boisterous pillow fights and waged mock battles. She was, though, a serious risk-taker. In 1998 she took William and Harry to her parents' home in Wales for two days. During their trip she let them both abseil without helmets, safety lines or any advance training off a 160ft high dam wall that was holding back 400 million gallons of water. The picture appeared on the front page of the now defunct *News of the World* with the headline MADNESS! She nearly lost her job, but the princes fought to save their surrogate 'mum'. That same year Harry was photographed hanging out of the back of a Land Rover on the Balmoral estate shooting rabbits through the roof of a moving car that Tiggy was driving while a cigarette was hanging from her lips. She was admonished for this lapse and also for giving Harry an enormous hug when they left church while staying at Sandringham, something the other royals considered inappropriate.

Diana was furious yet again when Tiggy was photographed smoking at the Eton Fourth of June holiday celebrations in 1997. The event is Eton's way of handling speech day and an occasion when family members and Old Etonians look round the school to see various displays of work, watch a cricket match, and the traditional parade of boats from the bank of the River Thames. That year William invited Tiggy to come as his guest rather than his parents, whom he told to keep away. Perhaps he was unsure as to whether they would behave. It was also a way of reducing the chance of the event becoming an embarrassing media scrum with him in the middle.

Tiggy resigned in October 1999 when she married Charles Pettifer, a former Coldstream Guards officer who had two sons from a previous marriage. Harry went to the wedding but was said to have behaved rather exuberantly by swallowing a goldfish from one of the table decorations. Tiggy went on to have two children of her own – Harry is godfather to her eldest son, Fred. She subsequently set up a renowned bed and breakfast business at her home in South Wales. Harry still stays in touch and took Meghan to meet her following an official engagement in Cardiff in January 2018 even though it meant a 40-mile detour.

Harry undertook his first royal engagement just before his eleventh birthday by attending the fiftieth anniversary of VJ Day at the Cenotaph. He was required to salute the officers in the military parade; it made him incredibly proud.

Meanwhile, as much as Diana tried to keep life calm and smooth for the princes, her own personal life was in chaos and she found it tough living alone at Kensington Palace. Once Charles was no longer around she began to free herself from what she regarded as the straitjacket of life as a senior royal. She made both major and minor changes. This included getting rid of cooks, housemaids, dressers and secretaries, often on a whim. She also promoted her butler, Paul Burrell, to run her household, and became increasingly reliant on him.

Against advice, in 1993 she gave up her police protection.

As a result whenever she and the princes were out in public they were hassled by paparazzi. 'They would shout at her and make her angry in the hope she would say something rude to make their story,' Harry told me in disgust, but he did like the way his mother tried to avoid them. 'A daily challenge was our mother driving a convertible BMW listening to [the Irish singer] Enya at full blast and trying to hide us from the press. She wanted to keep us safe.'

Here too Diana was inconsistent. Being in the newspapers more than Charles was part of the one-upmanship that went on during the separation and after the divorce. She would often contact journalists and tell them where she would be and what she would be doing so they would come along.

Dr David Starkey gave me an example of Diana's mixed views about the press. 'She always went on about being as thick as two planks, but she wasn't. She was very media savvy and even invented a new way of communication using posed photographs to get a front-page headline.' The best example is of Diana sitting alone on a bench in front of the Taj Mahal, the world's most beautiful monument to love, during a royal tour in February 1992, eleven months before the separation.

She changed her image by wearing clothes that were sleeker and sexier than would have been considered appropriate for a senior royal. She also reduced the number of charities she was involved with from about a hundred to six. She had had such a magic touch that many of the charities begged her to do just one event a year so they could retain her name on their notepaper and keep donations rolling in.

Unfortunately her thought processes became increasingly irrational to the point of paranoia. She began seeing conspiracies everywhere and as a result she abruptly dropped friends, family and staff, often without any explanation. She came to believe that individuals, including her brother-in-law Sir Robert Fellowes, then the Queen's private secretary, and Prince Philip, wished her dead. She felt the Palace was spying on her and wanted to take away her children. She also found it disconcerting that William and Harry, who were after all second and third in line to the throne, wanted to stay close to the Queen and their father. Her instability and waywardness became an increasing concern for politicians and senior royals who feared she could go completely off the rails and take the children with her. Some felt that the monarchy itself was at risk. A psychiatrist who treated her said: 'I suspect she would have been unwell whoever she was married to. Prince Charles may have exasperated her but ... he did not cause her underlying illness.'

As a result, in January 1994 Labour MP Frank Field, one of the House of Commons' most respected members and chairman of the Social Services Select Committee, pressed Prime Minister John Major to become directly involved in the welfare and upbringing of the two princes. He also requested that 'qualified' outsiders should intervene and assess what was best for them. It was both an appalling indictment of the royal couple and a gross interference on the part of the state. Mr Field was blocked from raising the matter in the Commons itself. Instead he approached *The Mail on Sunday*, which readily published his ideas. These included that the young princes' futures should be monitored by a group of 'wise men'. There was no mention of wise women and one of the potential 'wise men' made the following comment: 'Charles should influence them. They could become mummy's boys. Loving the boys as she does she must know that it cannot be good for their long-term development to be under her beautiful wing for much longer.'

Mr Field also wanted the Prime Minister to appoint 'people of stature' who could 'hold their own with the Court circle' to ask the princes if they were happy with their custody arrangements. He believed the boys should have a say on how they were brought up and the same rights as every child in Britain under the 1989 Children Act. This aims to ensure by various means that children are safeguarded and their welfare promoted. Had Mr Field's proposal been taken up it would have been the royal equivalent of the local council sending in a bevy of social workers to sort out warring parents by making decisions on custody and schooling arrangements. Mr Field had opened a royal Pandora's box that risked forcing a constitutional debate on the future of the monarchy. If William and Harry chose a life that was contrary to how the Queen or Prince Charles wanted them to be raised, and if it was in accord with the Children Act, there could have been a titanic conflict between the monarchy and Parliament. In early 2018 Mr Field spoke to me about his concerns around the welfare of the young princes in the mid-nineties and how his views have changed.

At the time Buckingham Palace kept tight-lipped and refused to comment except to say: 'Arrangements for spending time with their parents are worked out in advance and work very amicably.'

The whole business must have given both Diana and Charles a nasty jolt: shortly afterwards they met in the private apartments of St James's Palace to discuss long-term custody arrangements and the boys' schooling. William was eleven, Harry nine. It was agreed that they would both stay at boarding school and like so many children of broken families divide their holidays between their mother and father.

Unfortunately the jolt wasn't enough to stop both parents continuing to wash their dirty royal linen in public to the inevitable embarrassment of their children. In 1994 Charles gave a tell-all interview on ITV to Jonathan Dimbleby. *Charles: The Private Man, The Public Role* was meant to be a 'charm offensive' to rebuild his image after the damaging separation two years earlier. Instead he admitted he was unfaithful after his marriage 'became irretrievably broken'. Fourteen million people watched him confess to adultery with Camilla Parker Bowles.

The following year in November 1995 Diana conducted her own 'tell-all' hour-long interview on BBC's *Panorama* with Martin Bashir, which took place also in part to gain public sympathy. The day before the programme was shown she visited William at Eton and Harry at Ludgrove to warn them about it. In the bombshell interview she talked about her adulterous affair with James Hewitt, her depression and bulimia, how she cut her wrists with razor blades, the media, her love for her children, and the future of the monarchy. Viewers were agog as she anguished over her husband's relationship with Camilla and how it meant there were 'three of us in this marriage' – an infamous comment that became the most-used description of their failed marriage. She also said she didn't want a divorce.

In retrospect, it is hard to understand how two intelligent parents could continue to behave as they did. William and Harry were at an age when most boys couldn't bear to imagine that their parents even had sex. How much more destabilising and embarrassing for them when their father announces to millions of people round the world that he has returned to a previous lover, while their mother expects them to welcome various lovers, build a relationship with them, but end all contact when the next one turns up. It was bound to damage any feeling of trust. Harry watched the programme at school but loyally took his mother's part. One of his teachers allegedly said that he got very angry with Bashir for asking such intrusive questions. Overall, however, the princes' mood was largely conciliatory. William later said he understood why his mother had wanted to speak out, even though it meant he and Harry learnt things no child should hear about their parents along with the rest of the world via a TV screen.

The Queen reacted quickly and decided enough was enough. Charles and Diana's behaviour in public was becoming a threat to the monarchy. She told, rather than asked, them to end the marriage as quickly as possible. By July 1996 a settlement was reached that was thought to be worth more than £17 million. Diana was allowed to keep her apartment at Kensington Palace as 'a central and secure home for the Princess and the children'. (It is now the official residence and offices of the Duke and Duchess of Cambridge, their children, and Harry and Meghan). Diana was given access to the royal family's jets and was able 'to use the state apartments at St James's Palace for entertaining', as long as she asked the Queen's permission first. She was also permitted to keep all the jewellery she amassed during her marriage, with the exception of the Cambridge Lover's Knot tiara, which the Queen gave to her as a wedding present. (It was lent to the Duchess of Cambridge in both 2015 and 2016.) Diana could also retain the title Princess of Wales but could no longer be called Her Royal Highness, a title that shows that the individual has direct family connection to the crown and assures they will be automatically included in state occasions, which Diana was not. William has never accepted this snub.

Diana's sons were at the centre of her life. 'I love them to death,' she often said, but she did little to help them cope with the trauma of seeing their parents tear themselves apart in public. William, who accepted responsibility for his mother's wellbeing, became more reserved and wary and phoned her constantly when he was at school. Harry, however, gave the impression he was independent, intrepid, and a fun-loving rascal. 'Harry's the naughty one, just like me,' Diana said proudly. It seems he either fooled both his mother and some of the teachers into thinking he was fine or it was wishful thinking on their part. One member of staff added: 'If he is reprimanded by a teacher at school his usual ploy is to mimic his aggressor behind his back and run off laughing... While William is wary of the press, particularly photographers, Harry doesn't mind who watches him, in fact he enjoys it... Harry is fearless. He is so laid-back that very little seems to worry him. Although he looks nervy in photographs he is not in the least.'

What perhaps only Harry knew at the time was that the nervy child in photographs was the real him and the laid-back clown was his front for facing the world and coping with his family situation. Diana must also have felt some concern about how he was coping, as before the separation she went back to the psychiatrist she saw at the beginning of her marriage. The psychiatrist later told author Chris Hutchins that he advised her she could damage both children by involving them in her unstable love life. He said:

It would not be good for them, particularly for Prince Harry, who was already a fighter, and this might well affect him in later years. I never met her younger son but from what she told me he was already starting to rebel. She said he loved his father and admired James Hewitt, but it was obvious from what she told me that when other men came along he started to get not just confused but angry and she was especially worried that Harry was showing signs of the kind that lead in adult life to aggression and addictions of various kinds.

In December 1996, four months after the divorce became final, Diana who thought Harry 'might be unhappy', took him to see an alternative practitioner 'to help him externalise his feelings'.

Prince Charles was also concerned about how Harry was doing at school. He knew he was not a natural scholar, preferred sports to anything else and was struggling to make the grades. He arranged for him to have an independent assessment by an expert that confirmed his worst fears that Harry's performance in class and his general behaviour had been harmed by the manner in which he and Diana had made their private rows public and by their televised confessions of adultery.

These concerns were confirmed when in April 1996, Gerald Barber, headmaster of Ludgrove, told Prince Charles that Harry's school work was not good enough for him to pass the tough entrance exam to Eton. He suggested he stayed on for another year and worked harder, which Harry was not at all keen to do. William had had no problem with the Common Entrance exam, but Harry was struggling and his exam results so far were disappointing. Charles and Diana discussed the option of dropping Eton and considering less demanding schools like Radley College in Oxfordshire and Milton Abbey in Dorset. But Charles believed that having his sons boarding at the same school would enable them to support each other and keep the family bond close.

Diana also remained eager for Harry to go to Eton for two reasons. She was concerned that he would be labelled 'not good enough' if he didn't go there, so it was better that he did even if he struggled. She was also keen that he followed in the footsteps of her brother and father. Charles had been sent to Gordonstoun, Prince Philip's old school, largely because his father thought it would toughen him up. He had hated it at first and felt lonely and miserable. Although Diana and Charles disagreed about almost everything they both felt Eton would be the right place for Harry. Neither of them anticipated the tragic events that would shortly change so much in their young sons' lives.

Left: The Prince and Princess of Wales with Prince William and Prince Harry on the Royal Yacht Britannia in Venice. Harry is six months old, a time when Diana said her marriage was 'down the drain.'

Right: Harry, nearly two, in the uniform of the Parachute Regiment of the British Army with his mother in the garden of Highgrove House, the family country home. He had already decided to be a soldier when he grew up.

Below left: Harry and William sitting on the steps of Highgrove House. It was very difficult to persuade Harry, aged two, to wear anything other than his army uniform.

Below right: An apprehensive Harry waving to photographers as he arrives for his first day at nursery school in Notting Hill, London, one day after his third birthday.

Left: In 2017 Harry said how much he loved, remembered and missed his mother's hugs. Here he is snuggling up to her during a summer holiday at the Spanish Royal Palace just outside Palma.

(©Georges De Keerle/Getty Images)

Right: A more confident Prince Harry with his brother William as he starts Wetherby School in September 1989.

(©Tim Graham/Getty Images)

Left: Diana and ten-year-old Harry hold hands during the official celebrations of the 50th Anniversary of VE Day in London's Hyde Park.

(©Martin Keene/PA Archive/PA Images)

Right: Harry enjoying a toboggan ride on a ski holiday in Klosters, Switzerland in January 1997 with his father. It was less than five months after his parents' divorce and seven months before his mother died.

(©John Stillwell/PA Archive/PA Images)

Top: Harry, aged six, gets a ride in a tank during a visit to a British regiment in Germany. *(©Tim Graham/Getty Images)*

Below left: Harry, aged eight, running towards a tank during a visit to the barracks of the light dragoons in Hanover, Germany.
(©Martin Keene/PA Archive/PA Images)

Below right: Harry, aged eighteen, polishing his boots on his bed before taking part in the Combined Cadet Force at Eton College. CCF was one of the few aspects of school life he thoroughly enjoyed. *(©Kirsty Wigglesworth/PA Archive/PA Images)*

Above right: Charles, William and Harry look at the sea of flowers well-wishers brought for their mother at Kensington Palace two days before the funeral. *(©PA Archive/PA Images)*

Above left: Prince Charles holds Harry's hand as they look at the flowers and messages left in memory of Diana at the gates of Balmoral, Scotland.

(©Anwar Hussein/Getty Images)

Centre: (From left) Prince Philip, Prince William, Earl Spencer Diana's brother, Prince Harry and Prince Charles walk behind the coffin of the Princess of Wales on 6 September 1997 on the way to her funeral at Westminster Abbey. Harry told me 'no child should have been asked to do that.'

(©David Levenson/Getty Images)

Left: William and Harry bow their heads as their mother's coffin is taken out of Westminster Abbey at the conclusion of the emotional service.

(©Adam Butler/PA Archive/PA Images)

Above left: Harry shows his acting talent just before he left Eton College. He played Conrad in the school production of Shakespeare's play *Much Ado About Nothing*.

Above right: Harry plays polo for his school team at Cirencester Park Polo Club. A sport he was good at and still enjoys.

Below: Just before he left Eton College, Harry let press photographers into his room. Shortly afterwards he gave a two fist salute and a shout of 'Yes!' as he was driven away.

Left: Harry told his father it was 'the best day of my life' meeting the Spice Girls (L/R) Mel B, Emma and Victoria, at their concert in Johannesburg, South Africa in November 1997 three months after his mother's death.

(©John Stillwell/PA Archive/PA Images)

Below: The handsome Prince three days before his eighteenth birthday.

(©Anwar Hussein/WireImage)

Above: Harry chats to a young leukaemia patient at Great Ormond Street Hospital, London the day before his eighteenth birthday. *(©Toby Melville/PA Archive/PA Images)*

Right: Harry enjoys practical work and is using a wire cutter to help make a fence at the Mants'ase Children's Home for orphans in Lesotho during his gap year in 2004. Two years later Harry jointly set up the charity Sentebale to help vulnerable and HIV positive children of Lesotho and Botswana.

(©Tim Graham/Getty Images)

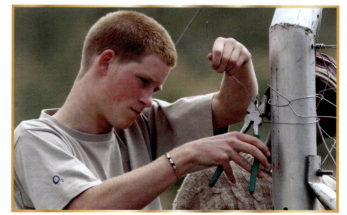

Left: Harry marches with fellow army cadets at the Royal Military Academy, Sandhurst in June 21, 2005, one month after he started the course. *(©Tim Graham/Getty Images)*

Right: The Queen and Harry beam at each other as she inspects soldiers at their passing out Sovereign's Parade at Sandhurst in Surrey in April 2006. *(©Tim Graham/ Getty Images)*

Left: Harry sits in a Spartan armoured vehicle in the desert in February, 2008 in Helmand province, Southern Afghanistan. *(©John Stillwell POOL/ Tim Graham Picture Library/Getty Images)*

Top: Prince Harry mans a 50mm machine gun aimed at Taliban fighters in January, 2008 in Helmand Province.

Below left: Harry practices his rugby skills during a work break in the desert in January 2008 in Helmand Province.

Below right: Harry in Turkey in April 2015 to mark the 100th anniversary of the Gallipoli campaign during World War One.

CHAPTER 5

The Loss of a Mother

William and Harry were on holiday at Balmoral with their grandmother, father and other members of the royal family throughout August 1997 and had not seen their mother for a month. Diana had spent part of this time in Greece on holiday with her close friend Rosa Monckton. This was followed by a cruise off the Sardinian coast with her millionaire boyfriend Dodi Al-Fayed, playboy son of the controversial businessman Mohamed Al-Fayed, who then owned the Knightsbridge store Harrods. Diana spent a lot of time posing on the deck of Dodi's father's £10 million yacht in a variety of stunning swimwear and had no qualms about openly kissing Dodi despite seeing photographers lined up to take her picture.

On Saturday 30 August, a year and two days after her divorce from Charles, she rang her sons at Balmoral for a chat, a call that causes them heartache to this day.

The world has changed beyond imagination in the twenty years since the death of the Princess of Wales. William and Harry are now mature men in their thirties and far more worldly than previous generations of royals. It has given them a different perspective not only on their mother's tragic death, but how it was handled. In the 2017 BBC documentary *Diana, 7 Days* they showed compassion and understanding for both their father and the Queen in the way they dealt with such an unexpected and overwhelming tragedy. Their own experience, however, was rather different.

Harry recalled: 'I think it was probably about teatime for us … I was a typical young kid running around playing games with my brother and cousins and being told, "Mummy's on the phone, Mummy's on the phone," and I was like, "Right, I just really want to play." And if I had known that was the last time I was going to speak to her, the conversation would have gone in a very different direction … And I have to live with that for the rest of my life, knowing that I was that twelve-year-old boy wanting to get off the phone and wanting to go and run around and play games rather than speak to my mum.'

In another TV documentary, *Diana, Our Mother: Her Life and Legacy,* William shared his brother's sense of guilt. 'If I'd known now what was going to happen, I wouldn't have been so blasé about it and everything else. That phone call sticks in my mind quite, quite heavily…regretting for the rest of my life how long that phone call was.'

Their comments show how, despite the passing of time, they still feel responsible for their mother and full of remorse that they didn't do enough for her. Rationally there is no reason why they should feel culpable. Nor was the accident in any way their fault. But just talking about it was obviously distressing for Harry who told me he believes 'there is still a lot of grief to be let out.'

What they didn't mention was that sometimes their mother's phone calls could be embarrassing. Diana often ignored the fact that they were with their father and that he might be in earshot. Instead, according to author Christopher Andersen, she would update the boys and especially William on how her latest romance was progressing and ask if they liked the sound of her new lover. It must have been awkward for them to speak and left them with a heavy emotional burden.

At the last minute, Diana and Dodi decided to spend the final day of their holiday in Paris before flying back to London. The princes were due to go back to school shortly and Diana wanted to be with them before they left, William for Eton and Harry for Ludgrove. There was scarcely time to ensure that protection officers were available, and swarms of photographers on motorbikes followed her and Dodi everywhere they went in the city. Shortly before midnight French time Diana and Dodi left the Ritz Hotel to go to Dodi's Paris apartment, just off the Champs-Élysées. Fayed's chauffeur Henri Paul, whose shift had ended three hours earlier, had downed five aperitifs on top of prescription drugs which were not to be taken with alcohol. Even after he was asked to drive the couple, he ordered another Ricard pastis – a liquorice-flavoured alcoholic aperitif – before getting into the car. The paparazzi gave chase and Paul crashed into a pillar in the Pont de l'Alma tunnel soon afterwards.

At 1am the British Ambassador in Paris, Sir Michael Jay, rang Sir Robin Janvrin, the Queen's deputy private secretary, to break the news of the crash. Dodi and the driver Paul had died instantly. Diana was injured but it wasn't immediately known how badly. In fact a vital pulmonary vein, which carries aerated blood from the lungs to the upper right chamber of the heart, was torn. Diana was first treated in the smashed Mercedes and then taken to the Pitié-Salpêtrière Hospital four miles away where surgeons tried desperately for two hours to save her life.

Janvrin immediately called Prince Charles and the Queen at Balmoral. Two hours later Charles received another call to hear that Diana had died from severe chest and head injuries. Charles was devastated and didn't know whether to wake William and Harry immediately to tell them. He talked it through with his mother, who suggested that they should be left to sleep. He then rang Camilla. He couldn't go back to bed and instead went for a solitary walk on the moors. His feeling of loss, guilt and personal failure overwhelmed him. He anguished over how to break such devastating news to his children and blamed himself for not trying hard enough to understand Diana's needs. As soon as Charles returned to Balmoral, he rang his private secretary, Stephen Lamport. 'They're all going to blame me,' he said. 'The world's going to go completely mad, isn't it? We're going to see a reaction that we've never seen before. And it could destroy everything. It could destroy the monarchy.' Lamport agreed it might.

Diana was only thirty-six years old and had become the most famous woman in the world. She was beautiful, charismatic, brave, unpredictable and flawed, an irresistible combination that made so many love her. Time went agonisingly slowly but at 7.15am Charles felt able to wake William. Before Charles could speak his son told him he'd had a very disturbed night. Charles conveyed the tragic news that there had been a terrible car accident and that every effort to save his mother had failed. William started to cry and wrapped his arms round his father. Charles, usually so emotionally inhibited, held him close. When he calmed down a little William expressed concern about Harry and how he would take such awful news. He wanted to go with his father to wake him up. Harry says his initial reaction was one of 'disbelief', and that there was 'no sudden outpouring of grief'.

In the 2017 TV documentary, Harry tried to put himself in his father's position. 'One of the hardest things for a parent to have to do is to tell your children that your other parent has died ... but he was there for us, he was the one out of two left and he tried to do his best and to make sure we were protected and looked after. But, you know, he was going through the same grieving process as well.'

When Charles felt his sons were able to leave their bedrooms he told them that the Queen and Prince Philip wanted to see them. All three held hands as they walked slowly to the room where their grandparents were waiting. Neither hugged them. Fortunately Tiggy Legge-Bourke was already at Balmoral. She had flown up the previous day to escort Harry and William back down to London. For most of the day Harry stuck to her like glue. Their cousin Peter Phillips was there, too.

Going to church on Sunday is a regular royal family ritual, and later that morning William, Harry and Tiggy were driven to Crathie Kirk, the local church close to the estate, with the rest of the family. By the time they left Balmoral the news of their mother's death had swept across the world and condolences began to pour in. The torrent of grief was unprecedented and would shake the nation, and the monarchy, to its core.

There was far more than the usual number of spectators waiting to catch a glimpse of the royals outside the church. They wanted to show sympathy and possibly also be part of the grieving process. A few perhaps had a prurient interest in the tragedy itself while others voiced how appalled they were that William and Harry were being put through the tough ordeal of being seen in public within a few hours of their enormous loss. There was no mention of their mother's fate during the service, much to the outrage of some of the congregation. The Rev. Robert Sloan's reasoning, explained afterwards, was that it would not have been appropriate so soon after the boys had been told of their mother's death. While some said the omission was at the Queen's request to spare her grandsons' pain. The omission, however, confused Harry who asked Tiggy: 'Are you sure Mummy is dead?'

Harry, who can't remember anything about the service, knew that going to church was 'the last thing' he wanted to do at the time, but looking back he now realises it was part of his and William's public role. Soon afterwards Prince

Charles flew in an RAF plane with Diana's sisters Sarah and Jane to Paris to collect her body. Millions of people watched television to see the plane land back in the UK at 7 o'clock that evening but the Queen refused to let William and Harry watch such a traumatic sight. On Charles's insistence Diana's body was taken to the Chapel Royal at St James's Palace rather than the local mortuary in Fulham as had originally been suggested.

Meanwhile, people in their hundreds if not thousands came that first day from all over the country to lay flowers by the gates of Kensington Palace and on the grass nearby. The date for the funeral was fixed for 6 September 1997 and for days after her death local florists sold out of flowers by lunchtime despite ordering vast amounts from overseas. Soon the whole area from Kensington Palace to Kensington High Street was awash with flowers that in some places were an astonishing 5ft deep. The combined smell of both fresh and decaying blooms was intoxicating. Candles, soft toys and passionate messages were left by the flowers or hung on the railings. On that first day most grieving well-wishers seemed too shocked to speak and those who did only whispered. A day or so later their shock had turned to grief and many wept unselfconsciously. This was followed by palpable waves of anger, when strangers shared fierce criticisms of the Queen who, they believed, was staying 'on holiday' and keeping William and Harry with her.

Prince Charles's press secretary, Sandy Henney, came to see the crowds and told Charles that William and Harry needed to be gently prepared for the extraordinary sight they would see. It wasn't until 2015 when Henney took part in a documentary on BBC2 that she admitted she also feared that public anger at the time threatened the future of the monarchy. It was subsequently understood that the royal family remained 500 long miles away within the confines of their Scottish retreat to try to help William and Harry begin to come to terms with the tragedy and to let them grieve in private.

In 2017, William and Harry showed a mature understanding of their grandmother's decision. 'It was a case of how do we let the boys grieve in privacy,' Harry explained, 'but, at the same time, when is the right time for them to put on their princes' hats and carry out duties to mourn not just their mother, but the Princess of Wales ... and a very public audience. When we go out and do things like that and not completely break down you have to put on a bit of a game face.'

William agreed: 'I think it was a very hard decision for my grandmother to make. She felt very torn between being a grandmother to William and Harry and her Queen role. She also wanted to protect our father. Our grandmother also deliberately removed the newspapers so we didn't know what was going on. And back then, obviously, there were no smartphones or anything like that so you couldn't get your news, and thankfully at the time to be honest, we had the privacy to mourn and collect our thoughts and to have that space away from everybody. We had no idea that the reaction to her death would be quite so huge.'

As each day passed there was a growing feeling that the

country was rising up against what was seen as the monarch's indifference to Diana's death. They were also angry that she had not mentioned a word about the tragedy in public. No one, not even the Queen, whose antennae is usually spot-on, had gauged the size of the reaction. One source believes that perhaps the Queen's initial reaction was, at some level, influenced by the anxiety Diana had caused. She had become a thorn in the royal flesh and her negative, non-negotiable behaviour must have affected a woman who placed duty above all else. It took the Queen several days to agree to lower the Union flag at Buckingham Palace to half-mast to acknowledge the nation's loss because, in the words of one courtier: 'She hadn't even done it for her father [George VI].' It was one of several royal protocols she broke in the wake of Diana's death.

Before they left Balmoral, William and Harry went with their father to look carefully at the flowers and anguished notes of condolence that had been left at the front gates. They read some of the messages and were all visibly moved. Harry grasped his father's hand and pulled him down to read one particular message. It was a touching moment of intimacy and symbolic of how the Prince of Wales was opening himself up to his grieving children. Their needs were taking priority and it marked the beginning of a warmer relationship between the children and their father. Something that was possibly easier for Prince Charles now that Camilla Parker Bowles, who loved, supported and made him happy, was back by his side.

Harry clearly remembers the event: 'Looking back the

last thing I wanted to do was read what other people were saying about our mother. Yes, it was amazing, it was incredibly moving to know, but at that point I wasn't there, I was still in shock. I was wearing a tiny little strange blazer with a horrible tie, and to read other people's outpouring of grief was quite odd, almost as if people are expecting you to grieve in public. To whose benefit would that be? Looking back on it I'm glad that I never cried in public. Even if someone tried to get me to cry in public I couldn't, and probably still can't. What happened then has changed me in that sense.'

Initially all the flowers left in memory of the Princess by the gates of Balmoral had been insensitively cleared away each day. This changed after a few days and they were subsequently allowed to pile up.

The Queen and Prince Philip flew back to London five days after the crash, shortly after Prince Charles, William and Harry who took an earlier flight. Normally, different generations of heirs to the throne are forbidden to travel on the same plane, but the Queen relaxed this protocol too. On landing the Queen and Prince Philip went straight to St James's Palace to visit the Chapel Royal and pay their respects to Diana. Then, when they arrived at Buckingham Palace, they climbed out of their limousine, much to the anxiety of their protection officers, to look at the flowers and cards by the gates. That evening, for only the second time in her reign, the Queen, dressed in black, broadcast live on BBC TV from Buckingham Palace to the nation. She spoke as 'a monarch and a grandmother' and fulsomely praised Diana: 'She was an exceptional and gifted human being. In good times and bad, she never lost her capacity to smile and laugh, nor to inspire others with her warmth and kindness … I admired and respected her, for her energy and commitment to others, and especially for her devotion to her two boys.'

She also explained her reasons for staying away and ended with the words, 'No one who knew Diana will ever forget her … I for one believe that there are lessons to be drawn from her life and from the extraordinary and moving reaction to her death. I share in your determination to cherish her memory.' Her return to London and her obviously genuine comments had come not a moment too soon. Public anger slowly subsided.

At the same time, the princes and their father came straight from their flight to inspect the sea of flowers in front of Kensington Palace. Charles once again held Harry's hand as he bent down to read some of the messages. William and Harry then bravely faced the grief-stricken crowds and began shaking people's hands. It is a memory Harry still struggles with and one that has left permanent scars. 'People were grabbing us and pulling us into their arms and stuff,' he said. 'I don't blame anyone for that, of course I don't. But it was those moments that were quite … shocking. People were screaming, people were crying, people's hands were wet because of the tears they had just wiped away from their faces before shaking my hand.' He was puzzled by the public grief, and remembers thinking: 'How is it that so many people who have never met this woman, my mother, can be crying and showing more emotion than I was feeling?'

There were furious rows during the days that led up to the funeral. The Spencer family and the Queen wanted a small private funeral. Prince Charles insisted on breaking with tradition and that Diana had a full royal funeral at Westminster Abbey. Then there was the question of who would walk behind the coffin. Earl Spencer wanted to do so on his own. Charles wanted to be there along with his sons as a mark of respect. Prince Philip volunteered to join them, partly because of the antagonism between Charles Spencer and the royal family and the growing fear that Prince Charles might be lynched by the angry, inconsolable crowd. As Charles suspected, many among the crowds believed that he was entirely to blame for all Diana's problems and the failure of their marriage. Halfway through my first meeting with Prince Harry at Kensington Palace in spring 2017, when we were chatting about his ideas for modernising the monarchy, he suddenly stopped talking, looked me straight in the eye and said quite unexpectedly, as if it was something he had long wanted to get off his chest: 'William and I were fifteen and twelve when our mother died and I had to walk a long way behind her coffin.' A look of grief and anger then swept across his face. 'No child should lose their mother at such a young age and then have his grief observed by thousands of people watching while millions more round the world did on television. I don't think any child should be asked to do that, under any circumstances. I don't think it would happen today.'

Sir Malcolm Ross, a senior Buckingham Palace courtier, who had five days to plan the funeral, revealed that in the end it was the Duke of Edinburgh who persuaded his grandsons to take part in the funeral procession by telling them: 'I'll walk if you walk.' Sir Malcolm died in September 2017.

The image of twelve-year-old Prince Harry, head bowed and fists clenched, walking at a slow, dignified pace behind his mother's coffin is one of the cruellest and most poignant images of mourning in modern times. If that wasn't enough for a boy of twelve, who was neither child nor man, and his adolescent brother a couple of years older but still in that tricky no man's land, both were expected to behave with control and dignity. It would have been unthinkable for either of them to cry when their family put so much value on a stiff upper lip. Their priority had to be to present the correct image to the world. It wasn't the first time in William's young life that he was required to behave like a man, but perhaps it was the first when he needed to act like a future king. The journey through the heart of London, from St James's Palace to Westminster Abbey, is almost a mile, but it must have felt more like a hundred. There were bouquets of lilies, white freesias and roses on top of the coffin. Alongside was a white envelope with the single word MUMMY written on it.

The almost unbearably moving funeral service in the Abbey was conducted with precision and style. The boys were not filmed while they were inside. Occasionally Charles held Harry close while William put a comforting hand on his shoulder. Harry insists he did not cry but admits it took an enormous amount of willpower. 'I refused to let myself down. Elton John's song [he played and sang 'Candle In The

Wind'] was incredibly emotional, and nearly brought me to the point of crying in public, which I am glad I didn't do.'

Diana's unaccompanied coffin, a tragic, lonely sight, was then driven slowly through the streets to Althorp, the Spencer family's stately home, for the private burial service on a tiny island in the middle of their lake. Charles, William, Harry and the Spencers made the same journey by royal train.

After Diana's body was buried, Charles, Harry and William went back to Highgrove, where Tiggy was waiting for them. They never spent another night at Kensington Palace, and instead moved into St James's Palace, the London home of several members of the royal family. Charles arranged for a suite to be designed for them replicating many of the features of the rooms they had in Kensington Palace. The building work was booked to take place while Harry and William were at school and Prince Charles on a royal visit abroad.

Well over 300,000 letters of condolence arrived within days of the funeral, mainly addressed to William and Harry. They promised to reply to them all and spent hours with their father, each at a separate desk, poring over the mountain of tributes poems and gifts they had been sent. A spokesman said: 'They were very touched and they just could not believe the many letters from all ages and from so many countries. The princes want to say a sincere thank you.'

Just before Prince Harry's thirteenth birthday he came across a letter saluting his bravery during the funeral procession from a boy of his own age who wrote: 'It's very difficult to put all this into words but I really wanted to write to you and tell you you're a real brave guy.' Overall it took a team of up to sixty volunteers more than four months to sort the mail.

Four days after the funeral the boys took their first step back to normality by returning to school. Harry was quieter and far less boisterous than usual and particularly so on his actual birthday, which occurred five days later. He must have hugely missed the usual loving birthday hug from his mother. It must also have been bittersweet when his aunt, Lady Sarah McCorquodale, visited him, bringing the PlayStation that Diana had bought for him in Paris. He sought comfort from the school matron, Vicki McBratney, who said: 'Every couple of weeks he'd come and knock on my door and we'd both go to the matron's lounge and I'd make him hot chocolate and we'd sit and talk and he'd share his letters from his mum. [He was] a loveable, friendly, nice boy, cheeky, but not naughty.' Vicki's duties included waking him up, laying out his clothes, tucking him up in bed and supporting him when he played sport. She said she was his 'counsellor and nanny' and for a short while became a surrogate mother. When he left the school he gave her a bottle of wine and a box of chocolates, plus a hug and kiss, and told her he would 'really miss' her. He saw her again seventeen years later in May 2015 during a walkabout in New Zealand. She was standing in a crowd of well-wishers with her husband and three children when he suddenly said: 'My goodness, I remember you. Long time no see.' He then bent over and gave her a kiss and stopped for a chat. She said: 'He's still got that same smile.'

Prince Charles was grateful for Tiggy's help but decided

that the boys also needed a male companion. He asked Mark Dyer, an ex-Welsh Guards officer who had been his equerry when the boys were younger, if he could help out. Mark and Tiggy knew each other and both got on well with Harry and William. Charles was particularly concerned about how the boys would spend their first half term at home, especially because it had previously been arranged they would stay with Diana as he was committed to a five-day tour of South Africa, Lesotho and Swaziland. Harry was such a shadow of his normal, boisterous self that Charles wanted to try to boost his mood by finding something exciting he could do.

By chance his old friend Geoffrey Kent, a travel industry leader he'd met when they were both serving in the British military, came to the rescue by offering to take Harry on safari in Botswana, leaving Prince Charles free to undertake his programme of engagements. Harry's schoolmate Charlie Henderson, Tiggy and Mike Dyer came too, but not William who didn't have the same half term. 'It was a sensitive time,' said Kent, 'but a successful one.'

He later wrote about the expedition: 'With a camera and binoculars in hand, Prince Harry is in his glory. For three days we cruised in an open-top Land Rover to view the animals.' It was Harry's first taste of Africa and the beginning of his love affair with the land, its people and its wildlife. Two decades later, working for animal conservation in Africa has become increasingly important to him and is one of his key causes.

They all went on to Pretoria for tea with President Nelson Mandela at his residence. The significance of the man and the meeting rapidly evaporated when shortly afterwards Harry met the Spice Girls, a pop girl group at the height of their popularity. He watched them sing in a huge stadium in Johannesburg and then joined them during the post-concert photo-call. Harry held hands with Victoria Beckham (Posh Spice) and Emma Bunton (Baby Spice) and was photographed grinning from ear to ear. He told his father meeting them was the best day of his life. The singing foursome were subsequently invited for tea at Highgrove. When they left Harry said it was the second best day of his life.

In January 1998 William and Harry made the difficult journey back to Kensington Palace to choose the keepsakes of their mother's they would like, and which of their own belongings they wanted in London and which in Highgrove. Tiggy accompanied them as they cut their childhood links with the family home.

* * *

Once Prince Charles and Diana had parted he'd begun gradually introducing Camilla Parker Bowles to the public and was biding his time waiting for an opportunity to introduce her to the princes. Unlike Diana, who involved her sons in her romances, Charles had ensured that Camilla was never at Highgrove when the princes stayed. He had tried to open up the subject of a meeting a couple of months before Diana died, but both boys went very quiet, so he immediately dropped the subject. He waited a year and then approached his objective in a more roundabout way by inviting Camilla's children, Tom and Laura, from her first marriage, to stay at

Birkhall, the Queen Mother's former residence at Balmoral. Prince Charles had inherited the 53,000-acre estate when she died in 2002. He also invited other guests to keep the atmosphere light. He was enormously relieved that, despite Tom being ten years older and Laura six years older than Harry, all four offspring seemed to get on well.

It was around this time that William and Harry decided to throw a surprise party for their father's fiftieth birthday. His actual birthday is in November, but they chose to have the party at the end of July as the school holidays had just begun but it wasn't yet time for the family to decamp to Balmoral. They knew their father would want Camilla to be invited and that it would be best all round for them to meet her privately first. They accepted that their mother had thought she was 'poison', but they wanted to make up their own minds. William asked his father to arrange a meeting. It took place on Friday 12 June 1998 at William's self-contained flat at the top of St James's Palace.

It must have been nerve-wracking for everyone but particularly for Prince Charles who so much wanted both his sons to get on with the woman he loved. In fact it went surprisingly easily. William was friendly and Camilla, who has an optimistic approach to life, was sensitive enough to let the relationship progress at his pace. They met again for lunch a few days later. Harry, who was much more laid-back about Camilla, met her with Tom and Laura a few weeks later over Sunday afternoon tea at Highgrove.

It was then full steam ahead for the party to be held in the Orchard Room at Highgrove. William and Harry enlisted the help of Tiggy and Prince Charles's former valet, Michael Fawcett, but the ideas, energy and enthusiasm all came from them. (Harry did, however, turn down his father's suggestion that Fawcett should help with the preparations for his wedding to Meghan Markle in May 2018.) He and William made enormous efforts to ensure that the party was kept secret, too. They sent handwritten invitations to the Queen, Prince Philip, Princess Anne, Prince Andrew and Prince Edward, and about a hundred of their father's friends. All guests were charged £25 each because they didn't want their father to pay for his own party. They arranged for the outside of Highgrove House to be decorated with wildflowers while Greek statues were placed in the walled garden. Entertainment was a *Blackadder*-style comedy starring Rowan Atkinson, Emma Thompson and Stephen Fry. Unfortunately one of the guests tipped off the *Daily Mirror*, which published details of the party. Both princes were angry and upset as yet again they felt press intrusion had destroyed something they cared about. In an unprecedented move, St James's Palace issued a statement condemning the paper for publishing details of their treat and 'spoiling' the surprise.

The birthday party itself, however, was a success. Charles was enormously touched by the trouble his sons had gone to and particularly that they had invited Camilla and sat her in a prominent place. The one embarrassment was that Prince Harry and William staged a mock *Full Monty*-style strip. Harry, then only fourteen, was said to have been so drunk that he didn't just take off a few items of clothing as was arranged, but stripped off entirely and ran around naked in front of the guests. One of the guests said: 'Charles was visibly shocked. In fact he turned crimson, but he told a group of us later that it was just teenage high spirits and he himself had done much the same. It was the only time in my life that I didn't believe him.'

Aside from themselves, the other people the princes haven't forgiven for their mother's death are the paparazzi. Although they were hideously intrusive, the final verdict in 2008 of the much-delayed £12.5 million inquest found that the crash that killed Diana was a failure of security and the 'grossly negligent' and drunk chauffeur Paul. Not least because the Mercedes 'struck the pillar in the Alma Tunnel, rather than colliding with something else'. In addition there was the contributory factor that neither Dodi nor Diana was wearing a seatbelt. It also concluded that there was 'not a shred of evidence' that Diana's death had been orchestrated by the Duke of Edinburgh or the security services, as endlessly alleged by Mohamed Al-Fayed. Nor was Diana pregnant.

Nonetheless, William and Harry's distain of the press continued. They hated how in the first year after their loss tabloids were revealing sordid details about their mother's love life and negative aspects of her behaviour during and after her marriage. For a while a dark cloud hung over Diana as the public realised she was not an angel or entirely innocent during her marriage. William was so angry he refused to go to a service of remembrance at Craithie Church to mark the first anniversary of her death unless newspapers stopped writing about her all the time. He wanted the media and the general public to move on.

CHAPTER 6

School Rebel

Harry should have started at his secondary school in the autumn of 1997, but, due to his poor exam results, he needed to repeat his last year at Ludgrove if he was to stand a chance of getting into Eton. The requirement was a 65 per cent pass in the Common Entrance exam, and his work in that extra year enabled him to meet the grade, much to everyone's relief. Harry said he was 'thrilled' and both Prince Charles and the headmaster Gerald Barber said they were 'delighted'.

Just before the first term at Eton started in September 1998, Prince Charles told Harry he wished to have 'an important conversation' with him. He had decided to tackle the intimate issue of James Hewitt for the first time, partly so Harry would be able to cope better if there were nasty comments from other pupils. He told Harry that without doubt he and not Hewitt was his father. Harry listened carefully but didn't say a word either while his father was talking or when he had finished.

Hearing the confirmation must have come as a huge relief for him, though, and given him one less thing to worry about. Harry had enough anxieties about how he would cope with both the academic demands and life in general at Eton, which was understandable. The devastating emotional trauma of losing a parent often distances a child from their peers. They are generally less trusting and can find making friends difficult. In addition, scraping into a top academic school by the skin of his teeth was hardly a confidence booster for Harry. Nor was it on his agenda to become a swot. He would need to rely on what he was good at: sports and clowning about.

Prince Charles accompanied Harry on his first day at Eton. The absence of his mother, who would have most certainly been with her adored son, must have been a painful reminder of her passing. It was a new start and on that day an official statement was made on the princes' behalf. Press Secretary Henny began: 'They have asked me to say that they believe their mother would want people now to move on – because she would have known that constant reminders of her death can create nothing but pain to those she left behind. They therefore hope very much that their mother and her memory will now finally be allowed to rest in peace.'

Eton College was founded in 1440 by King Henry VI and educates more than 1,300 boys (but no girls) aged 13–18. It has schooled nineteen British prime ministers, generations of the aristocracy, and star actors like Damian Lewis and Eddie Redmayne, but the school now makes a point of admitting some boys whose parents have only a modest income. Its situation in Windsor, Berkshire, close to Windsor Castle where the Queen usually spends her weekends, was a bonus as both princes could visit her for tea. As Harry became increasingly unruly at school, seeing his grandparents became a source of comfort.

The school is divided into twenty-five houses each holding about fifty boys, where they eat, sleep, socialise and study. Harry joined Manor House, the same house as William. It is known as the most prestigious of the houses and is situated next to the library. Each house has a housemaster who is referred to as 'Sir' and a matron who is referred to as 'Ma'am'. Harry's matron was Elizabeth Heathcote, whose job it was to look after the pastoral welfare of the boys and domestic issues. Prince Charles and Harry joined the other new boys and their parents for tea with Dr Andrew Gailey, their housemaster, and his wife Shauna. They had a young daughter and several pets, including two springer spaniels. Harry was destined to cause Dr Gailey a great deal of concern.

All the pupils have their own room with bed, desk and easy chair. They are expected to provide their own study chair and a trunk for storing sports clothes. Overall the timing of Harry's arrival was good. The practice of 'fagging', when a younger boy acted as a servant to an older pupil, had been dropped, as had corporal punishment, where the boys were caned on the buttocks with a birch rod while they lay stretched out over a wood block. Harry was taken to his room where he learnt he would have a maid to clean it and do his laundry. His royal protection officer had the room next door and was told to report to a superior if Harry's behaviour became a cause for concern. William's room was close by and after tea he took Harry to see the games room, which had a pool table, and the common room where they could watch TV and chill out on the sofas. Despite forcing himself to smile and walk with confidence, Harry felt uneasy. He knew there would be a big difference between his small, caring prep school and this vast public school. Like many in their first year he must have felt small against towering sixth-formers. The timetable for lessons was also confusing as it changed every week. Nor did he feel comfortable in the compulsory school uniform for lessons of black tailcoat, waistcoat, a stiff white collar and striped trousers.

He was apprehensive, not least because William was more academic and generally fitted in more easily. Harry was also fed up with being in his shadow and thought of as the stupid one, the spare who wouldn't go anywhere or do anything worthwhile. He struggled with the lessons from the start, and did not initially feel there were any other pupils on his wavelength. Even worse, none of the new boys showed a particular interest in befriending him. The result was that he felt frustrated and angry. A family therapist explained: 'Many traumas that a young child goes through only show themselves once they are teenagers, and anger is a common symptom.' There could have been many causes for this ongoing general distress, including hearing his mother weeping, the arguments she had with his father, the various men she brought home, or a combination of them all. Most of all he had to try to accept he had lost his mother, the most important woman in his life, who always loved him. For him life would never be the same again. Throughout Eton he was a teenager who was drowning in grief and crying for help. The question is, did anyone hear him?

Looking back, Prince Harry accepts some responsibility for why Eton didn't work for him. He told me with a smile that he chose to be 'a bad boy' while he was there. 'It was something my mother encouraged,' he said. 'Be naughty, but don't get caught.' He gave as an example that she would smuggle sweets into school in his football socks when he was at Ludgrove. He has always enjoyed playing pranks: 'I have a naughty streak which I enjoy.' Once he balanced a book above a door so that it fell on the teacher's head when he entered the classroom. He made William jump by leaping out from behind a tree during a cross-country race and shouting: 'Can I have your autograph?' William lost his concentration and as a result his chance of being among the winners. Harry also went to the barber and asked for a then-fashionable 'skinhead' haircut. Buckingham Palace pleaded with newspaper editors not to use any photographs of him looking too much like a delinquent.

According to clinical psychologist Alyson Corner: 'A young person who loses a parent suddenly and unexpectedly often finds it very difficult to cope with the intense emotions that arise. The feelings can be so overwhelming that they may bottle them up. This tends to happen if there is no one they can turn to to express what they are experiencing. Even if they are given care and support, they may end up getting involved in fights and arguments. As the teenager grows, their feelings may intensify rather than lessen and some might end up using alcohol or drugs to try and soothe their pain.'

Most teenagers experience extreme emotions during adolescence and these can cloud warning signs that something more serious is wrong. One former head teacher told writer Chris Hutchins: 'We used to say that Harry was like a firecracker and when other pupils saw him coming they used to pass a by now familiar warning, "don't light the blue touch paper"' In other words don't give him the slightest excuse to vent his spleen.' Harry's chronic anger meant he regularly got into fights and he was once photographed on crutches after kicking in a window following an argument with another pupil about a girl they both fancied. One Etonian said: 'His protection officers were always in the background so everyone knew who he was. But if you judged him by his behaviour you'd never guess he was a senior royal.'

He chose to sit at the back of the class and rarely finished his homework on time. One fellow Etonian described him as a 'rebel'. 'He gravitated towards the other boys who were often in trouble and didn't seem to care about getting on with schoolwork. Harry seemed to take the view that Eton was about having fun. He played the fool, going a bit further than anyone else. His group of friends were very similar but Harry was definitely the ringleader.'

Harry's lack of academic ability, combined with his

reluctance to work, not surprisingly resulted in him trailing at the bottom of the class at the end of his first year. It was not something he could keep to himself as Eton openly lists every pupil's overall marks at the end of each term. He was, however, good at art, which also seemed to calm him. He learned to do anatomical drawing from a skeleton and was particularly interested in aboriginal art, something he and his paternal grandfather share. His efforts were often included in school exhibitions. William praised his brother's skill. 'Harry can paint, but I can't. He has our father's talent while I, on the other hand, am about the biggest idiot on a piece of canvas.'

Sport was where Harry could shine. He was made House Captain of Games and was in the school teams for rugby, cricket and polo; he also enjoyed Eton's unique archaic wall game, which bears some resemblance to rugby. An early school report mentioned that he was often 'aggressive' when playing football, which was probably an outlet for his anger.

What is difficult to understand in retrospect is that despite the fact that his father, school staff, royal protection officers and all sorts of minders and mentors knew he was a vulnerable, desolate, grieving child struggling with the loss of his mother, no one person took ultimate responsibility for his welfare. It must have been difficult for him to know whom to turn to for emotional and psychological support. As a result, it took him nearly twenty years to confront his feelings about his mother's sudden death.

Harry did complain once or twice that William wasn't there for him, but he might have been teasing. Even if it was true, William at fifteen had barely any more experience of life than Harry did, despite spending years trying to be a parent to their mother. It was a grown-up's job and someone should have picked up that he needed professional help. Instead it is profoundly touching how hard he has tried to work out what to do to help himself. When we talked at Kensington Palace he explained that he effectively shut down all his emotions from the age of twelve. 'My way of dealing with it was sticking my head in the sand, refusing to ever think about my mum, because why would that help? I told myself: "It's only going to make you sad. It's not going to bring her back."' When that didn't work he would often try to divert the pain by pushing boundaries, alcohol and wild behaviour. He didn't however stop talking about her and many of his TV interviews are full of his love and admiration for her.

Drinking copiously is often used as a solution to problems an individual doesn't want to face. Harry was twelve when in July 1997 he first got drunk, just over a month before Diana died. He, William and their mother were on a cruising holiday on a boat owned by Mohamed Al-Fayed, just before he introduced her to his son Dodi. Harry went ashore whenever he could and tried out the local drink, which often happened to be brandy, and was drunk when he came back to the boat. He got drunk at his father's fiftieth birthday celebrations, and he was also caught drinking in August 1999 when he was with his father on the yacht *Alexander* owned by Greek shipping mogul John Latsis. He subsequently spent a lot of time weeping for his mother in Tiggy's arms, his despair no doubt partly fuelled by alcohol. Sometimes he drank until he was sick. He even vomited over a bar at the Duke of Westminster's home, Eaton Hall in Cheshire, during a shooting party. There are other allegations that include him being seen throwing bottles and acting in a drunken fashion during a surfing holiday at Rock, a coastal fishing village in Cornwall.

By the age of sixteen he was well in with a 'fast', young, wild and wealthy set, and in 2000 was invited to Spain to play in the annual Sotogrande Copa de Plata Polo tournament. While there, he spent his nights in various Marbella clubs, sometimes staying until 6am the following morning. After one long drinking session he went on to a local golf club, swerved around in a buggy and damaged the course by hitting the grass with a golf club as if it was a polo stick.

During school holidays Harry was often left on his own at Highgrove. He took the opportunity to drink and smoke to his heart's content, often with a bunch of rather disreputable friends. It was around this time that Prince Charles agreed to let William and Harry redevelop the cellar at Highgrove to create a private club, which they called Club H. Two adjoining rooms with high arched ceilings were painted black and a state-of-the-ark sound system was installed in addition to a well-stocked bar. It made a great venue for wild parties.

Harry and William used Club H a lot when their father was abroad on royal duty, but Prince Charles said he found them too noisy when he was at home. Instead Harry began going to the Rattlebone Inn, a local pub in Sherston, Wiltshire. At the time it turned a blind eye to under-age and after-hours drinking, and to cannabis being smoked openly at the bar.

Rumours grew that Harry was taking drugs, and his occasional erratic behaviour and sudden rages led some to believe he had tried mind-altering substances. In addition, a couple of his drinking sessions ended up in fights and he was thrown out of the pub. At Eton his nickname became Hash Harry because of the sweetish odour that seemed to emanate from the direction of his room, although it wasn't easy to gauge the exact origin of the smell. It is difficult for a parent to keep tabs on a wayward teenager, but once again a situation seems to have arisen where there were plenty of helpers but no one person to look out for an increasingly troubled adolescent.

Journalists, however, were aware of what Harry was up to, but in 1999 new rules were introduced to stop them from reporting on the young royals. It was agreed that while William and Harry remained in full-time education they were not to be photographed, except by accredited photographers. It was a concession almost all UK editors agreed to.

Prince Charles finally became aware that Harry was experimenting with drugs when he was sixteen. He might have heard sooner if the armed royal protection officers who accompanied Harry everywhere had passed on what they were seeing. They, however, argued it was their responsibility to guard him, not to exert parental control. In any event Harry could deny their allegations, which could lead to them losing their jobs. Some say Charles eventually found out what was going on through a member of his staff at Highgrove, others that he was told by a MI6 officer who by sheer chance was observing someone else who was a regular at the pub. The story appeared in the papers and wasn't denied by senior royal officials. Instead they confirmed that Harry had subsequently spent a day at Featherstone Lodge rehabilitation centre in Peckham, South London. It was later revealed that he had indeed been to the centre, but before the story of his drug-taking appeared in the newspapers. The two events were unrelated but the trip to the centre was used to give a positive slant to the scandal.

Mark Dyer, by now Harry's mentor, had gone with him to the centre, where he was chaperoned by a 'buddy', a former heroin addict, to learn about the possible consequences of starting to take cannabis. In theory the media had been banned from reporting and photographing Harry. In practice the story was too big to hide and made headline news. The public was largely sympathetic: the general belief was that lots of adolescents go off the rails during the tricky time of growing up. Harry confessed that he had experimented with cannabis and drank to excess, and apologised for the trouble he had caused. There then followed a run of statements to try to put an end to the matter. Senior aides to Prince Charles hoped that the public and the media would look upon Harry's potential drug problem 'sympathetically', stating: 'Unfortunately, this is something that many parents have to go through at one time or another.' A spokesman for the Home Office said it was unlikely that the police would bring charges because he had not been caught in possession of or using marijuana.

Eton headmaster John Lewis stated there were clear rules about drug use by Eton students: 'Any boy possessing, using or selling drugs at school during term time can expect to forfeit his place. In cases where concerns exist about a boy's possible involvement in drugs he will be counselled and warned, and urine tests are sometimes used to clarify the situation and if possible to put the boy in the clear, which is in fact the usual outcome.'

Prince Charles issued a statement: 'This is a serious matter, which was resolved within the family. It is now in the past and closed.' The Queen was 'dismayed' to hear about Harry. Her statement read: 'The Queen shares the Prince of Wales's views on the seriousness of Prince Harry's behaviour and supports the action taken. She hopes the matter can now be considered as closed.' One practical outcome was that Prince Charles tried to ensure Harry wasn't left on his own so often at Highgrove.

The details about Harry's GCSE results were not made public, but he did so poorly in his AS levels that he dropped History of Art and had to retake Geography, leaving him with just two A level subjects, Art and Geography. As a consequence he was for the second time in his school life demoted to a lower year. Harry had already decided that, unlike his brother, he didn't want to go to university, but he was very keen to get into the Royal Military Academy Sandhurst, the training centre for British and overseas army officers, and knew he had to pass two A levels to be accepted. His father tried to encourage him to work harder by offering him a gap year playing polo if he got good A level results.

Harry's problems with drink and drugs also destroyed his chances of following William and becoming a prefect.

Although his name was originally one of fifty considered by a committee of outgoing prefects, the older boys voted against him being put on the shortlist. One of the prefect's duties was to catch pupils slipping out to drink illegally in pubs. Since that was one of Harry's habits, it was felt inappropriate to elect him.

Harry's salvation came at last when he joined the Combined Cadet Force (CCF) in his third year at Eton. The CCF is sponsored by the Ministry of Defence and can be found at many schools round the country. It aims to encourage leadership skills and endurance through military and adventurous activities. Harry had longed to be a soldier since he was two and at last he could put his dreams into practice. Being part of the CCF involved, amongst other things, practising with live ammunition at a rifle range, learning how to handle weapons, first aid, target reconnaissance, camping out all night and learning how to march. Discipline, obeying orders and total concentration were vital requirements. One might have imagined such demands would go right against Harry's rebellious nature. The reality was quite the opposite and instead they sowed the first seeds for Harry to find himself and come into his own, not least by adding much-needed structure to his chaotic life. Being part of the CCF also inspired Harry for the first time at Eton to give of his absolute best. Perhaps he realised that doing well here was his only chance. Or perhaps he knew he had found his vocation and wanted to show just what he was made of.

In March 2002, when he was seventeen, he took part in an escape and evasion training exercise and offered to be the hostage. It was a good opportunity to test himself and see how he might cope in a real-life situation. He thrived on the tough challenge. Five students dressed as Taliban fighters, complete with assault rifles, 'captured' then removed him to a barn in Boveney, a small village in Buckinghamshire. While other pupils were searching for him, his 'captors' kept him hooded while they interrogated him intensely for twelve hours. This included making him both kneel in front of them and stand for hours. They also did their best to first disorientate him and then crack him mentally by shouting vile abuse. He was released at 5am the next day, by which time he had only revealed his name, date and place of birth. A bystander said: 'He did exactly as a soldier should have done, and didn't crack. He had a great time. He loves this sort of thing.'

Harry's natural skill combined with training hard and coping with difficult field exercises led to his promotion through the ranks and he became the most senior cadet in Eton's 140-strong cadet force. He was both Cadet Officer and Parade Commander, which was even better than his brother. As a result it was Harry's prestigious duty to take command of the annual tattoo – Eton's version of Trooping the Colour. His boots shone, his uniform was immaculate and his bellowed orders ensured that the entire corps marched in unison onto the College Field parade ground. The mighty finale was an assault on a mock castle using a real Scimitar tank from Windsor Castle, while Harry led the defence. It was watched by hundreds of parents including his proud father. It went flawlessly, which was not just a remarkable achievement but also an indication that Harry had a promising future in the military should he want it. As a result he went into his last year of school feeling better about himself. One school friend said: 'He has certainly cleaned up his act.' He surprised some friends by voluntarily attending several Holy Communion services in the college chapel. The rebel seemed to be growing up.

Harry's success in the CCF was one of the few bright spots in 2002 for the royal family. Early in the year the Queen lost her sister, Princess Margaret, who died on 9 February following several strokes. Six weeks later she lost her mother, Queen Elizabeth the Queen Mother, who passed away in her sleep aged 101. Prince Charles adored his grandmother, it's said that he got on with her better than he did with his mother. He was heartbroken at her loss and immediately flew back with William and Harry from their skiing holiday at Klosters. Both princes wore morning dress to walk behind the horse-drawn cortège along with other members of the royal family. It must have evoked tragic memories of their mother's funeral five years previously. Harry also attended the memorial service in commemoration of the 9/11 terrorist attacks of the previous year just a couple of weeks before he turned eighteen.

His father had offered Harry a party at Highgrove to mark his birthday but he turned it down. Instead he decided to take advantage of the occasion to change the world's view of his mother. He had felt over the years that the focus had become far too negative and diverted attention away from her achievements and the barriers she had torn down. He wanted to use his first official press interview on his birthday to do something about it. He reminded the world about her humanitarian work, how more than twenty years earlier when irrational fears about being infected with HIV/Aids were at their height, her simple gesture of touching the hand of a HIV-positive man altered public attitudes. He spoke of her pioneering work to get rid of landmines, and how her example would influence his own future path. 'She had more guts than anyone else,' he said. 'I want to carry on the things that she didn't quite finish. I have always wanted to but was too young.' It seemed that in theory at least Harry was maturing and seeking to mend his ways by following in his mother's footsteps.

Shortly before the end of his final year at Eton he appeared in a school performance of Shakespeare's *Much Ado About Nothing*. Harry played Conrad, gentleman follower of Don John, the evil brother of Don Pedro, Prince of Aragon. He appeared in only three scenes, but he looked very dapper in his chestnut-brown knee breeches and white shirt and acted with enormous enthusiasm, including in the masked scene when he danced with girls from a local school. It was performed for three nights and both the Queen and Prince Charles came to support him.

To mark the end of his time at Eton he allowed photographs to be taken of him in his room, which looked so clean and tidy it must have been done especially for the occasion. Doubtless too he had taken away anything he didn't want the public to see. Aside from obvious typical teenage possessions, the objects he chose to have around him gave a fascinating insight into his tastes and interests, many of which remain with him today. In pride of place on his desk was a photograph of his mother, possibly from the last photoshoot taken by Mario Testino before she died. There was a bottle of his father's Duchy Original mineral water and a photograph with his father and other members of the Highgrove polo team. It's a game he still loves.

There were several posters on the walls including one of actress Halle Berry who had starred in the James Bond movie *Die Another Day* and who looks remarkably like Meghan Markle. Another is a portrait of Caprice, the former Wonderbra model, who looks a little like Harry's former love Chelsy Davy. There was an Indian wall-hanging of elephants, a favourite animal of the young Harry, as is still the case. In addition, there was a Union Flag, Lynx deodorant – famous for its sexy boy-meets-girl commercials – and a book of Mario Testino's portraits.

After sitting his final A level paper in Geography Harry returned to Manor House, his home for the last five years, to clear his room. Photographs showed his left arm bandaged as the result of a 'bang'. He exchanged a few words with Dr Gailey and kissed his wife. He then hurled several large black bin bags into the boot of a waiting Land Rover, and with a wave, a two-fisted salute and a shout of 'yes!' he was driven away.

CHAPTER 7

Gap Year Surprises

Harry spent most of summer of 2003 partying and clubbing while waiting to hear how he had done in his A levels. He managed a D in Geography and a B in Art, a poor result by Eton standards as more than 90 per cent of pupils gain A or B grades and take more than two subjects. Nonetheless, Sandhurst had only demanded two A-level passes, so Harry once again had managed to scrape through. Prince Charles did, however, withdraw his offer of letting him play polo for a year as he didn't think his results were good enough to deserve it.

There was also a cloud hanging over his B grade in Art. Just before he left Eton, Sara Forsyth, one of his art teachers, accused him of cheating and claimed that she had ghostwritten his A level coursework. Miss Forsyth, whose contract was not renewed by Eton at the end of a two-year probation period, took her case to an education tribunal where she made the claim. She also maintained that she had been unfairly dismissed, bullied by staff and had been the victim of sexual discrimination. The allegation of cheating was dismissed but she was awarded £45,000 in damages for being bullied. Harry commented on the accusation in his twenty-first birthday message to the country in September 2005: 'Maybe it's just part of who I am. I have to deal with it. There's lots of things people get accused of. Unfortunately mine are made public.'

In order to be accepted by Sandhurst, Harry also had to go through some wide-ranging assessments to see if he was officer material. He sailed through the first Pre-Regular Commissions Board assessment, in September 2003, a sign perhaps that he could do well if he really wanted to, and that most of the subjects at Eton hadn't interested him. It also meant he could have gone straight to Sandhurst from Eton, which in retrospect might have helped him fight his demons by giving him a firm structure. It would also have kept the press away. The Press Complaints Commission Code of Conduct protected the princes up to the age of eighteen as long as they were still in full-time education, after which it was no holds barred.

However, Prince Charles felt it was important that Harry took a gap year. He wanted him to start afresh, get away from bad influences and have new experiences. In practice Harry took a double gap year, a significant slice of which was taken up by hard partying. Lots of gap-year students run a little wild, but unlike Harry they don't have the world's press itching to report their bad behaviour.

Prince Charles asked Mark Dyer, his senior aide, to help organise Harry's time overseas, keen that he went to both Australia and Africa. Harry left the UK shortly after his nineteenth birthday. First stop in Australia was Tooloombilla Station, a 40,000-acre ranch near Roma in central Queensland, where he was to work as a jackaroo, an Australian term for a cowboy, for two months. The ranch was owned by Noel and Annie Hill, who had impeccable royal connections. Noel's wealthy father, Sinclair Hill, a successful polo player, had coached Prince Charles, while Annie had been one of Diana's flatmates before she married. They were both delighted to host Harry. His duties would involve rounding up livestock in the scrub, branding animals, and doing chores such as fencing, for which he would be paid about £100 a week. He stayed in a weatherboard-clad cottage.

The world has long been fascinated by Harry and what he gets up to. William is more reserved and his life has been carefully mapped out, whereas Harry is an unpredictable rebel, liable to break the rules and potentially have much more fun. The naughtier he got, the more the public seemed to love him.

As a result, as soon as he arrived at the ranch, reporters, photographers and cameramen swarmed over the cattle station and wouldn't go away. Harry was furious. He couldn't get on with his work and for several days refused to go outside. Instead, he spent most of his time watching videos. He had come to Australia in search of action and adventure but instead was a prisoner of intense media scrutiny. His press team issued a statement to try to get the press to ease off. 'He wants to learn about outback trades not dodge the cameras,' they said. Mark Dyer pleadingly told reporters: 'I've got a young man in there in pieces.' The pleas made little impact. Harry felt so exasperated and angry that he decided to go home. Seats were booked for him and his bodyguards to fly out of Roma airport and back to London. Another jackaroo said Harry told him: 'I can't do what I came here to do so I might as well go home.'

Prince Philip was not amused and told Harry he was not to quit as the public reaction would be similar to what his uncle Prince Edward faced when he found life too hard with the Royal Marines and gave up. His grandfather's unshakeable belief in the stiff upper lip approach to life was not Harry's; like his mother, he has always worn his heart on his sleeve. A call was made from Buckingham Palace to enlist the help of Peter Beattie, the then Premier of Queensland, who in turn asked the media to give Harry some peace. Initially there was no reaction and a planned trip to a nearby rodeo had to be cancelled as the number of newsmen expected to attend was too large for the local security forces to handle. After a while the press agreed to back off on the promise of arranged photo-shoots in the future.

Harry also had trouble with screaming girls who behaved as if he was a pop star. On one occasion when he managed to sneak out, two teenage sisters aged seventeen and fifteen rushed up to him and pleaded for a kiss. Instead he shook their hand and said: 'Sorry, I've been told I'm not allowed to do that.'

He eventually settled into a work routine. His day began

at 7.30am and lasted until around 6pm with a two-hour lunch-break when the Australian heat was at its fiercest. While he was there he managed to slip out to watch a nearby bull-riding competition, sitting untroubled on a grass hill and sipping a soft drink rather than anything alcoholic. Harry kept his word with the media and let himself be photographed riding with other cattle hands. Dressed in an open-neck blue shirt, jeans and a brown Akubra hat, he rode a chestnut-coloured horse called Guardsman and guided a herd of thirty shorthorn and Charolais cattle round part of the property.

He found time to lead the Young England polo team to a 6–4 victory over Young Australian Polo, and to meet up with his cousin Zara Phillips at the Manly Wharf bar in Sydney. Mike Tindall, who was a member of the England squad that won the 2003 Rugby World Cup, was also drinking there. Harry introduced them. They subsequently became an item and married in July 2011.

When his two months in Australia were up, Harry gave a short statement: 'I have had a great time working out here, meeting people and learning a bit about how to be a jackaroo, and of course the rugby was absolutely fantastic. It's a great country.' He didn't however stay to answer any questions.

He was still in Australia when Paul Burrell's memoir, *A Royal Duty*, was published. Diana's butler had included personal details about William and Harry as well as explicit details of their mother's love affairs. William, still at university, was furious and got in touch with Harry. They issued an icily polite statement: 'We cannot believe that Paul, who was entrusted with so much, could abuse his position … It is not only deeply painful for the two of us but also for everyone else affected and it would mortify our mother if she were alive today and, if we might say so, we feel we are more able to speak for our mother than Paul. We ask Paul please to bring these revelations to an end.'

Harry returned home for Christmas. Prince Charles felt relieved that after the initial hassle Harry's time in Australia had gone well, but if he believed that it was the start of a clean new chapter for his son he was going to be disappointed. Harry described his subsequent life to me as a 'roller coaster'. The ride lasted for more than ten years.

Harry approached his next trip in a different way. 'I thought, "Right, I've got a year off. I want to do something really constructive with my life that makes my mother proud."'

It was Prince Charles's idea that Harry went to Lesotho, a tiny country encircled by South Africa that is so small it sometimes doesn't appear on maps. It is also one of the least-developed countries in the world. Nearly half the population lives below the poverty line and it has the second highest rate for Aids in the world. Life expectancy is forty-one years and one in three children of the nearly two million residents are orphans. Prince Charles wanted Harry to see how hard life can be, especially for children, and hoped the experience would help him appreciate his own life. The prince could not have made a better choice but it wasn't going to be a cure-all experience.

Harry flew out to Lesotho for an eight-week stay with his friend George Hill, and Patrick Harverson, a communications secretary for the royals. The last part of the journey was by truck and soon after he arrived he was set to work building a wire mesh fence around the orphanage compound. He also played with the children. Small children, whatever their background, have a sixth sense that tells them if an adult seems genuine or someone to be wary of. There was no doubt about Harry. The children, some shy, others boisterous, crowded round him, smiling broadly or staring at him wide-eyed. He had brought along some rugby balls and footballs, and quickly playing with them helped them to bond.

Over a short period of time he built up an extraordinary rapport, and unusually for his age had no qualms about cradling tiny babies and picking up toddlers to cuddle. He clicked particularly with one four-year-old boy, Mutsu, who'd been orphaned by Aids. He followed the prince everywhere and refused to take off a pair of blue Wellington boots Harry had given him. Harry was smitten. 'He was tiny,' he said 'but he just took my hand [and also] helped me plant a tree.' The children had an almost equal beneficial effect on Harry. He loved that they had no idea who he was, as it made it easy for him to relax, be himself and even reach back to his inner child.

He spent a lot of time doing hard manual work too: he painted walls at the Mants'ase Children's Home in Mohale's Hoek and even volunteered to do the washing-up. He felt good as he was fulfilling the promise he made in his TV interview to mark his eighteenth birthday to carry on the work of his mother.

Harry not only instantly took to the country and its people. He also got on well with the mini-kingdom's Prince Seeiso who was eighteen years his senior. Years later Seeiso, who calls Harry 'H', admitted he was initially apprehensive at the thought of looking after the unruly prince on his gap year but the feeling quickly evaporated. 'While we grew up in very different countries I think we have a lot in common and have a really close bond and similar values,' Seeiso said, going on to explain: 'Before I met him I had total sympathy for him because I am a second son as well. Being number two has an effect on you and the way people perceive you. I knew how it felt to be judged against someone who is squeaky clean, quiet, reserved and perfect. My brother, like H's brother William, ticked all the right boxes, and I ticked all the wrong boxes. Fortunately, we do not have an aggressive media in Lesotho because I am sure if we had there would have been stories about me rather like the ones printed about H.'

Both princes had also lost their mothers in tragic circumstances. Prince Seeiso's mother, Queen Mamohato, had died not long before Harry arrived. Both she and Diana had campaigned against Aids and cared about vulnerable children. Harry agreed it gave their relationship 'a special bond'.

Seeiso also took him on an extensive tour of the country. Much of the population live in highland villages that can only be reached on foot or horseback. Life by necessity is very simple and education is not a priority. In winter most of the country is covered in snow. In summer some families send herd boys as young as five into the hills on their own for months at a time to graze the precious livestock.

Harry was aware that the country's financial resources were very limited and that ironically the only way to make people aware of the plight of so many orphans was to invite the media along for a photo opportunity. One of the journalists who flew over was Tom Bradby, then ITN's royal correspondent. The two men talked and Harry agreed to take part in a documentary. *The Forgotten Kingdom: Prince Harry in Lesotho* was shown on ITV in 2004. It chronicled Prince Harry's visit and included private videos that Harry himself had taken to build a visual diary. The documentary helped raise nearly £2 million for the British Red Cross Lesotho Fund. In it Harry talked about his contribution: 'I am not going to be some person in the royal family who just finds a lame excuse to go abroad and do all sorts of sunny holidays. I've always been like this. This is my side that no one gets to see. I believe I've got a lot of my mother in me, basically, and just think she would want us to do this ... Obviously it is not as easy for William as it is for me. I think I've got more time on my hands to be able to help. I always wanted to go to an Aids country to carry on my mother's legacy.'

Looking back in a later documentary, he said about his initial visit: 'At that stage I had no mechanism to be able to start a charity or make any more of an impact than just literally being the ginger, white prince who has come to try to make these kids laugh.' He was underestimating himself.

In 2006, he co-founded a charity with Prince Seeiso. They called it Sentebale, which in the local language means 'forget me not', in memory of both their mothers. It aims to support the mental health and wellbeing of children and young people who are the victims of extreme poverty and are affected by HIV/Aids in Lesotho and more recently in Botswana.

The next challenge Harry had to overcome was to ensure his entry into Sandhurst by passing the Regular Commissions Board entrance exams that were set for July 2004. It involved four tough days of physical, mental and emotional aptitude tests. General Sir Richard (now Lord) Dannatt, former Chief of the General Staff, admitted: 'It is tough. They are not looking to see whether you are a fully rounded leader at that moment. They are looking to see whether you've got the potential to become an effective leader and an effective army officer of which leadership is the core activity.' Harry passed and was told he could begin his training as an army officer in 2005. In addition he spent six weeks as a volunteer assistant rugby development officer with the Rugby Football Union, helping to coach young children at schools and clubs to play rugby, one of his favourite sports.

Unfortunately, when Harry has a long run of generally doing well, he often then trips up and bruises his reputation. In October 2004 he was involved in a nasty fracas outside Pangaea, a smart nightclub off Piccadilly, central London. Harry was leaving at 3.15am when he was surrounded by about fifteen photographers. He was angry and witnesses heard him say: 'Why are you doing this? Why don't you leave me alone?' It ended with Harry being bundled into the royal limousine by his protection officers and driven home. One of the photographers, Chris Uncle, was left with a cut lip. At the time Uncle said: 'Suddenly he (Harry) burst out of the car and lunged towards me as I was still taking pictures. He lashed out and then deliberately pushed my camera into my face. The base of the camera struck me and cut my bottom lip.' Around this time Harry was also pictured giving press photographers a one-finger gesture during a polo party and was seen canoodling with a former topless model at the Chinawhite nightclub.

★ ★ ★

Prior to his start date at Sandhurst there was a family wedding. It couldn't have been easy for Prince Charles to tell his sons that the woman blamed for the break-up of his marriage to their mother was going to become their stepmother, but in the autumn of 2004 that's what he did. Harry accepted that Camilla had been in his father's life for a very long time and had grown to like her. Since he was a small child he has been able to see things from other people's point of view and was quoted as saying: 'To be honest, she's always been very close to me and William. She's not a wicked stepmother. Look at the position she's coming into. Don't feel sorry for me and William, feel sorry for her. She's a wonderful woman and she's made our father very, very happy which is the most important thing. William and I love her to bits.' Camilla, ironically, like Diana is a people person and skilled at making people feel comfortable in her presence.

Their wedding plans were announced by Clarence House

on 10 February 2005 and William and Harry released a joint statement: 'We are both very happy for our father and Camilla and we wish them all the luck in the future.'

More than 20,000 people watched Charles and Camilla, in an oyster silk basket-weave coat and chiffon dress, arrive at Windsor's Guildhall on 9 April for their private civil wedding. At the time the Church of England were reluctant to let divorced people marry in church. Harry and Meghan fared better and were given the all-clear for their marriage in 2018. Afterwards, the newly-weds returned to Windsor Castle for a service of blessing led by the Archbishop of Canterbury, a ceremony attended by about 800 of the couple's friends and family, including the Queen and Prince Philip. Just to ensure the Queen felt at ease in what could have been an awkward occasion, Harry kept making her laugh by imitating the facial expression she uses when seeing something she disapproves of. He has a knack for taking the sting out of tricky situations. The Queen made a speech in which she described how 'proud' she was of Charles, and wished the couple well. After an afternoon tea of smoked salmon sandwiches, cakes, tarts and fudge, the couple drove off in a Bentley and spent their honeymoon in Scotland.

Harry had another positive life-changing experience in Africa during his double gap year. In April 2004 he flew out to Zimbabwe and renewed acquaintance with Chelsy Davy, a striking, clever, ambitious blonde, whom he had met a couple of years previously when she was at Stowe school. Several of her friends knew Eton boys and she was introduced to Harry at a party. She was eighteen then, a year younger than

Harry, but not much happened between them. When they met again, she was in her first year at Cape Town University studying Politics, Philosophy and Economics with a view to becoming a lawyer. She was living with her younger brother, Shaun, in her parents' beachfront apartment in Camps Bay.

Chelsy was nothing like any previous upper-class girl Harry had met. Born in Zimbabwe on 13 October 1985, she was the daughter of South African safari operator Charles Davy and his wife Beverly, a former Miss Coca-Cola Rhodesia. Her wealthy family owned 1,300 acres in the Lemco safari area and charged significant sums for expeditions to shoot wildlife. She grew up surrounded by a vast wilderness. Her lessons at school were often interrupted by monkeys stealing pupils' pencils, or students chasing wild animals out of the classroom. Once, when Chelsy was a child, a poisonous snake fell on her head.

When she was thirteen her parents enrolled her at Cheltenham College in Gloucestershire and she moved to England. It was initially a huge culture shock as the other thirteen-year-olds in her class were, in her eyes, far more sophisticated than she was. She said: 'I'd never worn make-up and suddenly everyone was in make-up. My eyes were like little saucers. I wore ridiculous things and I didn't know anything about fashion. The girls scared me a bit as everyone was more grown-up than me. I was this innocent stunted child who had been brought up in the bush.' She quickly caught up academically and then moved to Stowe where her sense of humour and generous smile made her lots of friends.

Harry got to know her parents when they were first

courting. He got on well with her father, but caused a major security alert by leaving the family ranch one evening without informing anyone first, after he had drunk 'one too many'.

He and Chelsy shared a love of outdoors and Africa. He relaxed in her company and liked the fact that she was both funny and tough and could even ride bareback. What's more, she didn't seem in the least interested in his royal status. In fact she seemed to love him despite rather than because of it. They also both enjoyed parties and drinking vodka. Harry seemed equally relaxed with her brother and their friends. He could feel ordinary with them, chill out and know they totally got his rather whacky sense of humour.

For the first few months Harry was determined to keep their relationship secret, something which Chelsy, and later Meghan, initially didn't understand. She discovered why when in an abandoned moment they kissed in a polo field in Durban and were spotted by a photographer. From then on, Chelsy was harassed by the media, eager for a story on Harry's love life. She hated all the attention.

Harry fell head over heels and wrote to a trusted former school friend to say that Chelsy was 'the love of my life – this one's unreal'. Three months later he flew back to London and told his father he had fallen in love. Charles listened and then quietly told him that he had his final Sandhurst entrance exam to study for and should put the relationship on the back-burner. But for Harry this was no holiday romance. He was determined to see Chelsy as often as possible and didn't think twice about the twelve-hour flight.

Falling in love didn't, however, stop him enjoying

himself at home. In January 205 he turned up to a friend's party in Wiltshire with a 'colonial and native' fancy dress theme. Harry chose to wear a German desert uniform with a swastika armband. It caused ructions. The next day the *Sun* carried a photograph of him on its front page with the headline 'Harry the Nazi'. It also reported that Prince William came to the party dressed as a lion. Clarence House issued a statement: 'Prince Harry has apologised for any offence or embarrassment he has caused. He realises it was a poor choice of costume.'

It wasn't enough. Harry faced condemnation all round for his total lack of judgment and sensitivity, not least because Holocaust Memorial Day would occur in that same month and his behaviour would be very awkward for Prince Edward who was attending the commemoration. Harry was wholly distraught and turned to Chelsy, who agreed to fly over to be with him. He appreciated her total support, clear-headedness, intelligence and warmth. It made him feel that not everyone was against him.

He realised too that he would always be under constant scrutiny from the press and there would be no such thing as a hiding place. In practice, however, slowly but surely he has turned media interest to his advantage, particularly when it comes to promoting the causes he cares about – just like his mother.

CHAPTER 8

Soldier and Prince

On 8 May 2005 Prince Charles drove Harry to the Royal Military College, Sandhurst in Berkshire to begin his forty-four-week course to become an officer. It was five months later than originally planned because of a knee injury Harry had sustained while teaching children how to play rugby. Prince Charles was introduced to the top brass, then gave his son a friendly punch on the arm before taking his leave.

Harry had dreamt of being a real soldier in the British Army since he was two and now at last his chance had come. He knew that, like Eton, he had only been accepted by the skin of his teeth. Unlike him, more than 80 per cent of his fellow officer cadets were university graduates. His age was a disadvantage too: at twenty he was a year or two younger than the rest and lacked the experience and maturity that comes from spending three years at university. As the course was aimed at graduates he was bound to struggle and he found it physically, emotionally and, what worried him most, academically challenging. Attending lectures and writing essays on subjects that included military history and international relations were compulsory, but unwelcome. He just hoped that his experience in Eton's Combined Cadet Force, where he had been promoted to the highest rank of cadet officer, would count for something even though the overnight exercises and shooting at rifle ranges had been designed for schoolboys.

In a TV interview with Sky TV to mark his twenty-first birthday later that year he talked about how he tried to toughen himself up physically and mentally before the term started by doing some rugby coaching, and '[I] got my brain to work every now and again by doing some work experience with land management ... I wanted to have fun during my last week but had to get my brain to work ... otherwise it would have been even more difficult.' He also managed to squeeze in a holiday with Chelsy and her family on the island of Bazaruto off the coast of Mozambique. It is an idyllic place with white beaches, clear water and a rich marine life.

In advance of Harry's arrival, the Sandhurst instructors were told that the prince's protection officers would be around both at the base and when he was out on training exercises, but that they were to take no notice of them. Harry himself was to be treated just like everyone else on his course and anyone caught giving him special treatment would be in trouble. His royal title would not be used. Instead he would be known as Officer Cadet Wales. This pleased Harry.

He enrolled along with 270 other recruits and was told

he was to join twenty-nine of them in the Alamein squad. He was given a name badge, and his name was also printed in white capital letters on his luggage. Before term started, Harry, in common with all the new cadets, had been given a list of what he needed to bring. This included a boot-cleaning kit, a specific number of coat hangers, padlocks, an iron and an ironing board. Like all the other cadets he also had his head shaved. His allocated room was not much bigger than a prison cell. Unlike Eton, where a maid cleaned and tidied up after him, Harry was expected to keep his own room spotless and do his own ironing. He admitted it was the first time in his life he had used a lavatory brush. One former cadet said: 'On the first day of the new intake in Sandhurst it's a sea of ironing boards. Getting your ironing board in the door you have to remember is only the first step.' The second was learning how to iron out every single crease in the uniform. The penalty for failing to do so is not just being on the receiving end of a stream of vile abuse from one of the instructors but an added penalty of press-ups for the entire platoon.

Harry was given sheets and blankets and told perfect hospital corners were expected when he made his bed. His immaculately ironed uniform had to be precisely folded and his boots polished until they shone. There was an inspection each morning and he was obliged to be standing in the corridor outside his room dressed and ready by 5.30am. Harry was familiar with the hour as it regularly marked the end of a long night out, but not at all for the start of his day. He joked to one of the new cadets: 'I was never up this early unless I was going to bed this late.' It was a real shock to his system and some days he didn't make the 5.30am call. His punishment was a ferocious dressing-down.

Some cadets expected Prince Harry to be an arrogant snob: 'We were looking forward to knocking him down,' said one. Instead, to their surprise, they found that he didn't complain or try to pull rank. What they couldn't have known was how much he wanted to fit in. Just one cadet tried his luck mocking him. 'He picked on the wrong man,' a witness recalled. Apparently Harry punched his private parts hard and was not picked on again.

The safety of the third in line to the throne was an important issue for the top brass. Increased precautions had been made before he arrived, but a month after he started there was a major security alert. A British tabloid newspaper claimed an undercover reporter had wandered round the buildings with a fake bomb.

The first five weeks at Sandhurst are known to be exceptionally rigorous and demanding. New recruits are always sworn at by the NCO and on the receiving end of a stream of instructions and rules, but Harry knew that in the army you don't answer back when rebuked. It was initially touch and go whether Harry, an instinctive rebel who likes to push boundaries, would cope. Despite wanting to be one of the guys, he was used to being addressed as 'Sir' or 'Your Royal Highness'.

During the initial training period cadets were not allowed off base. Laptops, mobile phones, TV and alcohol were banned and all radios were tuned so that only BBC Radio 4 could be listened to. Harry wasn't even allowed to put a framed photograph of his mother on display. His days consisted of non-stop physical training interspersed with barked commands and rebukes. There was little time for meals: cadets had to stop eating the moment a bell rang. Evenings were taken up with mundane but essential chores like polishing kit and cleaning rifles.

There were two significant reasons for the harsh start. It was a quick and efficient way to remove cadets' previous habits and instil different ones in their place. It also encouraged the cadets to bond through shared experiences. Some cadets just couldn't cope: as is usual there was a small exodus on the second day of training and about a 15 per cent drop-out after the first week. Harry stayed put and coped with all the physical demands. Perhaps he welcomed the obligatory routine imposed on his life as he had done when he joined the Combined Cadet Force at Eton. Instead of being defiant he grasped the challenges and bonded with the other cadets. Above all, he discovered how much he enjoyed working in a team. He told me about this in 2017. 'If you want to be a success you have to be a team player,' he said. 'You get taught in the army that you can't get anywhere without the support of other people. I agree.' It has been a crucial element of his subsequent success in making things happen, such as his African charity Sentebale, and particularly the Invictus Games, a multisport international event for wounded, injured and sick service personnel.

He also talked about his state of mind at the time. 'I was at a stage in my life [when] I was probably lacking a bit in guidance.' Although he initially found it hard being mocked by a NCO he came to understand it had value. 'He was someone who teased me at the right moments and gave me the confidence to look forward … have that confidence in yourself to know who you are, to push forward and to try to help others.'

Life was much harder when his platoon left the confines of Sandhurst. Early on in the course the cadets were taken to Ashdown Forest in Sussex for a three-day exercise. The instructors failed to take on board that the area is public land, and, not surprisingly, several journalists and photographers were eagerly awaiting Harry's arrival to take the first pictures of him in military uniform. A reporter from the *Daily Mirror* even rushed up to him as the cadets were marching and tried to get a quick interview. Harry was livid and let rip. 'This isn't a joke you know,' he shouted. Members of the public also began to gather and point at him. His protection officers were not concerned, but the military instructors were and the exercise was abandoned.

In his twenty-first birthday interview, Harry opened up a little about how tough the first five weeks had been. 'You are marched around for the first week in a green overall, half like a gardener half like an inmate.' He didn't have to wear a 'ball and chain,' he said, but 'it's pretty close to that.' He said that everyone had to start from scratch, whether it was learning how to march or being told exactly how to wash and shave. He admitted it had been 'a bit of a struggle but I got through it.' There was some fun too. 'I do enjoy running down a ditch full of mud, firing bullets. It's the way I am. I love it.'

He couldn't forget about royal matters altogether during

his training. In his first term it was announced that he had been appointed a Counsellor of State to whom the Queen delegates powers and functions when she is unavailable or unwell. By law they must include the Sovereign's spouse and the next four people in line of succession who are over the age of twenty-one. Their jobs, for example, would be to attend Privy Council meetings, sign routine documents and receive the credentials of new ambassadors to the UK.

Having shown the guts, strength and determination to manage the physical demands of the training, Harry had to prove himself academically. Cadets who didn't reach the grade had to repeat the term. The work included writing essays on famous battles, accumulating a working knowledge of international affairs, and studying both military law and the rules that governed armed conflict. In addition he had to prove he could be articulate in group discussions and deliver a lecture to the other cadets. He also had to answer a list of multi-choice questions so his instructors could evaluate his reasoning, general knowledge and, above all, intelligence. His overall score was four out of ten, one of the lowest marks of his intake and the minimum acceptable.

Meanwhile, because the press couldn't get access to Harry while he was at Sandhurst they chose to follow Chelsy Davy, and her life in Cape Town, where she was studying at university, became unbearable. A friend of the couple revealed: 'Photographers were putting tracking devices on her car and following her everywhere she went. It was a serious intrusion into her life.' Chelsy didn't speak about the ordeal until much later, when she was thirty and wanted to promote her new line of ethical jewellery. Talking to *The Times* in 2015 she revealed that she found it 'terrifying. It was so full-on: crazy and scary and uncomfortable. I found it very difficult when it was bad. I couldn't cope.' She added it was a particularly tough thing to handle while she was still only in her teens. 'I was trying to be a normal kid and it was horrible.'

In his twenty-first birthday interview Harry also spoke about Chelsy, acknowledging how protective he felt about what she had to endure only because of her connection to him. He said: 'It does irritate me because obviously I get to see how upset she gets and I know the real her, but that's something we deal with in our own time and unfortunately it's not something I can turn round to people in the press and say "she's not like that, she's like this." That is my private life. I would love to tell everyone how amazing she is but once I start talking about that I have left myself open.' Despite the 6,000-mile distance between them they tried to stay as close as they could and she came to stay with him at St James's Palace the first time he had some time off.

Harry, who sat on a low wall in front of a line of stables for his birthday interview, looked fresh-faced but uncomfortable and restless. He explained he would not be at Sandhurst itself on his actual birthday. 'I will probably be in a ditch somewhere on an exercise,' he said, and that his fellow cadets would 'probably do something crude' to celebrate the occasion.

One of the things he was really looking forward to at the end of the course was William having to salute him. After graduating from St Andrew's University, William was due to follow in Harry's footsteps and start his officer training at Sandhurst in January 2006. 'It will be very amusing,' said Harry. 'He is determined not to salute me but it is the army and you have got to do things.' Not that the prospect marred their relationship. 'Every year we get closer,' he went on, 'and we've even resorted to hugging each other now after not seeing each other for long periods of time. He is the one person on this earth that I can actually talk to about anything and we understand each other.' The physical warmth they originally learnt from their mother had not only become part of their brotherly relationship but was also steering them to a much more emotionally led approach to life Although they may not have realised it at the time, their feelings for each other marked the beginning of the end of a stiff-upper-lip approach to life.

Harry also emphasised continually how important it had been for him to feel 'normal' during his training, adding that it was a great relief to have made 'very good friends' among the cadets: 'Being who I am it's difficult to trust people, but it hasn't been the case.' He called his fellow cadets 'really good guys' who treated him 'normally' and 'always give me support if some rubbish comes up in the papers'. It made him feel 'really lucky'; one of the best things about Sandhurst, he said, was knowing 'you've got a platoon of guys, that everyone's going through the same thing and the best thing about that is being able to fit in as just a normal person.' He was determined to fight on the front line and saw himself 'spending thirty-five to forty years in the army'. It was an ambition that would be dashed all too early.

A few months into the course Harry found himself for the second time accused of cheating in his exams with a *News of the World* front-page headline that read: 'Harry's aide helps out on Sandhurst exams'. The story alleged that Harry had contacted Jamie Lowther-Pinkerton, his private secretary, for help with an essay on how the SAS successfully handled the 1980 London siege of the Iranian Embassy. In fact Harry asked for an information source on the siege. He wrote: 'I need to write an essay quite quickly on [the siege]. I have got most of the stuff and if you've got any extra information or websites that you know please, please, please e-mail it to me.' As only Harry and Pinkerton knew about the communication it was baffling as to how the paper had information about his request. It was the start of a period lasting several years when both William and Harry became increasingly mystified and worried about how details of their private phone calls found their way onto the pages of national newspapers. As a result they found it progressively more difficult to trust members of their staff or even close friends. The mystery was only solved eight years later in 2013 during the phone-hacking trials when it was revealed that the *News of the World* had hacked the private voicemails of several members of the royal family.

Harry completed the last exercise at Sandhurst in April 2006 and could look back with pride on his achievements. He had thrived there, which he hadn't done at Eton. He had shown that he was a natural leader, and felt comfortable with the military's embedded ethos of duty and teamwork. It was therefore a shame that his bad-boy impulsiveness took over just a few days before the passing out ceremony where he would parade in front of his grandmother, the Queen.

Cadets had had to be back in barracks for a 10pm curfew throughout the course, but this was lifted after the last exercise as the only thing left for the cadets to do was prepare for the passing out parade. Harry, four cadets and two protection officers took advantage of the extra free time and went to a local bar to celebrate the end of ten months of strict military training. Harry felt so relaxed and uninhibited with his pals as they had so many shared experiences that when one of the group suggested they went on to a club for a bit of fun, he agreed. They turned up at 3am at Spearmint Rhino, a strip club in Slough, a large town on the western fringes of Greater London. It was naïve of Harry to imagine that he wouldn't be recognised by the door staff and within seconds a message whizzed round the club that Prince Harry had turned up with a group of friends. He had achieved the dubious honour of being the first senior royal to visit a lap-dancing club. The next day the *Sun*'s front-page headline read: 'Dirty Harry'. Another tabloid called it his 'night of shame'. Dancers asked for £10 to dance topless and £20 for a nude lap dance in a private room. Mariella Butkute, a titivating Lithuanian in yellow hot pants and a matching bra, was apparently the first to approach the prince, seize her few minutes of fame and be quoted in newspapers worldwide. 'When I saw him I didn't know who he was,' she began. 'One of the other girls said it was Prince Harry. I went straight over to him and kissed him on both cheeks. I asked if he wanted a dance and he said he didn't because he had a girlfriend he was really in love with.' The newspapers alleged that he did let her sit on his lap for a ten-minute chat. The group left an hour later. Contacted for a comment by the rest of the press, Prince Charles's office declined the invitation.

A few days later, in April 2006, twenty-one-year-old Harry marched in the passing out parade as a second lieutenant in the Household Cavalry (Blues and Royals). The Queen took the Sovereign's Parade in person for the first time in fifteen years. There were 220 graduates but she reserved her biggest smile for Harry, who beamed back. Harry had at last found his vocation and for the first time achieved something significant before his brother. It also meant that Prince William had to salute him, as Harry had wished.

Also present at the parade were the Duke of Edinburgh, Prince William, then a mere cadet, his father and stepmother, ex-nanny Tiggy Pettifer, and Jamie Lowther-Pinkerton, his private secretary. Chelsy flew to London to be with him, but stayed away from the formal part of the day as she didn't want to distract attention away from Harry. She was apparently 'livid' about his high jinks in the lap-dancing bar, but was understandably silent when a clutch of reporters and photographers asked her for a comment. They were very much together during the evening at the Sandhurst Ball as was William's then-girlfriend Kate Middleton. The extravagant event was held in the gymnasium, which was decorated with white flowers and scented candles. There was also a casino and chocolate fountains. Harry, however, only had eyes for Chelsy who looked stunning in a backless, clinging turquoise satin dress. He was so elated to see her he kissed her passionately on the dance floor while an energetic jazz band played in the background. Together they watched a firework display, drank champagne and ate hamburgers. On the stroke of midnight, as tradition decreed, he took off the velvet covers from the insignias on both shoulders to proudly show his rank of second lieutenant, also known as cornet, the most junior commissioned officer rank in the army. He would receive an annual salary of £22,000.

He felt just as proud when Clarence House announced that as part of his training he would serve as a troop commander in an armoured reconnaissance unit. It cleared, albeit temporarily, a gnawing anxiety that after all his hard work he would not be allowed to go to a war zone. He explained his feelings in the way perhaps only Harry could. 'There is no way I'm going to put myself through Sandhurst, then sit on my arse back home when my boys are out fighting for their country.' Specialist training began in May 2006. It involved team building, team bonding, training for operations, maintaining the team's light tanks and being in charge of eleven men, all of whom had to be ready for combat.

When Harry had a free weekend or was not on duty he would go back to London to party at bars and clubs. He regularly pressed his self-destruct button while frequenting the VIP room in Boujis in Kensington, where he and his friends would drink copious amounts of luxury brand Belvedere vodka mixed with Red Bull, magnums of champagne, or vodka and passion fruit juice topped with champagne. The drinks were free as the prince's presence was tremendous publicity for the club. He also liked to go to Raffles in Chelsea and a pub called Public, which was part owned by his friend Guy Pelly. Once the clubs and pubs closed, Harry and friends would go on to private parties or hang out with his male and female friends at Mark Dyer's house, while his protection officers would hang around outside until he was ready to go home. There were regular stories in the press about his dubious behaviour and womanising, which upset Chelsy. As a result their relationship often became turbulent.

Once Harry finished the training course he was gung-ho to be sent to Iraq. Sorting how where and when gave the Ministry of Defence a relentless headache, particularly as the country was becoming increasingly dangerous. If Harry had been an ordinary cadet it wouldn't have been an issue, but as third in line to the throne his wishes had to be balanced against his safety. Month followed month until a MoD spokesman finally made a non-committal statement: 'Prince Harry's deployment to Iraq, as we have always said, is under constant consideration. It is still our intention that Prince Harry will deploy as a troop leader.'

Conservative MP Patrick Mercer, himself a former army officer, believed that Harry should be treated as an ordinary citizen. He told BBC's Radio 5 Live: 'There's no doubt that the situation is deteriorating, more soldiers are being killed and it would be quite wrong for us to value a member of the royal family's life more than we value the life of a humble private or a humble trooper. I think it sets an outstanding example to the ordinary people of this country that a member of the royal family is prepared to do this.'

The final decision of whether or not Harry would go to war lay in the hands of General Sir Richard Dannatt, then Chief of the General Staff. He decided that Harry's wish would be his command and in April 2007 the MoD and Clarence House issued a joint statement confirming that Harry would be posted to Iraq in May or June. The announcement read: 'We can confirm that Prince Harry will deploy to Iraq later this year in command of a troop from A Squadron of the Household Cavalry Regiment. While in Iraq Cornet Wales will carry out a normal troop commander's role involving leading a group of twelve men in four Scimitar reconnaissance vehicles each with a crew of three. The decision to deploy him has been a military one. The Royal household has been consulted throughout.'

There was an almost immediate response from Abu Zaid, commander of the Malik Ibn Al-Ashtar Brigade, who boasted: 'We are awaiting the arrival of the young, handsome, spoiled prince with bated breath. He will return to his grandmother but without ears.' The Shia leader also said if plans to abduct the prince failed, then militias would try and assassinate him. In addition, he claimed he had spies who would know where Prince Harry was as soon as he arrived. Also of concern was that intelligence leads had revealed that a sniper who had killed six British soldiers had been allocated the task of assassinating the prince. Dannatt decided the risk to Harry's life was too great and on16 May 2007, just before his men were due to leave, his own deployment was cancelled. According to Jamie Lowther-Pinkerton: 'Harry went boiling mad' and 'went out and got blotto'. It was a terrible blow that having given his all during the training it looked as if he wouldn't be able to put his skills into practice.

His grandfather wasn't sympathetic. The Duke of Edinburgh had disapproved of the fact that Prince Harry had chosen the army rather than adhering to royal tradition and spending time in the navy; he believed the navy would have been a far more secure environment. Others bemoaned the 'waste of public money' spent on the prince's training. Harry contemplated quitting the army. 'Well, if I'm going to cause this much chaos to people then maybe I should just, well, bow out and not just for my own sake, for everyone else's sake.' It was a threat rather than a promise and his commanding officer and military mentor Edward Smyth-Osbourne quickly came to the rescue. He told Harry: 'You're coming to Afghanistan with me. I do know you haven't been able to go to Iraq but I'm going to make sure that you get to Afghanistan, so hang on in there.'

Dannatt endorsed Smyth-Osbourne's offer and said he too would try to get him to the front line. An ordinary cadet would not have stood a chance of such high-ranking commanders trying to help him fill a wish nurtured since childhood. As a senior royal Harry was different and on top of this, despite being academically weak, he had the capacity to be an outstanding soldier. There was also concern that if he didn't go to war he could go off the rails in a major way.

A draft military plan was therefore made for Harry to leave for Afghanistan in December 2007. Harry was hugely relieved but now faced several months on hold to see if his deployment would actually come to fruition. The Ministry of Defence suggested still more training and sent him off to the British army training unit in Suffield, 160 miles from Calgary, Canada, where he spent three months training to be a battlefield air controller.

It would be an additional expertise that would give him a better chance of getting to the front line. Harry soon showed his strong leadership skills and how much he was committed to his men. Although the ban on gay and lesbian servicemen and women had been lifted in 2000 there remained considerable anti-gay prejudice in the forces. In 2008, Trooper James Wharton, twenty-one at the time and under Harry's command, suddenly found himself faced by six squaddies from a rival regiment who taunted and insulted him about his sexuality. He fled to find Harry and told him what had happened. Harry confronted the tormentors, warning them they would face severe discipline if they were violent either physically or verbally. He and Wharton spent several weeks together in their tank and, according to Wharton, even swapped details of how they had lost their virginity.

When off-duty Harry liked to spend time at the Calgary Cowboys bar, renowned for its scantily clad staff. One of them made lurid allegations about him to the *News of the World*, saying she was hoping to become a model on the back of what happened. The newspaper report was again very upsetting for Chelsy who tried to believe it was largely due to being in a long-distance relationship. She wanted to be a lawyer, so enrolled on a postgraduate degree in law at Leeds University. Unfortunately the lure of Leeds was not nearly as enticing as South Africa for Harry. He was an hour late picking her up at the airport when she arrived for her course and subsequently failed to help her celebrate her birthday. Instead he went to Paris to watch England play South Africa at rugby. On the one occasion he did visit her in Leeds he felt uncomfortable with her new friends. Their relationship was slowly crumbling.

At the time, Harry's attention was also diverted because he and William had decided to organise a memorial concert to mark the tenth anniversary of their mother's death at the end of August 2007. Harry wanted a massive celebration of her life, which he also saw as a significant fundraiser for charity. He persuaded William to agree. The Queen, however, felt a quiet dinner with close family and a few friends was more appropriate. The princes decided that they were old enough to assume responsibility for their mother's legacy and stuck to their decision that it was about time the positive side of their mother's work with charities was highlighted, something they felt the Palace had failed to do. It showed that Diana's boys had become young men, that they still loved and admired her, and were now in a position to show the world just how much they cared.

The plan was to have a concert of live music performances and dance, which they knew she would have loved. Any money raised would be split between Centrepoint, William's favourite charity, Sentebale, Harry's favourite, and the Diana Memorial Fund. They chose the date of 1 July, which would have been her forty-sixth birthday, and to hold it at the new Wembley Stadium. Diana's favourite band Duran Duran agreed to play. There was a segment of *Swan Lake* performed by the English National Ballet, and songs from Andrew Lloyd Webber's musicals. Performers included Sir Elton John, Lily Allen, Andrea Bocelli and Sarah Brightman.

The concert was opened by Sir Elton John, who introduced the princes to the audience. Harry and William were dressed casually in jeans, jackets and open-necked shirts and stood in front of a huge screen illuminated by a giant D. The stadium held 63,000 people while about 500 million watched the concert on television in 140 countries. Harry, fearless, determined and obviously in his element, began his speech with two simple words: 'Hello, Wembley!' It was enough to galvanise the crowd who roared their approval by standing up, clapping, cheering and stamping their feet.

The young royals who attended included Princesses Beatrice and Eugenie, and Peter and Zara Phillips, plus Kate Middleton, who had recently reunited with William after a short break-up, and Chelsy, who sat next to Harry. Harry also used the event to send a message to his Household Cavalry squadron serving in Iraq who were listening to a live simulcast. He said: 'I wish I was there with you. I am sorry I can't be. Stay safe.' The Queen watched the concert on television and told Harry afterwards that his choice of commemoration had been right. She could hardly do otherwise. Throughout her reign she has emphasised how important it is that when the royal family is at a significant event, it is covered by the media and ensures their popularity. Harry's idea resulted in a huge boost for the royals, money for the charities as well as a touching personal tribute from her sons.

In an interview on the American TV channel NBC to commemorate the anniversary, Harry, speaking from Clarence House in London, revealed he and his brother thought constantly about how their mother died. He said: 'For me personally whatever happened, that night, in that tunnel, no one will ever know. I'll never stop wondering about that.' He described his mother as 'a happy, fun, bubbly person who cared for so many people. She's very much missed by not only us but by a lot of people and I think that's all that needs to be said really.' William added: 'We were left in no doubt that we were the most important thing in her life.'

Harry then gave an agonising glimpse of what they felt they had to overcome. 'It's weird because when she passed away ... there was never that sort of peace and quiet for any of us due to the fact that her face was always spattered over the papers the whole time. Over the past ten years I personally feel... she's always there. She's always been a constant reminder to both of us ... it still upsets me... that we didn't have as much of a chance as other children to spend time with her.'

He continued: 'She wasn't always herself in front of the cameras. She was more natural behind the scenes when there was no one else there and she could be herself. I don't know whether it's the right thing to say but she was quite good at acting. She wasn't acting as though she was trying to be someone different, but very much trying to appear as normal as she could in front of the cameras which she hated so much.'

He then revealed how upset she was when her body was

criticised and that she leant on him and William to make her feel better. It apparently happened regularly and he gave as an example an insinuation that she had cellulite. 'There were many times when we had to cheer her up and tell her she was the best thing ever.' He also criticised the media for the amount of coverage they were giving the inquest into her death as it made it more difficult for him and William to move on. 'When you're being reminded about it, [it] does take a lot longer and it's a lot slower.'

Harry and William insisted that after the concert there would be a more private memorial service on the actual tenth anniversary of her death. This took place two months later on 31 August and was held in the Guards Chapel at Wellington Barracks in London. William had the nightmare task of sorting out the seating plan of the Fayed, Spencer and royal families, and became exasperated by the bickering over who sat where. Harry, obviously keen to show his leadership skills, rang his father and rattled off where everyone would sit and then asked: 'Right. Are you happy?' Prince Charles replied: 'I suppose so.' Harry's solution was to sit William and the Queen next to each other in the front row, while he sat with the Spencers.

At the service, Harry delivered a moving address, which he wrote himself, paying tribute to their mother on behalf of them both. He said:

William and I can separate our lives into two parts. There were those years where we were blessed by the physical presence beside us of both our mother and father. And then there are the ten years since our mother's death ... When she was alive we took for granted her unrivalled love of life, laughter, fun and folly... she was quite simply the best mother in the world. We would say that, wouldn't we? But we miss her. She kissed us last thing at night. Her beaming smile greeted us from school. She would laugh hysterically and uncontrollably when she remembered something silly she might have said or done that day.

To lose a parent so suddenly at such a young age, as others have experienced, is indescribably shocking and sad. It was an event that changed our lives for ever, as it must have done for anyone who lost someone that night. What is far more important to us now and into the future is that we remember my mother as she would wish to be remembered, as she was, fun-loving, generous, down-to-earth and entirely genuine. We both think of her every day, we speak about her and laugh together at all the memories. Put simply, she made us and so many other people happy. May this be the way she is remembered.

If, during the memorial service, the Queen recalled being at Balmoral at the time of Diana's death and balancing her position of grandmother and Queen, she now had a similar situation to weigh up. As Queen she was Commander-in-Chief of the armed forces and could sort out a posting, but she was also the grandmother of a young man she wanted to protect who was desperate to fight for his country on the front line. What was the right thing to do?

CHAPTER 9

Harry's War

While Harry waited impatiently to hear the exact date of his departure, his grandmother was having several meetings with General Dannatt to try to make it happen. It took a great deal of planning and effort. He needed to be posted where there would be some action but where his presence wouldn't put his fellow soldiers in even more danger. Although it couldn't have been easy for the Queen to help send her much-loved grandson into a dangerous war, she, more than most, understood the concept of duty. She also knew that the effect on Harry if he was rejected could be devastating.

It quickly became obvious that it was crucial the British media was on side because even if Harry got out of the UK without being recognised, soldiers stationed with him would immediately know who he was and could be tempted to sell their story. The only way it could work was if there was a complete media blackout throughout the time he was in Afghanistan. There is a precedent for this in kidnap cases, where the British press has for many years agreed on a total news blackout while the case is ongoing in return for a full briefing and access to everyone involved once the victim has been released. Senior newspaper, radio and TV executives were called to a meeting and were told that if they agreed to a blackout, a reporter and photographer would, in exchange, be given access to Harry in the war zone as long as nothing would be revealed until he returned safely home. Some of the left-wing media were reluctant to go along with the plan but eventually agreed.

Only a very tight group knew about Harry's placement both in the UK and in Afghanistan and Dannatt sighed with relief as he told the Queen, and subsequently the Prime Minister, Gordon Brown, the good news. The ambassador in Kabul was not informed. Des Browne, the Secretary of State for Defence, who was also in the secret, did not believe the agreement would hold. 'You'll never get away with it,' he said. General Dannatt, the Queen and Prince Charles knew for Harry's sake they had to try. It's hard to imagine anyone else being so indulged by the top brass.

Later Harry commented: '[The Queen] was very pro my going then, so I think she's relieved that I get the chance to do what I want to do. She's a very good person to talk to about it. Her knowledge of the army is amazing for a grandmother – I suppose it's slightly her job.'

A senior officer explained to me what was worked out:

'We decided not in the end to give Harry the position of troop commander that he had trained to be as it involves a bunch of soldiers and it's more complicated to find the appropriate time to send them all over. Instead we went with forward air controller, which we sent him to train for in Canada. We felt it was the best specialist role at this stage in his career. As it doesn't involve any other servicemen it gave us flexibility. It is much easier to fly one individual into the campaign. It is also an important job and highly technical.'

The plan worked and Harry, dressed in desert fatigues, quietly left the UK on 14 December 2007 from a makeshift departure lounge at RAF Brize Norton. With him were royal military police officers to protect him while he was at base camp and SAS men who would take over when he was on active service. The flight on the C-17 transport carrier to Kandahar airport in Afghanistan took twelve hours, briefly broken by a refuelling stop in Cyprus. Once they entered Afghan air space Harry and the other soldiers on the flight put on body armour and helmets. When the plane landed everyone on board was told to rush to a waiting Hercules troop carrier, which, under cover of darkness, would take them to Camp Bastion, the British and American base in the heart of Helmand Province in southern Afghanistan.

When the plane took off Harry began to feel that at last he had a chance to fulfil his destiny and prove to himself and anyone else that he could succeed at something worthwhile. The most dangerous part of the journey was the descent to the runway, as the plane was at risk of being blown up by rocket-propelled grenade attacks from the ground. As a result the followed procedure is that the plane stays as high as possible for as long as possible, then at the last moment spirals down so the landing is short and quick.

After a briefing they were then taken by Chinook helicopter to forward operating base Dwyer, an isolated desert outpost six miles from the front line in the middle of Helmand Province. It had been named after a young officer who had been killed the year before. It was just what Harry wanted – no special privileges or protection. Life was basic and like the rest of the men he slept under a mosquito net in rough bunkers built from blast-proof mesh cages filled with rubble and topped with corrugated iron and sandbags. Robert Jobson in his book *Harry's War* added that there were no hot showers, just freezing cold water from a bag hung up in outdoor wooden cubicles. Water usage was rationed, which is why Harry could only shower and shave every three or so days. He used the rounded ends of missile cases as shaving bowls. Bottled drinking water was airlifted in each day and was also rationed. If he was particularly thirsty he had to make do with metallic-tasting chlorinated water, often mixed with a flavoured powder called 'screech'. He also had to get used to desert conditions with boiling hot days, and freezing nights when the temperature could go down to minus 10 degrees. Around the base was flat, sandy, unpopulated land as far as the eye could see. The only gratifying sight was a glamour girl calendar Harry had brought with him and fixed above his bunk. Meals largely consisted of military ration packs plus anything local the men might find. The risk of dysentery was always a concern. Breakfast was usually a mixture of mashed biscuits, jam and margarine. Main meals were usually either boil-in-the-bag chicken tikka masala, or corned beef hash. Harry's treats were peanuts or biltong that Chelsy sent by post. Once a week, Harry, in common with everyone else, could use the satellite phone to call home for a maximum of thirty minutes.

Harry's role as a forward air controller meant he was responsible for controlling military air movements from the ground. Sometimes he would also react to insurgents and targets close to the base. He spoke for hours over the airways to the pilots but was known only as Widow Six Seven. One sharp-eared pilot mentioned that he thought Widow Six Seven 'had a rather plummy voice, although he was obviously trying to tone it down'.

Harry was in his element. The adrenalin was pumping and he preferred living on the edge to the various shades of grey his life had been until now. He particularly enjoyed the camaraderie between the men, saying later: 'This is what it is all about, what it's all about is being here with the guys rather than being in a room with a bunch of officers ... I think this is about as normal as I'm ever going to get.' He was also pleased to be doing something important for his country.

A senior military figure told me they were pleased with his performance. 'The other soldiers out there were almost universally impressed that he wanted to serve his country and wouldn't break the confidence about where he was. He was a genuinely admired and respected young soldier. He had a strong sense of what he was doing and helped to save lives.'

Some days were quieter than others but the ever-present

danger kept him alert and made it easier to concentrate. Like every soldier in Afghanistan he knew that the biggest risk he faced was leaving the forward operating base and treading on one of the many explosive devices that had been planted by the Taliban. It was a daily task for soldiers to go on foot patrols through the sandy tracks close by to reassure local Afghans of their presence and let any insurgents, who regularly planted explosive devices wherever they could, know that British troops were nearby.

Harry is not someone who does things by halves and this was just as true in the army. As an officer he didn't pull rank but led by example. He was brave, sometimes to the point of being foolhardy. He mucked in, and could be the life and soul of his group, but he was always concerned about any of his men who were justifiably finding life difficult.

On Christmas Eve Harry asked to be posted to Gurkhas FOB Delhi. This was a tiny base on the edge of Garmsir, a bombed-out ghost town in the southernmost corner of Nato control in Helmand. It formed a buffer zone and any unknown person found in the area was treated as a threat. 'I asked the commanding officer if I could come down ... and spend Christmas with the Gurkhas because I spent some time with them in England on exercise in Salisbury.' He was given the go-ahead.

His experience could not have been more different from the traditional royal family festivities in Sandringham. The Queen, however, made sure he was not forgotten and before the family sat down for Christmas lunch said a prayer for her grandson and his safe return. Harry meanwhile was having a great time away from all the formality and routine. One of the Gurkhas had somehow managed to get hold of a goat, which became the basis of a Nepalese curry cooked over an open fire for Christmas lunch.

The only print journalist allowed to record Prince Harry in action, as agreed by Dannatt, was John Bingham, who worked for Press Association news agency and arrived a couple of weeks after Harry. By chance that night insurgents launched missiles from a trench about 500 yards away from the Garmsir base. Bingham reported: 'The base was under daily attack, from rocks or firearms. There was no way this was staged for our benefit. Harry was in the war zone and the dangers were all around. On the second day there, we went up a nearby hill, which had been turned into an observation point. Things got a bit hairy when a firefight broke out on the way down the hill. Harry was already back at the base when we returned and just laughed: "I see you got contacted."'

Bingham told journalist Duncan Larcombe for his book *Prince Harry: The Inside Story* that he saw 'the prince at home in a setting as far removed from the nightclubs of London as it is possible to imagine'. Instead his social life was spent hanging out with the Gurkhas and eating various small animals they managed to slaughter and transform into a curry. Bingham was also impressed by Harry's attitude: 'It was clear that he had made a point of learning everyone's name from the cooks and the most junior soldiers to the captains and officers of a more senior rank. He came across as being very natural. There're no issues about him being a royal and he acted as if he was just one of the men doing your job in a different environment.'

Harry's closest brush with death wasn't revealed until 2016 with the publication of a book, *Coldstream Guards, 10 Years in Afghanistan, Guardsmen's Stories,* that recounted the stories of officers and soldiers fighting the Taliban. In it, Sergeant Tom Pal, from an anti-tank platoon, recalled his stopover at the forward operating base Dwyer. 'I was sitting chatting with … Prince Harry about random stuff when the camp was hit by a Chinese 107mm rocket... whoosh bang wallop.' It struck 'a breath-stopping' fifty metres from where they were sitting. They put on protective body armour and their helmets. 'It was a bit late but we did … At that time of year where we were working, it was pretty mental. Various checkpoints were getting attacked every single day. It wasn't anything new – the thing that was new was that you were sat next to a royal, chatting random stuff. Then all of a sudden all hell breaks loose.' Harry, he revealed, was 'rather shaken'.

Some of the men found the strain of being under attack overwhelming. When this happened Harry would quickly switch from being one of the lads and cracking jokes to being paternal and compassionate. He often advised a young soldier to 'think of the folks back home. You will see them again. Focus on what a wonderful moment that will be and don't forget they're longing to see you, too.'

On 30 December Harry was watching his monitor when the Taliban opened fire on a small British observation post. As a result he guided an aircraft in to drop their bombs accurately. It was a success. On another occasion a possibly misfired Taliban rocket hit the home of some Afghan civilians. Harry went to help and comforted a soldier as the charred remains of young children were removed. When morale was down he assumed responsibility to cheer everyone up. He once tied a pair of purple and yellow knickers to the front grille of an armoured vehicle. The piece of underwear had been sent to him by post but he refused to say whether it came from Chelsy.

Harry had only been in Afghanistan for ten weeks when an Australian women's magazine, *New Idea*, leaked his whereabouts. They later claimed that they had no idea there was a news blackout. Initially the revelation wasn't picked up, but the German daily tabloid *Berliner Kurier* then ran the story that he was with his regiment in Afghanistan. Shortly afterwards, on 28 February, the same story appeared on the American news website The Drudge Report. General Dannatt felt let down. 'I am very disappointed that foreign websites have decided to run this story without consulting us,' he said. In retrospect it is amazing that Harry's whereabouts weren't revealed earlier. General Dannatt's deal had been done with the British media alone, so was by no means watertight, and the foreign press knew nothing about it. Nor, it turned out, could they have been controlled. The feeling was, I was told, that Harry's posting was specifically chosen because it was not an area the foreign media were interested in. Nonetheless, it was a risk and a sign perhaps of how determined high-ranking military personnel were to give Harry what he wished for.

One officer told me: 'The truth is we didn't think we could keep it as quiet for as long as we did. We had confidence in the integrity of the newspaper editors, but in the days of social media there is always the danger that some soldier might try to make money from the press. In fact someone did, but with a paper that was in on the deal so nothing came out. Also about a month before the story really broke a social comment column in a German magazine mentioned that they hadn't seen Harry coming out of a nightclub in the early hours for a while and speculated he could be in Afghanistan. We held our breath but it wasn't picked up.'

Dannatt rang the Queen immediately he heard what Drudge had published and told her that Harry had to be brought home straight away. She agreed, adding, 'Please bring him home safely.' The hot news spread like lightning round the world and instantly put the lives of Harry and his fellow soldiers in danger and vulnerable to orchestrated suicide attacks. Dannatt immediately sent the order to Helmand to get the prince home. Harry was monitoring radio conversations on the morning of 29 February when he heard one that didn't mention any names but sounded as if it was about him. Shortly afterwards a Chinook helicopter, kept on standby for emergencies, took off from Camp Bastion. It was joined by an Apache helicopter that hopefully would deter any Taliban fighters from trying to bring the Chinook down. Six of Harry's heavily armed SAS men flew in while the Apache hovered above with the co-pilot keeping his hand on the trigger. Harry was told he had less than an hour to pack up and hand over his high-tech equipment.

He and his royal military police officers were guided to the rear of the Chinook. The ramp was lowered and they were told to climb aboard as fast as they could. It then took off for Kandahar. From there Harry was transferred to an RAF TriStar passenger jet for the journey back to RAF Brize Norton. He kept asking what was going on but no one said a word until he had been flown out of Afghan airspace.

A senior military officer explained why he was not disappointed that Harry's deployment was curtailed so soon. 'The aim was for Harry to be deployed for at least twenty-eight days. The minimum for him to be eligible for a campaign medal, and every day after that was a bonus. Ideally we wanted him deployed for six months but hoped we could keep him for at least half that period. We very nearly achieved that.'

Perhaps Harry hadn't known details of the plan. It certainly was not enough for him and he told me rather sadly: 'I felt very resentful. Being in the army was the best escape I've ever had. I felt as though I was really achieving something. I have a deep understanding of all sorts of people from different backgrounds and felt I was part of a team... I also wasn't a prince. I was just Harry.'

Nearly ten years later he publicly articulated his feelings about leaving his men behind in Afghanistan. In an interview with the TV show *Good Morning America* in 2016, he said: 'I have done everything I could to get out there. All I wanted to do was prove I had a certain set of skills. Literally being plucked out of my team, there was an element of me thinking, "I'm an officer, I'm leaving my soldiers and it's not my own decision." I was broken. I didn't know what was going to happen to them and then suddenly I find myself on the plane that is delayed because a Danish soldier's coffin had been put onto the plane.'

He related his experience of his flight home. 'While I'm sitting there, I look through the curtain in the front, and there's three of our lads wrapped up in plastic, missing limbs. One of the guys was clutching a little test tube or whatever it is of shrapnel that had been removed from his head and he was in a coma, clutching this thing. And I suddenly thought to myself, "People don't get to see this." In those ten weeks, I never saw the injury part. I only heard about it.'

Before he landed he vowed to do his best in future to help these physically and psychologically wounded ex-servicemen. Little did he know at the time but the experience would help him sow the first seeds of what would eventually grow into the acclaimed Invictus Games, that would also help put his own life into perspective. At the opening ceremony at the Toronto Invictus Games in 2017, he described the revelation that occurred on his flight home, when he realised 'that it was my responsibility to use the great platform that I have to help the world understand and be inspired by the spirit of those who wear the uniform.'

The plane landed briefly at Birmingham airport so that the injured soldiers could be taken to Selly Oak military hospital. One of these was Royal Marine Ben McBean, twenty-two, who suffered a head injury and extensive burns as well as losing an arm and a leg in an explosion. Doctors had feared he might die from his injures, but he managed to pull through. Harry wrote to him regularly and said he was 'humbled' by his bravery. Five years later he turned out to encourage McBean as he completed a gruelling 31-mile run on behalf of the Poppy Appeal. McBean was 'in shock' seeing him. 'I didn't expect to,' he said. '[Harry] said, "Well done" and that I'd raised lots of awareness for a good cause. He then told me to go have a bath and a well-deserved beer.'

Harry was still wearing his combat uniform covered in desert sand when he arrived back at RAF Brize Norton. His father and William were at the airfield waiting for him. Harry turned to his father and said: 'Got your Christmas card the other day.' He then threw his baggage into the boot of the waiting car and without a shower or change of clothes talked to the press. He initially concentrated on the wounded soldiers who were on his flight. 'Those are the heroes, not me,' he insisted. 'The ones who have lost limbs and will never be able to live a normal life again.' He was asked how he felt. 'Angry would be the wrong word to use,' he replied not entirely truthfully, 'but I am slightly disappointed. I thought I could see it through to the end and come back with our guys.' He even thanked the British media for 'keeping their side of the bargain … there was stuff they [the British press] did behind the scenes to stop stuff coming out, which was massively kind of them.'

A reporter asked him what he would do next. William, who knew this would be the last thing Harry would want even to think about, turned to Miguel Head, Chief Press Officer at the MoD, and ran his finger across his throat. Head immediately ended the interview. Harry, Charles and

William then got in the car for the short drive to Highgrove. Harry didn't say a word on the journey and on arrival went to have a bath where he stayed for over an hour, no doubt trying to absorb the reality that yet again something he really cared about had been torn away. It was hard at that moment to believe that he could ever make something of himself, if he was never given a proper chance.

When he was feeling slightly more human he rang Chelsy and told her he had a three-week break from the army and would come to Africa to see her if she was free. She was and he flew out to Botswana. She hired an old houseboat that they had been on before and planned a trip along the Okavango Delta, one of the ecological wonders of the world with amazing wildlife. As well as hippos, elephants, crocodiles, lions, rhinos and monkeys, the Delta also has over 400 species of birds and about 70 types of fish. The houseboat was the opposite of luxurious, which so soon after Harry's time in Afghanistan suited him well. There was a small gas cooker for simple cooking and at night they climbed up a tin ladder to sleep in a tent on the houseboat's roof. There could be no better way to forget the pressures of both war and royal life.

Their relationship seemed on a solid base again and in May Harry asked Chelsy to watch him receive his service metal from his aunt the Princess Royal, who was Colonel of the Blues and Royal. It was Chelsy's first official royal engagement. Shortly afterwards she was with Harry at his cousin Peter Phillips's marriage to Canadian-born Autumn Kelly. Their wedding ceremony took place at St George's Chapel in Windsor (where Harry would marry Meghan Markle in 2018). The celebrations provided the ideal opportunity for Harry to informally introduce Chelsy to the Queen and the rumours grew that perhaps their four-year relationship was now more serious. Instead it remained on and off until 2010.

Nothing, however, could distract Harry for long or stop him feeling less tense and restless. His few weeks in Afghanistan had been nowhere near long enough to satisfy his life-long passion to serve his country. He had to get back to active service. Once more Harry took advantage of his high-powered connections. He, General Dannatt, who also lived in Kensington Palace, his wife Pippa, and Jamie Lowther-Pinkerton talked about how to get him back. Dannatt, who had been made Commandant of the Army Air Corps a few years earlier, had already thought through Harry's plight. Although some senior military men were dubious about Harry's often impulsive behaviour, he saw a rather immature young man struggling with his demons and the weight of media and public intrusion that came with being third in line to the throne. He also believed that in his short time on deployment he had proved to be a good leader who had gained the respect of his men. In addition he saw his placement in a positive light: 'I thought the definition of success was getting into Afghanistan.' Dannatt suggested to Harry that he consider becoming a helicopter pilot. Harry initially wasn't keen because the training lasted about two years and he wanted to get back to the front line far more quickly. In any case it would mean more studying and even then he might be refused because he didn't have the aptitude.

But he quickly realised he didn't have much option: the MoD would never risk sending him to the front line again.

Harry thought about what he should do over the summer of 2008 and decided he would follow Dannatt's advice. In October 2008, it was announced that Harry was to follow his brother, father and uncle in learning to fly military helicopters, and he began the process of switching regiments from the Blues and Royals to join the Army Air Corps. There was a gap between his application to do so and the MoD giving it the go-ahead and Harry felt too on edge to hang around. As a result, in October he and William took on the physical challenge of taking part in Enduro, a charity motorbike trek of 1,000 miles in Africa, to raise funds for his charity Sentebale. Both princes had been taught to ride motorbikes by their Metropolitan Police bodyguards. Harry hugely enjoyed it, not least because with his helmet and visor on no one could recognise him. He once spontaneously decided to ride at speed to Kent to eat fish and chips by the seaside. As he neared Canterbury he and his two plain clothes protection officers were pulled over by two local policemen who had registered that they had exceeded the speed limit. The protection officers showed their Metropolitan Police badges but the local police were determined to press charges. Then Harry lifted his visor and smiled at the police. His magic ability of making strangers instantly warm to him did not let him down and the officers decided that on this occasion a verbal warning was all that was needed.

The trek gave him something physically demanding to focus on and shortly afterwards the MoD gave the go-ahead for Harry to train as a helicopter pilot. His limited academic ability, lack of concentration and bouts of inappropriate behaviour did however cause concern. Chief flying officer Lieutenant-Colonel David Meyer told biographer Penny Junor in her biography *Prince Harry: Brother, Soldier, Son*: 'When I first heard that Harry was going to come flying I had two thoughts: first, very simply, that's fine; second was, there was a standard to be met and we weren't going to cut corners.' The main issue was motivation. Would Harry have the staying power and could he cope with the inevitable criticism of his performance during training?

'It wasn't so much are you quick-witted, have you got good hand-eye coordination?' Meyer explained. 'Those were going to be found out very quickly. It was: can you see it through to the end? The motivation has to be there to get up every morning and perform to the best of your ability and then do it again the next day and the next day and the next day, despite the fact that somebody's saying you're not good enough... It's one of the longest professional qualification courses in the army, and nobody sails through it. We're not talking about flying from one airport to another, we're talking about doing this at night in some pretty hostile environments. There's a lot of competition so it takes quite a lot of courage just to put your head above the parapet and give it a go.'

When he met Harry, however, he changed his mind. 'He came in, I thought, remarkably under-confident and very reserved. I was expecting somebody to fill the room more than he did, to be quite cocky and self-assured, and I was pleasantly surprised. I thought that's interesting, so you're like anybody else because those interviews are not easy and I don't think he thought he was going to get through it without problems.'

The course was divided into three phases and took place in three different locations. There was lots of flying and weeks of pure study that lasted from 9.00am to 5.30pm, plus homework to be done overnight. Harry worked hard and whether he felt getting through the work was like swimming through treacle or incredibly boring, he kept at it. He also enrolled in an army diversity course to make him more racially aware.

He neglected Chelsy, though, who felt so abandoned that in response she changed her Facebook relationship status to 'not in one'. It seemed to mark the end of a loving and rewarding relationship. Although she was a guest at Prince Charles' sixtieth birthday, and she and Harry stayed in touch, the spark and determination to stay together no matter what was over. She worked for a while as a solicitor at the London firm Allen & Overy, but in 2010 went back to Zimbabwe and later launched her own jewellery line. She has said since that she'll always 'be good friends' with Harry. Perhaps the break-up was easier for Harry to cope with because he was on the way back to war.

The Defence Helicopter Flying School at RAF Shawbury on the Welsh borders was where Harry concentrated on the specific requirements needed to fly a helicopter. It became obvious almost from the moment he started flying that he was a natural and had at last found his vocation. Being abruptly withdrawn from front-line duty in Afghanistan had ironically created an opportunity for him to unearth qualities and skills within himself that he had no idea he possessed. His dark cloud had a silver lining, after all.

Lieutenant-Colonel Meyer believed Harry's mild dyslexia was a contributory factor to his success. 'There are a lot of dyslexics flying and it's to do with spatial awareness and ability to visualise things in 3D, which is a strength of dyslexics apparently. [It needs to be] coupled with good strong hand-eye coordination. I for one was rubbish at school but I was quite a good sportsman – as is Harry – and so when people said to me, "He's not very bright", no, but he's a bloody good polo player, he's a good shot, he makes decisions pretty quickly: actually he's a really good pilot, that's good enough for me. Lots of people have said, "Oh you got him through, didn't you?" Absolutely not. He got himself through and I think a lot of it is that innate quick-wittedness and basic skills. I know he found some of the academics challenging, but to my mind that was absolutely not as important as, could he do the job at the other end?

'Harry's course was incredibly well-galvanised and they tended to galvanise around him. That was one of his key strengths, as he wasn't better than anyone else at flying, or anything like that, but he just understood the whole team ethic, how to win together.'

Coincidentally, William, who wanted to become a search and rescue pilot, had been sent to RAF Shrewsbury for six months' training. Rather than live at the base he and Harry decided to share a small cottage near the village of Clive, less than three miles away. The brother-bonding was seized on by the media as an opportunity for a joint interview. They weren't keen but remembered their grandmother's wise words that royalty needs to be seen by the British public to survive. Instead, they seemed to have worked out a comedy duo act, which they have often repeated, that makes an amusing broadcast and neatly sidesteps difficult questions.

Harry's reply to the obvious question of how they were coping sharing a home was: '[It's] for the first time and the last time I can assure you of that.' William, who Kate devotedly cooked for and even ran his bath, insisted he did all the cooking and had to tidy up after his messy brother. 'He does do the washing up but then he leaves it in the sink.'

'Oh, the lies, the lies,' Harry chuckled. William then complained that he was kept awake by Harry's snoring. So Harry quipped: 'They're going to think we're sharing a bed now!' It was entertaining but equally obvious that the two princes were determined to stay in control and avoid probing questions. There was one touching moment when Harry admitted: 'Exams have never been my favourite and I always knew that I was going to find it harder than most people.' William immediately showed his caring side, in a way that was reminiscent of how he tried to help his mother when she was in despair, by lavishing praise on his younger brother. Although the brothers are very unalike in character and temperament they are bound together by their unique position and the experience of losing their mother very young. But they don't live in each other's pockets, and while William was at university, they didn't see much of each other.

Left: Prince Harry and four-year-old orphan Mutsu Potsane preparing to plant a peach tree at the Mants'ase Children's Home. Mutsu adored Harry and followed him everywhere. They are still in touch fourteen years later.

Above: Harry in Mokhotlong, Lesotho in 2014, a decade after his first trip. He shows his camera to a group of herd boys who from the age of five can spend months away from their families in the mountains where their precious livestock can graze.

Centre: William and Harry join celebrities and members of the public for a one-mile fun run along the River Thames to raise money for the charity Sport Relief.

Right: Harry joins the disabled war veterans UK team against the USA during a volleyball exhibition match during the Warrior Games, Colorado Springs, USA in May 2013. It inspired him to launch the Invictus Games.

Left: Harry and his then girlfriend Chelsy Davy in the royal box at The Concert for Diana in July 2007 in London to mark the tenth anniversary of her death.

Right: Prince Charles, Harry and Chelsy at Harry's pilot course graduation in May 2010, at the Army Aviation Centre, Andover. Charles, Colonel in Chief, presented flying badges to the students, including Harry.

Left: Harry and his then girlfriend Cressida Bonas at the WE Day UK, a charity event that brings young people together, held at Wembley Arena in March 2014 in London. Their relationship ended shortly afterwards.

Left: Harry dancing hard during his visit to a youth project in Kingston, the capital of Jamaica.

(©POOL - Julian Parker/UK Press via Getty Images)

Right: Harry teases William with an African rock python during their visit to Mokolodi Education Centre in June 2010 in Botswana, a country he loves.

(©Chris Jackson/Getty Images)

Left: Harry is first out of the blocks against Olympic sprint champion Usain Bolt, at the University of the West Indies, in Jamaica during his first solo royal tour to mark the Queen's Diamond Jubilee in 2012.

(©John Stillwell/PA Archive/PA Images)

Right: Prince Seeiso of Lesotho and Harry on stage with the Basotho Youth Choir at the Sentebale Concert at Kensington Palace, London in June 2016. It marked the tenth year since Sentebale was founded.

(©Jeff Spicer/Getty Images)

Left: US First Lady Michelle Obama and Harry take tea together at Kensington Palace in June 2015. Michelle was on a global tour to promote her 'Let Girls Learn Initiative'.

(©Amanda Lucidon/The White House via Getty Images)

Right: Harry on the Buckingham Palace balcony with the Duke and Duchess of Cambridge and their children Prince George and Princess Charlotte during the Trooping the Colour ceremony to mark the Queen's 90th birthday on 11 June 2016.

(©Samir Hussein/WireImage)

Left: Harry attends The Sovereign's Parade at the Royal Military Academy, Sandhurst in December 2017 in Camberley. The occasion brought back many memories of his own time at Sandhurst eleven years earlier. As he has a beard, he couldn't wear military uniform.

(© Richard Pohle/AFP/Getty Images)

Left: Kate, William and Harry spearheaded a campaign called Heads Together to break the stigma around mental health. It prompted Harry to reveal his own 'near breakdown' and long-term grief over his mother's death.

(©Nicky J Sims/Getty Images for Royal Foundation)

Right: Harry plays handball with children in East London in July 2017 as part of the Fit and Fed campaign to provide them with free access to activity sessions throughout the summer holidays.

(©Max Mumby/Indigo/Getty Images)

Left: Harry always seeks out the elderly, infirm and handicapped to talk to on his walkabouts. He has the ability to connect with people of all generations.

(©Andrew Yates - WPA Pool/Getty Images)

Right: Harry during the Opening Ceremony of the 2017 Invictus Games at the Air Canada Centre in Toronto, Canada. Meghan Markle was sitting close by but not in the VIP box alongside Harry for reasons of protocol.

(©Danny Lawson/PA Wire/PA Images)

Left: Harry hugs gold medallist Maurice Manuel of Denmark after defeating team UK in the wheelchair rugby final during the 2017 Games.

(©Justin Heiman/Getty Images for the Invictus Games Foundation)

Right: Barack Obama and Harry enjoy chatting together. Here they are watching the wheelchair basketball at the 2017 Games.

(©Chris Jackson/Getty Images for the Invictus Games Foundation)

Left: Harry and Meghan Markle at their first joint public appearance. Harry whispered in Meghan's ear and they laughed together as they watched a wheelchair tennis match. It helped change the question from 'if' they would get engaged to 'when.'

(©Danny Lawson/PA Wire/PA Images)

Top left: Harry outside the Help for Heroes centre talking to wounded war veterans who were building a wooden outhouse in January 2017   (©*Angela Levin*)

Top right: Harry talking to a once traumatised paramedic at the Emergency Operations Centre for London Ambulance Service in February 2017.   (©*Angela Levin*)

Bottom left: Harry in Nottingham playing with nine-year-olds, who were thrilled to see a 'real prince' in October 2016.   (©*Angela Levin*)

Bottom right: Harry at the Community Recording Studio, St Ann's, Nottingham in October 2016 with leader Trevor Rose and a bunch of young people with difficult backgrounds. They warmed to him instantly.   (©*Angela Levin*)

Left: Prince Harry and Meghan Markle during an official photocall to announce their engagement at the Sunken Gardens at Kensington Palace on 27 November 2017. (©Samir Hussein/WireImage)

Above: Prince Philip, the Duke and Duchess of Cambridge, Meghan Markle and Prince Harry after the Christmas Day Church service at Church of St Mary Magdalene, 2017 in King's Lynn, England.

(©Chris Jackson/Getty Images)

Below: Prince Harry and his new fiancée Meghan Markle choose Nottingham for their first joint official royal visit less than a week after announcing their engagement. The crowds shouted Meghan's name as she clung on to Harry's arm. (©Karwai Tang/WireImage)

Advanced flying training at the Middle Wallop army base in Hampshire followed on from the basic course. This included forty or so hours of flying and covering the more advanced aspects of flying such as night-flying, flying in bad weather, emergency drills, and more advanced handling techniques. Here Harry would also be assessed on whether he would fly a Lynx or Apache helicopter. I was told by an military expert that: 'all prospective pilots are trained on the Lynx and only those who show a particularly strong aptitude will be allowed to train on the Apache because it is so complex. Harry had that natural aptitude.'

Harry also had his heart and mind set on flying the attack Apache helicopter, worth £35 million, as it would mean he would get back to the front line, but knew it partly depended on what was needed. He concentrated hard, so much so that he barely acknowledged his twenty-fifth birthday, a day when he would receive the first instalment of his multi-million-pound inheritance from his mother's estate, most of which came from the divorce settlement. Without touching the capital the interest was thought to give him a very comfortable £300,000 a year spending money. Perhaps he also felt that at this stage in his helicopter course it was safer to have nothing to drink rather than risk going astray. His hard work again paid off: Meyer told him he had not only passed the necessary tests but he was second top of the group. He had amazed everyone and probably himself by making the grade as one of the army's elite Apache plots.

In May 2010, Prince Charles as Army Air Corps Colonel-in-Chief, presented Harry and eight of his fellow trainees with their distinctive pale blue berets and wings at a ceremony at Middle Wallop. The Duchess of Cornwall, his two maternal aunts, Lady Jane Fellowes and Lady Sarah McCorquodale, came to watch. So did Chelsy, which kick-started speculation that their on-off relationship might be on again. Harry gave a short speech. 'It is a huge honour to have the chance to train on the Apache, which is an awesome helicopter. There is still a huge mountain for me to climb if I am to pass the Apache training course. To be honest, I think it will be one of the biggest challenges in my life so far. I am very determined though, as I do not want to let down people who have shown faith in my ability to fly this aircraft on operations. It is a seriously daunting prospect but I can't wait.'

It was a personal as well as professional breakthrough. Harry was so lavishly praised for passing the necessary exams that it seemed he would be whisked off to Afghanistan at the first opportunity. In fact he faced two more years of intermittent training that were not long enough to keep him fully occupied, or short enough to make space for some-thing else significant. So at twenty-five, an age when most men were making their way in the world, Harry whiled away much of his time, getting drunk in expensive nightclubs, staying up until dawn, and sleeping through the morning.

The first of his additional courses took place in April 2011 when Harry was sent to America for an Apache conversion to role course in Arizona and California. The focus was on aviation environmental training, judgmental training, and handling the aircraft both by day and night in mountainous and desert conditions. There were also live firing exercises. Then it was back to the UK for more flying practice. On 16 April 2011, it was announced that Harry had been promoted to captain. He was subsequently asked if he felt more comfortable being Captain Wales than Prince Harry: 'Definitely,' he said. 'My father's always trying to remind me about who I am and stuff like that. But it's very easy to forget about who I am when I am in the army. Everyone's wearing the same uniform and doing the same kind of thing. I get on well with the lads and I enjoy my job. It really is as simple as that.'

In June 2011 Clarence House announced that on completion of his training conversion course to use Apache helicopters in the war arena, Harry would be available for deployment, including in current operations in Afghanistan, as an Apache pilot. It was probably also a nudge to the military to hurry things along. Harry was getting increasingly fed up and during an interview on American television threatened to leave the army if he wasn't sent back to Afghanistan. He pointed out: 'You can't train someone and then not put them to the role they need to play... these people [who said I shouldn't go] live in a ridiculous world.'

CHAPTER 10

Pilot Officer Wales

There was joy and relief all round when on 16 November 2010 Prince William and Kate Middleton announced their engagement after an eight-year relationship that had a short break in the middle. Harry spoke generously, saying he was 'enormously pleased' that William had finally popped the question. 'I've known Kate for years and it's great that she is now becoming a part of the family. I always wished for a sister and now I have one.'

The wedding was set for Friday 29 April 2011 at Westminster Abbey with Harry as best man. It was a venue that held painful memories for both William and Harry as thirteen years earlier their mother's funeral had been held there; now the place could also hold joyful occasions. The two princes spent the night before the wedding together at Clarence House. The streets were already packed with hundreds of well-wishers keen to secure a good spot for the following day's proceedings. To everyone's surprise and delight, at 8.30pm William and Harry suddenly appeared among them. For ten minutes they joked, laughed, shook hands and thanked many of them for coming. It was an inspired idea that they only told the police about five minutes before they left Clarence House. It was significant too, as it showed William's wish, encouraged by Harry, to share such an important and personal day in his life with his future subjects, so that they too could feel involved.

After an evening meal with William, Prince Charles and Camilla, Harry went along to the nearby Goring Hotel, which Kate's parents had taken over for a few days before the wedding. It was a happy occasion to celebrate and he stayed in the hotel bar until 3am when he leapt from one of the hotel's balconies on to the pavement and apparently hurt his ankle. A friend said he tried to persuade him not to jump but he allegedly said it would be quicker than going down the stairs. The friend added that Harry was 'showing off' and 'pissed'.

There was no indication of either alcohol or a bad ankle when, a few hours later, he arrived with his brother at Westminster Abbey. Rather they both looked immaculate in military uniform. Harry was in the ceremonial colours of his regiment, the Army Air Corps. A pocket had been specially sewn into it so he could keep the wedding ring safe. William was dressed in the ceremonial uniform of Colonel of the Irish Guards. On the way to the Abbey, William told his brother that he'd only slept half an hour the previous night because the crowds outside had sung and shouted endlessly, and due to his own nerves. Harry is known to rise to an occasion and knew just how to support his brother on this, one of the most important days of his life. It was also a way to show William how much he appreciated the support he'd given when needed. Harry gauged that the most difficult time for his brother would be standing in the Abbey waiting for Kate to arrive. So Harry walked him slowly down the aisle and straight into a private room where he could keep him calm until they heard that Kate had arrived.

She looked stunning in a close-fitting satin and lace dress with a nine-foot train and a veil of ivory silk tulle, held in place by a tiara loaned to her by the Queen. She had four little bridesmaids and two pageboys. Her sister Pippa, whose bottom became an overnight sensation, was maid of honour. There were 1,900 guests in the Abbey for the service, and more than two billion people worldwide watched the second heir to the British throne marry a middle-class girl of his choice.

The ceremony had been organised within an inch of its life and, apart from Prince William struggling a little to push the wedding ring down Kate's finger, it went very smoothly. The radiant newly-weds then travelled in an open-topped carriage for the fifteen-minute journey from Westminster Abbey to Buckingham Palace where the Queen and Prince Philip hosted a canapé reception for 650 guests. Prince William and Kate also went out on to the balcony of Buckingham Palace. When they kissed each other gently on the lips they were cheered by about 500,000 well-wishers outside, who also watched RAF planes fly past in honour of the new royal couple. The Queen and Prince Philip then left the celebrations, missing Harry's best man's speech in front of about 300 friends and relatives at a dinner and disco hosted by Prince Charles. Harry had read it out first over the phone to Chelsy in South Africa who, despite no longer being his steady girlfriend, had also been invited to the wedding. She suggested he remove some of the racier anecdotes, including a reference to Kate's 'killer legs', as she didn't think the Queen would take kindly to laddish humour. Harry was also obliged to submit the final version to Palace courtiers.

By all accounts Harry was at his absolute best and had the guests crying with laughter. He gently teased William with anecdotes about his childhood, how he had behaved with girlfriends and his increasing hair loss. He also described him as 'the perfect brother' and repeated that Kate was 'the sister I always wanted'. It also included a moving tribute to their mother. Harry then took over the compere's role and introduced other speakers, including Kate's father Michael Middleton and William, with jokey one-liners. The newly-weds danced until 3am then left the proceedings. Harry was up for more fun and led anyone who wanted to join him onto a waiting coach that took them to the Goring Hotel. This after-party went on until about 5am when Harry felt it was time to go home.

If at any moment he wondered what Chelsy felt as she watched William and Kate take their vows, a friend revealed that seeing the enormity and pomp of the day convinced her that she and Harry had been right to separate. Although they had a lot in common, she saw clearly that because they came from such different worlds it could never have worked, especially as she valued her privacy and guarded it so carefully.

The wedding might, however, have spurred Harry to move on, and a few weeks later he began dating a beautiful blonde model-turned-actress, Florence Brudenell-Bruce. They had known each other for years and she had girlfriend potential. She liked being in the limelight and her father, a wine merchant, had gone to Eton, but their relationship barely lasted a season. Someone close to Florence, whose friends call Flee, said she soon realised that Harry had a wandering eye and was a practised flirt. She wasn't interested in dealing with that kind of relationship.

Harry talked to an American TV channel about how difficult it was to find a suitable girlfriend and how for the moment he had decided to prioritise work over his love life. He also admitted that media reaction to him merely talking to a female gave him 'massive paranoia'. 'Even if I talk to a girl, that person is then suddenly my wife and people go knocking on her door,' he grumbled. 'If or when I do find a girlfriend, I will do my utmost to ensure that me and her can get to the point where we're comfortable before the massive invasion that is inevitably going to happen into her privacy.' He put this into practice with Meghan Markle and managed to keep their budding relationship a secret for six months.

He added that he tried not to blame himself too much.

'To be fair, I haven't had that many opportunities to get out there and meet people. At the moment my focus is very much on work. But if someone slips into my life' – a phrase he also used when describing how he met Meghan – 'then that's absolutely fantastic. When people finish work in the City or wherever work is, if you want to have a bit of downtime, you might go to the pub with your mates. I do that less because it's not downtime for me. I don't know who I am going to bump into. I don't know if someone's going to try and grab a selfie. So there is very little private life.'

The truth was that Harry, who is expert at mixing being both dutiful and a rebel, had no trouble finding the here-today-gone-tomorrow type of girlfriend. Long-term relationships were, however, much more of a problem due to the demands of the royal family and the intense media spotlight.

★ ★ ★

The next celebration was the Queen's Diamond Jubilee in 2012. Although the actual anniversary that marked sixty years since she succeeded her father, George VI, was in June, throughout the year visits to different Commonwealth countries had been fixed for senior royals to represent her Majesty and mark the occasion.

Harry asked if he could go to the Caribbean, and the Queen picked Belize, the Bahamas and Jamaica as the countries she would like him to visit. It was to be his first solo royal tour and some courtiers were worried about whether he could be trusted to behave properly during the more formal part of the tour, to not go off the rails or get drunk even when not on duty, and above all not shame his grandmother. Even a careless off-the-cuff remark could have been a disaster. There was particular concern about the timing of his visit to Jamaica as Prime Minister Portia Simpson-Miller, an ardent republican, had just called for Jamaica to become a republic and 'achieve full independence'. She also asked for the Queen to be removed as head of state and said she expected Britain to apologise for slavery. How Harry behaved and how she reacted would be scrutinised intently by politicians and courtiers alike and could have long-lasting diplomatic repercussions either way.

Harry took his first tour seriously, thoroughly researched what he would be doing and also asked for advice from the Foreign Office and his grandmother on possible pitfalls. In the event, he did more than rise to this occasion, opening up a little to the public and letting them see his good side, feel the warmth of his personality, and discover his natural sense of humour, his instinct for saying the right thing at the right time, and his innate ability to make people feel good about themselves. It was as if at last he had released the charisma that he had kept bottled up inside for so long.

It was particularly on show when Harry met up with the Olympic gold-winning sprinter Usain Bolt, the fastest man on earth. The event was also a typical example of how Harry is a risk-taker and likes to push boundaries. He challenged Bolt to a race and managed to beat him by getting him to look the other way when they were about to start and then making a wild dash across the finish line. He then cheekily adopted Bolt's famous lightning pose. It was something that no other royal would even consider let alone pull off. Royal tours are valuable because if they go well they can improve international diplomatic relations and increase trade. If his prank had annoyed Bolt, the hero of his country, it could have ruined the entire trip. Instead, the Jamaicans loved it and Harry's stunt filled two pages in most of the British newspapers the next day.

His biggest challenge began with the arrival of his motorcade outside the governor-general's residence where he was to meet the prime minister. When I spent time with him I noticed he always got out of his car with his hand outstretched to greet his host. This time, perhaps by instinct, he just smiled as he walked towards Prime Minister Simpson-Miller. That small gesture must have brought out the mothering instinct in her, something he seems to have a knack of doing with women of all ages. Mrs Simpson-Miller beamed back and the next thing you knew she was giving him an all-encompassing hug followed by a kiss on the cheek. She then took his arm to lead him inside. As they walked arm in arm together the imp inside Harry made him turn to face the cameras and say with a smile: 'This is my date for tonight.' The sixty-five-year-old Prime Minister beamed with delight. She was later seen dancing enthusiastically with him, which delighted the royals at home.

On his last day in Jamaica, Harry went to a morning beach party at the Montego Bay resort where there were younger beauties including the current Miss Jamaica. There was also dancing and singing, and Harry was seen to mouth the words of the Bob Marley hit 'Three Little Birds' as a violinist played the tune.

Harry took home many happy memories, and a present of a bottle of thirty-year-old Jamaican rum for himself and another for his brother. As far as the UK was concerned, his trip had been a diplomatic tour de force. A report in the *Daily Telegraph* called it 'one impressive royal debut' that would give him 'a huge number of new fans, and,' it added, 'rekindled, for Britain, the bond with former colonies. This was a prince coming into his own.' As well as being a huge relief for his family, the Palace and senior army officials, it also pinpointed the moment when Harry's popularity soared around the globe. It was obvious that Harry was charismatic and had a magic touch but at this stage he could only show it in fits and starts. Internally, he told me, he was still struggling with his past and the loss of his mother.

Along with Prince William and Kate, Harry also played a significant part in the 2012 London Olympic Games, despite initially being completely outsmarted by his grandmother. The Games opened on 27 July with a formerly unimaginable stunt, devised by the film director Danny Boyle in the newly built Olympic Stadium at Stratford in East London. Suddenly, in the middle of the opening show giant screens throughout the stadium cut to the actor Daniel Craig who, as secret service agent James Bond, arrived at Buckingham Palace and made his way along the red-carpeted corridors to the Queen's study. Looking up from her desk she turned to him and said coolly, 'Good evening, Mr Bond.' She then got up and, with the corgis following her, left the palace and walked purposefully to a waiting helicopter. Moments later spectators at the Olympic stadium heard the roar of a Westland hovering overhead and to the total amazement of everyone, including members of the royal family who were not in on the secret – although some later said that Harry had persuaded the Queen to play along – a figure dressed identically to the Queen parachuted into the arena closely followed by 'Mr Bond'. It was an indication that Harry's love of mischief is inherited not only from his mother but also from his then eighty-six-year-old grandmother.

Harry was later interviewed by the BBC's sports commentator Sue Barker, and called the Queen 'an unbelievable good sport'. The three young royals, all sports enthusiasts, turned up on more occasions than had been anticipated to cheer on the UK teams. Harry also made sure he was there to support his cousin Zara Phillips, who won a silver medal as part of the British equestrian team. The achievement made her the first member of the royal family to win an Olympic medal. Harry was thrilled. 'We as cousins are very, very proud,' he said, adding with a smile, 'It now explains why we never get to see her because she's always riding.' Harry is less judgmental of his family than William and is known as a peacemaker.

Harry also joked that his money was on Usain Bolt to win a gold medal in the 100 metres 'because I'm not allowed to compete'. He went on to talk more seriously about the positive effect the sprinter had had on young people: 'There are kids back in Jamaica now who started running ... simply because they look up to him ... he is a wonderful example to his country for the nation for the world ... we hope these Olympics and their efforts would encourage and inspire future generations to get involved in sport rather than sitting in front of the TV and playing computer games.'

It was also left to Harry to preside over the closing ceremony, as William had returned to work as an air ambulance pilot in East Anglia. It was a powerful endorsement of his now widely recognised ability to connect with people, although he would not often have to talk to the billions of individuals watching globally. He said he believed the Games would 'stay in the hearts and minds of people all over the world for a very long time to come. I congratulate all the athletes who have competed. They have shown us that there are few boundaries to human endeavour.' He added that the spirit of the Olympics represented 'a magnificent force for positive change', and that it had 'captured the imagination of the world'.

The year 2012 was also memorable on a personal note as Harry's cousin Princess Eugenie introduced him to a beautiful blonde at an early summer festival in Hampshire. Cressida Bonas, a granddaughter of Edward Curzon, 6th Earl Howe, and daughter of Lady Mary Gaye Georgiana Lorna Curzon had, like Harry, a fractured upbringing. Her parents divorced when she was five. She was a gifted dancer and spent several years at the Royal Ballet School before being awarded a sports scholarship at Prior Park College in Bath. She moved on to Stowe School, where Chelsy had been, and like Chelsy went to Leeds University but to do a dance degree rather than Law.

When Harry met her she was working as a model but longed to be an actress. Harry was instantly smitten and took the unusual step of being seen with her in public only two weeks after they met at the premiere of the Batman film *The Dark Knight Rises* in July 2012. Soon afterwards they flew to Necker, Sir Richard Branson's private Caribbean island, to celebrate his son Sam's twenty-seventh birthday.

Unfortunately Harry wasn't quite besotted enough. The following month he went to Las Vegas with a group of male friends, got drunk and took a group of about twenty-five people, mostly girls he didn't know, to his luxury suite on the thirty-fourth floor of the Encore hotel. The suite included three master bedrooms, a gym, butler service, whirlpool hot tub, 72-inch TV screen and a pool table. Someone suggested a game of strip billiards, where each player takes it in turns to pot a ball and if they miss they remove one piece of clothing. As Harry was only wearing swimming trunks, when he missed the first pot he went naked apart from an African necklace and his Rolex watch. One of the scantily clad girls captured him on her mobile phone both on his own and embracing a young woman who was also nude, and sold them for an estimated £10,000 to the American showbiz website TMZ. The British press picked up the story but initially used more modest photos of Harry to illustrate it. The headlines, however, were not so subtle and included 'Harry Grabs the Crown Jewels', 'Palace Fury at Harry Naked Photos', 'Harry's Naked Romp'. The *Sun* decided to use the real photographs on its front page with the headline 'Here It Is! Pic of naked Harry you've already seen on the internet.'

Harry accepted he had done wrong but also blamed the press for the intrusion: 'I probably let myself down, I let my family down, I let other people down. But at the end of the day I was in a private area and there should be a certain amount of privacy that one should expect. It was probably a classic example of me probably being too much army, and not enough prince. It's a simple case of that.' He also felt it was unfair. 'The papers knew that I was going out to Afghanistan anyway, so the way I was treated by them I don't think is acceptable.' He added: 'Certain people remind me, "Remember who you are, so don't always drop your guard".'

According to some reports Cressie, as Cressida is often called, found the whole episode rather amusing. And a group of military servicemen showed their support for Harry by stripping off and forming a group, with guns concealing their nether regions. They posted the image online. His behaviour did nothing to lower his popularity with most young people who felt that what he did in private was no big deal and he should be able to behave as he wanted.

Such open-mindedness could not be expected from senior army ranks and no doubt much pleading was done behind the scenes to ensure the 'mishap' didn't ruin his army career. Lord Dannatt later revealed: 'At the time, I thought, "Oh my goodness, this is quite unnecessary and, given recent behaviour, rather out of character. Disappointing ... an Army officer does not appear in public with no clothes on – section 64, conduct unbecoming."'

To Prince Harry's enormous relief he soon heard that he

would leave for Afghanistan on 7 September. He arrived back at Camp Bastion as part of the 100-strong 662 Squadron, 3 Regiment, Army Air Corps to begin his four-month combat tour as a co-pilot and gunner of an Apache. If he hoped for a similar experience to his first deployment he was in for a bitter disappointment.

Unlike his first placement the authorities didn't ask for another press blackout because he would be spending most of his time flying a helicopter and well away from threatening insurgents. It soon turned out, however, that he was not immune to sinister death threats. Three days after he arrived, Taliban spokesman Zabiullah Mujahid contacted Reuters and was quoted as saying: 'We are using all our strength to get rid of him, either by killing or kidnapping ... We have informed our commanders in Helmand to do whatever they can to eliminate him.'

Worse was to come. At the time, Camp Bastion was a sprawling, well-fortified British-run base, almost like a small town and believed to be impregnable. However a week after Harry's arrival a gang of nineteen Taliban attackers broke through into the camp, despite the fact that it was ringed by 30ft-high wire fences topped with triple-concertina barbed wire. They were armed with rocket-propelled grenades, mortars and automatic weapons, and proceeded to attack the airfield inside the base. Two American Marines were killed and five aircraft were either destroyed or damaged before Nato soldiers led by British troops killed all but one of the attackers, whom they took prisoner. A Taliban spokesman subsequently said they had been inspired to attack the camp because of an amateur American-made film that they claimed insulted the prophet Mohammed and also because they knew Prince Harry was there.

The British Defence Secretary Philip Hammond later admitted that as soon as the attack began Prince Harry was moved to a guarded location, while Nato confirmed that he 'was never in any danger'. But the last thing Harry would have wanted was to be wrapped up in cotton wool. He also hated being a celebrity soldier. He told me he always 'just wanted to be treated as one of the guys', so he must have felt annoyed and self-conscious being singled out because he was a senior royal and rushed to safety.

As a co-pilot of an Apache, Captain Wales had two important roles. One was to provide air cover for the troops on the ground when they were being attacked, locate the enemy and annihilate them. The second was to lead specialist medical aircraft to a wounded soldier on the ground and protect them from the air while they received medical care. The combination wasn't enough for Action Man Harry when compared to what he had experienced on the ground during his first placement, and he felt disconnected from day-to-day manoeuvres. When on duty he had to remain in a state called Very High Readiness, VHR, so that when he was needed he could be in the air within seven minutes. In practice Harry said that entire days could be spent 'sat inside a tent and playing computer games, watching films or playing PlayStation waiting to be called to action'.

Harry had agreed to be interviewed for television and newspapers while he was on tour as long as the reports were embargoed until he returned home. In one interview he described in fascinating detail what happened when he was called to action. 'It is probably the most rewarding if you're busy,' he said. 'You can fly up to seven and a half hours in a day. We did seven hours ten [minutes] the other day, which is exhausting. On other days you can be in and out of the tent eight or ten times doing half-an-hour here, forty-five minutes there, et cetera …[But] as soon as we get a shout, we get to the aircraft as quick as possible – about six and a half, seven minutes is the quickest we've got it going. You can't lift off until certain things are done in the aircraft and then as soon as you've got clearance from the ops room … off you go as fast as you can. Once you're there, who knows what the situation is going to be like.

'Every time you run to the aircraft you get that adrenalin rush and when you get to the aircraft you've got to try to slow yourself down because if the adrenalin is pumping too much and you rush, you're going to miss something. There's a lot of pressure obviously when we go and support the Americans or when there is a wounded soldier on the ground.'

The prince admitted he had fired on the Taliban during operations to support ground troops and rescue injured Afghan and Nato personnel, adding that he was only doing his job. 'When you fire … the whole floor vibrates and when you fire a missile the whole aircraft shudders. If there's people trying to do bad stuff to our guys, then we'll take them out of the game, I suppose. Take a life to save a life … everyone's fired a certain amount.' He also confirmed he had come under fire. 'Yes, you get shot at.'

Harry's admission that he had killed Taliban militants echoed round the world. It also made him a target for terrorist attacks in the future and is one reason why he remains heavily guarded by protection officers. Ironically, if he had dodged the question he might have avoided becoming so frustrated by their constant presence.

He added that most of the time the helicopter acted more as a deterrent. 'Because the guys [insurgent fighters] recognise the sound and the shape of the aircraft, it's a case of "right, they're above so we are not going to do anything".' He also talked about how much he disliked being at the camp. 'I hate it, being stuck here. I'd much rather be out with the lads in a PB [patrol base]. The last job was, for me personally, better. Obviously lots of guys like the luxury and comforts of Bastion, but what's weird is we're stuck in Bastion and what's going on out there is completely separate.'

Although he hadn't felt self-conscious about his royal status during his first deployment, he did in Camp Bastion. It irritated him when it became obvious that bored off-duty soldiers would spend time trying to 'spot Harry'. On one occasion two girls from the RAF asked if they could have a picture taken with him. He refused and walked away.

His annoyance went further: 'It's a pain in the arse … going into the cookhouse with hundreds of people … [having] a good old gawp and that's one thing that I dislike about being here, because there's plenty of guys in there that have never met me, therefore they look at me as Prince Harry and not as Captain Wales, which is frustrating. Which is probably another reason why I'd love to be out in the PBs away from it all.'

He admitted his negative comments on being an Apache pilot would not go down too well. 'That sounds quite spoilt when I'm standing in front of this thing [an Apache], £35 million-worth – but I think hopefully my friends and family back home know exactly what I'm talking about.' His resentment was indeed rather indiscreet, not least because the British taxpayer had invested more than £1 million in training him to fly a helicopter, a skill he put to use for little more than four months.

To my surprise I was told by a senior military figure that his short time in Afghanistan wasn't considered by those in charge to have been a waste of taxpayers' money. 'It was still a very good turn on investment. He turned up to serve Queen and country and went out and flew the hours just like every other pilot in Afghanistan. It was also wonderful for the general rank and file to see him there. He has since occasionally flown a helicopter. '

But Harry wasn't all gloom and resentment. In another broadcast, one that was transmitted to Afghanistan, he was full of praise for the military. 'It's often said of our armed forces that they are ordinary people doing extraordinary things,' he began. 'Well, I don't buy that. Ordinary people don't run out under withering enemy rockets and heavy machine-gun fire to rescue a wounded comrade. Ordinary people aren't described by their platoon as being "the rock" who held them together. Ordinary people don't brave monsoon conditions dangling on a winch line to rescue thirteen people each in turn. For that matter, ordinary people don't put their lives on the line for distant folk such as the Afghans who need our help and are now turning their country round because of it.' It's guesswork as to how much credit he took for his own actions, but his bravery and attitude also makes him the opposite of 'ordinary'.

On 21 January 2013 it was announced that Harry was returning home. He felt angry and disappointed when he was brought back from his first deployment. This time he felt lost and had little idea what he would do next. Interviewed in Cyprus by ITN on his way back he opened up to say: 'Normal for me? I don't know what is normal any more. I never really have done.' His outspokenness highlighted that he wasn't in the mood to offer the sort of jokey answers that in the past had let him off the hook. Not only did his return home mark the beginning of the end of Harry's army career, the combination of thinking about what the future held for him and his unresolved grief was the start of a downhill path that led to the mental health issues he spoke about publicly in 2017. He hadn't just enjoyed the physical side of army life. The army had become his alternative family. He trusted his fellow servicemen and felt at home. When the army was wrenched away in one sweeping moment he also lost feeling part of a team, the easy camaraderie that develops from shared experiences plus the dark humour he so enjoys. It had also provided 'a hideaway' from his public role.

Once Harry had safely returned to the UK, a military official told me there was considerable nervousness in the upper echelons of the forces about how the Arabic world would react to his deployment in Afghanistan. 'Once Harry was back all the websites and Twitter feeds possible in the Arabic world were monitored to see their reaction. We half-expected a jihad to be announced against the House of Windsor. But to everyone's surprise almost every Twitter feed was full of admiration for a royal prince who could have lived a life of luxury and not done much but instead put himself on the line for his country. It was very favourably received and some countries were quite scathing about their own royal families for doing so little. It was completely unexpected. No one had thought anyone from the Islamic world would praise him.'

Harry didn't quit the army immediately. Kensington Palace announced that he would take up a staff officer role in HQ London district. It was a job that kept him employed by the army but in reality meant his active military career was all but over. Instead, he would help coordinate 'significant projects and commemorative events' for the army. The job was completely unsuitable for his temperament and skills, and stood as much chance of working out as getting a tiger to give up meat.

In a rather rambling interview with Sky TV during a visit to New Zealand in May 2015 he was asked how difficult it was to leave the army. He replied: 'It is a crossroads. I'm in the same position now as most people in my year group or my rank would be in and most of the guys I joined with have left for numerous reasons. If we move on ... more responsibilities come and I suppose with wanting to take on slightly more of this [royal] role I don't really feel as though I would be in the right position to take on the careers of more soldiers and to take on the responsibility of continuing to fly, for instance. So I've been trying to get the balance right over the past six months to a year before I finished and it was getting hard. Inevitably what happens as you climb the ranks is that you will do more of a desk job.'

He told me he found being desk-bound sitting in front of a computer and applying himself to warfare skills unfulfilling. 'I get very agitated if I am stuck in front of a computer for long,' he said. He is a practical man who prefers action.

One positive thing about being home was that his relationship with Cressida resumed. Over the next two years the couple were often photographed together attending events including Glastonbury music festival and a society wedding. They also accepted an invitation from Princesses Eugenie and Beatrice to join them on a skiing trip in the exclusive Swiss resort of Verbier with their parents, the Duke and Duchess of York. Although they had divorced twenty years earlier they remained friends.

Harry, who is very demonstratively affectionate, was uninhibited about kissing Cressida publicly in a restaurant or while they were waiting for the ski lift. One loving moment was captured by a French photographer and published round the world and was assumed to mean Harry had fallen in love again. Cressida later joined Harry to watch an England ruby match at Twickenham, London, and in March 2014 Harry persuaded her to join him for what would be her first official royal engagement. The event was a WE Day concert organised by the charity Free The Children, which encourages young people to help others. It took place at Wembley Stadium, London. Speaking to 12,000 largely screaming young students from 400 schools Harry described voluntary work as the 'coolest thing in the world'. He was again seen kissing and hugging Cressida, and commentators interpreted his public behaviour to mean they were on the verge of getting engaged.

Instead, within a month they had parted. The Press Association reported the couple had decided to go their separate ways to allow Cressida to focus on her acting career. Harry believed the collapse of their relationship was also due to media intrusion. Ingrid Seward, a friend of Cressida's mother, revealed at a subsequent Henley Literary Festival that twenty-seven-year-old Cressida told friends she split from the prince because she received too many negative comments whenever they went out together. 'She just said it was awful because every time she walked down the street she could hear people criticising her.' Cressida was also distraught by comments on social media.

It must have upset and infuriated Harry that yet again living under the glare that comes with being royal had contributed to the failing of another important relationship. It helps explains why in 2016 he was so angry when his relationship with Meghan Markle was discovered and she and her family were hounded by the world's media.

CHAPTER 11

Ups and Downs

By 2013 Harry was finding it increasingly difficult to cope. Although he managed to put on a good front and fulfil his royal duties, he was falling apart inside. But it wasn't until 2017 that he confessed that the previous few years had been a real struggle, that he'd bottled up his emotions for two decades but waited until he was twenty-eight before seeking help.

At the time he'd felt trapped by his royal life and grief-stricken over the loss of his mother. He badly needed someone to talk to about this but it was hard to find anyone emotionally available he could lean on.

It was not a subject he felt able to raise with his father who was very happy with Camilla Parker Bowles and had made a new, more contented life for himself. Harry was pleased for him, but how could he pour out his heart about how much he missed his mother, longed to feel at peace in her arms, when he knew full well how devastated she had been by Camilla's presence. Nor could he open his heart to the Queen and Duke of Edinburgh who had mixed feelings about the charismatic but troubled princess and believed that emotions should be kept under control. While Harry, like his mother, does not.

Nor did it help that once he'd left active duty in the army it was hard for him not to feel aimless, particularly as he'd hoped it would provide him with a life-long career.

If you add a mental health problem to all these pressures and disappointments, he showed great courage to continue with his royal duties, make a huge success of his first solo tour in the Caribbean, be involved in the London Olympics, fly an Apache helicopter in Afghanistan and have a romance with Cressida Bonus. He also had to deal with the fall-out of his indiscretions in Las Vegas.

He told me that losing his mother had 'quite a serious effect' on both his personal and professional life and left him in 'total chaos'. He also told the *Daily Telegraph* that his mental health issues were not a result of his time in Afghanistan. 'I can safely say it's not Afghanistan-related,' he stated. 'I'm not one of those guys that has had to see my best mate blown up next to me and have to apply a tourniquet to both their legs. Luckily, thank God, I wasn't one of those people.'

He also experienced panic attacks. 'Every time I was in any room with loads of people, which is quite often, I was just pouring with sweat, like heart beating – boom, boom,

boom, boom – and literally just a washing machine. I was like, "Oh my God, get me out of here now. Oh, hang on, I can't get out of here, I have got to just hide it."'

In retrospect there had been small but significant signs for some time that all was not well, perhaps indicative that he had not come to terms with losing his mother and didn't know how to handle his grief. A therapist says: 'This can affect someone outwardly by being hostile and aggressive and inwardly through low self-esteem, anxiety and depression.'

'At times,' remembers someone who knows him well, 'he ghost walked through his royal duties. He was very diminished from the Harry everyone knew.' So much so that during his week-long royal visit to the US in May 2013, even the *Washington Post* noticed that his spark had gone and commented that he was 'painfully well behaved'.

It was his first trip to America since his infamous visit to Las Vegas, when he was photographed naked during a game of strip billiards. If he hoped the regretted incident wouldn't be brought up, he was mistaken. It was the first thing Governor Chris Christie referred to when he took Harry to see areas in New Jersey that had recently been damaged by Hurricane Sandy. 'Believe me, nobody's going to get naked if I'm spending the entire day with Prince Harry,' he said, adding more positively: 'the Prince has said he apologises for his conduct back then. Lots of young people make mistakes … I'm thrilled he wants to come and see the destruction himself first-hand and he wants to be helpful.'

The main reason for Harry's tour was to promote the rehabilitation of injured American and British troops. At times, however, he was greeted like a huge pop star. His week began with a look round an exhibition at Capitol Hill organised by The HALO Trust, a landmine-clearing charity that was close to his mother's heart. She was also its patron. Senator John McCain accompanied him and as both men entered the rotunda of the Russell Senate Office Building where the exhibition was on show, 'hundreds of screaming women' were waiting for him. They made so much noise that security guards asked them to leave. Harry's female fans continued to make their presence heard throughout the week.

When McCain was asked what Harry thought of his superstar reception he replied: '[He] just kind of seemed to be a little ... the word isn't embarrassed, but ... I'm sure it's not the first time that he's had that experience.'

Later that day Harry made what the American TV programme *Today* called 'a most charming appearance' at a Mother's Day tea at the White House hosted by first lady Michelle Obama. When Harry walked in Mrs Obama shouted: 'Surprise!' The mothers and grandmothers, many of whom were attached to the US armed forces, were initially astonished and then thrilled and thronged round him.

As well, Harry laid wreaths at the Tomb of the Unknown Soldier at Arlington National Cemetery, and for military personnel killed in Iraq and Afghanistan. He visited wounded veterans at Walter Reed National Military Medical Center, where he also saw the facility's prosthetics centre. He visited 'socially, economically challenged' parts of New York and attended a smart dinner for American Friends of the Royal

Foundation where he gave a short speech. He spoke with feeling about the effects of HIV and Aids on children in Africa before sitting down to a meal of beef tenderloin with a salad made up of green leaves, peas and baby carrots.

He captained a polo playing team in Connecticut to raise funds for his Africa-based charity Sentebale and stopped off in Colorado to visit the British Armed Forces team, which was competing for the first time in the Warrior Games, an annual sporting event for wounded US servicemen and women aimed at helping them overcome their debilitating injuries. It was run by the US Olympic Committee and in this fifth Games had over 200 servicemen and women competing including, for the first time, a British contingent.

Watching the courage and determination of the competitors had an immediate and life-changing effect on Harry. One that was similar to what he'd felt when he first visited Lesotho and saw countless abandoned orphans with HIV. It made him think he could maintain a link with the army and bring royal support for these games that he believed not enough people were watching.

'I wanted to do it on a massive scale,' he told me when we met. 'I want people to watch and then change how they think about wounded servicemen and woman.' Few could disagree this is what he has succeeded in doing. It was therefore all the more surprising that when he gave a speech praising the Games there was none of the usual animation in his voice or expression. His tone was flat, his face blank and he let out several small sighs as he spoke as if it was all rather an effort. Perhaps they were indicative of how low he was feeling. He began by explaining that his interest in the Warrior Games began the previous year, adding a touch cynically: 'I was in Washington on the ambassador's lawn to plant a tree which is what most of our family do nowadays.' There he met ex-servicemen and women who were just returning from the fourth Warrior Games and told them he was sorry to have missed it. He spoke too about his own experience in Helmand Province where he saw both individual bravery and the 'devastating consequences and life-changing wounds' of the injured.

It made him decide to try to bring the concept of a similar sporting event to the UK. When Harry has an idea he embraces it completely and wants quick results. Once he returned home he secured the backing of then Mayor of London Boris Johnson, the London Organising Committee of the Olympic and Paralympic Games and the Ministry of Defence. He launched the Games on 6 March 2014 saying that they would take place 10–14 September. It took an enormous amount of effort and determination but Harry put his heart and soul into getting it up and running. He pulled it off and a mere six months later he stood proudly beside Prime Minister David Cameron, Prince Charles, William and Kate at the opening ceremony in London's Olympic Park. It was named the Invictus Games – '*invictus*' is Latin for undefeated – a word that Harry was struggling to feel about himself.

Former army captain David Wiseman, who was shot by the Taliban in 2009 and played a major part in organising those first Games, told me: '[Prince Harry] has tremendous commitment to the men and women in uniform and is able to use his celebrity status to highlight the remarkable things they do. I have never seen anyone do it better.'

Broadcast by the BBC, around 300 competitors from 13 countries competed in the Games, and many of the events took place at venues used during the 2012 Olympic Games in London. They were a great success, highly competitive and, as Harry was involved, also good fun. As well as gold, silver and bronze medals, there were also medallions for every competitor, so everyone's participation could be recognised. Harry was delighted: 'Sport is surely the best way to support recovery of mind and body,' he suggested. 'The premise is simple: set yourself a target, take your mind off all the negative thoughts and concentrate on the challenge in front of you, all while relearning to use your body.'

Of course it's easier said than done and a sporting success won't make a soldier suffering from post traumatic stress disorder (PTSD) or who has lost one or more limbs suddenly feel themselves again. It is more a confidence booster to help them move on in other areas of life. Harry's involvement earned the praise of countless ex-servicemen. Mike Goody, who lost a leg in Afghanistan and swam in the 2014 and 2016 Invictus Games, voiced what many felt: 'Harry was an absolute legend. He was everywhere. He was literally boosting everything, pumping everything, getting everyone going, really encouraging.'

There was excitement too on a personal level. At 16.24 on Monday 22 July 2013 Kate gave birth to George Alexander Louis – Prince George of Cambridge. He was William's and her first child. The birth took place in the private Lindo Wing of St Mary's Hospital, Paddington, where both he and Prince William had been born. Prince George immediately became third in line to the throne while Prince Harry slipped down to fourth. The twenty-eight-year-old prince talked about his newborn nephew a few days later while on a visit to a photographic exhibition in London documenting the work of Sentebale. He said he had cuddled the baby prince who was 'crying his eyes out' when they met, how it was 'fantastic to have another addition to the family', and that 'I only hope my brother knows how expensive my babysitting charges are.'

When asked what his role was as an uncle he replied: 'To make sure he has a good upbringing, keep him out of harm's way and to make sure he has fun. The rest I'll leave to the parents.'

Harry experienced a similar rock star reaction to the one in New York when he made a two-day visit to Sydney and Perth in Australia to commemorate the 100-year anniversary of the arrival of the Royal Australian Navy's fleet. Prime Minister Tony Abbott accompanied him and publicly apologised that many Australians were anti-monarchists, adding that you wouldn't know it, judging by the huge crowds that had gathered to greet Harry. 'Today everyone feels like a monarchist,' he said.

Harry has always enjoyed extreme sporting challenges and is patron of Walking With The Wounded charity. He had to withdraw early from a successful North Pole expedition in 2011 to attend his brother's wedding, but in the winter of

2013 he joined a 200-mile trek to the South Pole with a team of injured service personnel from the UK, all of whom had physical or cognitive injuries. There was a similar team from the United States and one from the Commonwealth. The walk was originally going to be a race but the competitive element of the expedition was dropped because of 'difficult terrain'. The UK group left London for Cape Town on 17 November to acclimatise at Novolazarevskaya Station, an Antarctic research station, and the expedition itself began on 30 November. It was estimated that it would last around 15 days with the teams trekking between 15km to 20km per day. Temperatures went as low as -45°C with 50mph winds. In addition, each individual pulled a 70+kg Arctic sledge.

Ed Parker, the expedition's director and co-founder of Walking With The Wounded, said: 'We always knew that this wasn't going to be easy, but that is what makes the challenge so exciting.

'Our aim was to show that, despite injury, young men and women from our armed forces can still achieve great things.

'We came down here, determined to get ... to the South Pole, and this is what we have done. The feeling is incredible.'

Prince Harry spoke on a voice blog just before they reached their destination. 'The wind has dropped down, which is nice. We get to the South Pole on Friday 13th, unlucky for some, lucky for us.' He added all those on the trek were in 'high spirits', but that he thought 'everyone is feeling a bit tired'. The successful trek meant that Harry became the first member of the royal family to reach the South Pole.

He praised everyone but particularly his UK teammate,

Sgt Duncan Slater, from Muir of Ord, who lost both his legs in Afghanistan in 2009 when his vehicle was blown up by an improvised explosive device. '[He] simply doesn't find walking to the South Pole a big enough challenge, which is why he really enjoyed the race. I think everyone back home will appreciate the fact that just being able to walk … in these conditions with no legs is a pretty amazing feat in itself.'

Another of Harry's long-term relationships with former soldiers has been with Kirstie Ennis, a young blonde American marine who served in Afghanistan as an aerial door gunner. In June 2012, the helicopter Sgt Ennis was flying in crash-landed for no apparent reason. She was lucky to survive but suffered traumatic injuries to her brain, spine and face, as well as severe damage to her shoulders and her left leg. Harry got to know her in 2015 when she was the only woman competing in an exhausting 1,000-mile 72-day walk from the north of Scotland to Buckingham Palace to raise money for Walking With The Wounded. It was an agonising trek – doctors had told her three years previously that she would never walk again. At the time she still had both legs, having postponed the amputation of her injured left leg in order to take part.

Harry joined the walkers at various milestones en route, much to her delight. 'He seems so engaged and committed,' she stated. 'He wanted to know my story and I felt I could open up to him and that he really listened. It was just like walking with a friend, or a brother.

'The military is a family in that respect. It's a brotherhood. It really meant something to have Harry walk with us. I told him about my time at Camp Bastion because we were serving in the same place at the same time.

'He's so down to earth and very easy to get along with. He's also very kind and when people came up to say "Hi" he made time for them, especially the kids, and you could see it really made their day.'

She also recalled how the group teased him when he dared to complain that his knees were aching at the end of one 15-mile walk. 'He was limping at the end and complaining a bit, but quietly as he knew we would give him grief,' she laughed.

The group of six found walking up to 18 miles a day a huge challenge, but she said having him alongside lifted their morale. 'It's not been easy. With my injuries I deal with pain constantly and it affects me physically and emotionally. I've never felt as disabled as I have done on this walk. It has been so hard. It was great when Prince Harry joined us.'

Despite her injuries she heard on the walk that she would be part of the US team competing at the Invictus Games in Orlando in 2016. 'Confirmation about the national team came through while I was walking with Prince Harry in Norfolk. He was really proud and very excited for me. He loves to see veterans excel and overcome their disabilities, that's what drives him and you can really see that.' She competed in rowing, swimming and outdoor events.

The weary group reached Buckingham Palace in October 2015, where Prince Harry was waiting to congratulate them on their amazing achievement. The following month Ennis had her leg amputated, initially up to her knee, but due to an infection she had to have a second amputation above the knee. Prince Harry kept in touch with her progress both in and out of hospital.

'I don't think of him any differently than as my friend. I know he is caring about my situation and concerned and is compassionate about absolutely everybody.' Prince Harry has meanwhile saluted her 'absolutely incredible' courage.

In 2014, Harry made several short royal visits abroad including to Estonia, Italy, Brazil, Chile, Belgium, Oman and Abu Dhabi, plus a visit to Lesotho to stay close to what was happening with his charity. Key events included attending on 4 August the unveiling of the Folkestone Memorial Arch in Kent to mark the World War I centenary. On 14 November he opened the Royal British Legion's 86th Field of Remembrance at Westminster Abbey on behalf of the Duke of Edinburgh, and three days later was at Remembrance Sunday Service at Kandahar Air Base in Afghanistan to represent the Queen.

In January 2015, it was reported that Harry would take on a new role supporting wounded service personnel, a Ministry of Defence initiative in partnership with Help for Heroes and the Royal British Legion. The motive was to ensure that wounded personnel had the 'right sort' of recovery plan. Working with the unit and listening to both men and women talk about mental health as well as physical issues helped his understanding of what was involved and that it was good to talk.

After two years working in an administrative capacity for the army Harry had had enough. The timing almost coincided with him attending a commemoration service at St Paul's Cathedral on 13 March 2015, to mark the end of the Afghanistan campaign. Shortly afterwards Kensington Palace announced that Harry would be moving on from the armed forces in June. But before then, he would spend four weeks seconded to the Australian Defence Force while also being available to represent the royal family at military occasions.

Harry flew into Sydney and went straight to Canberra where he laid a wreath at the Tomb of the Unknown Australian Soldier. He then officially reported for duty to Air Chief Marshal Mark Binskin, Chief of the Defence Force. He presented him with a letter from his grandmother, which reading between the lines sounds very much as if she was rather worried about Harry and decided to send the Chief Marshal a note to ask in the subtlest of royal terms if he could look out for him. The letter expressed how delighted she was about 'military secondment of my grandson, Prince Harry', adding, 'I know that Captain Wales will benefit greatly from spending time with the Australian Diggers [soldiers] and I thank you for welcoming him into your ranks.'

Harry trained with Australia's elite special forces, the SAS in Perth and spent time at bases in Darwin and Sydney where he co-piloted an army Black Hawk and participated in counter-terrorism training in Sydney Harbour with Royal Australian Navy clearance divers. Some felt it was odd for him to train for something he would not do again and that it would underline what he was missing. Others believed it was merely an opportunity for him to have a good time.

The placement was briefly interrupted by a quick visit to Turkey to join his father and mark the disastrous allied campaign at Gallipoli in 1915, in which thousands of allied soldiers including those from Australia and New Zealand died.

While in Australia, Harry released a rigorously upbeat statement: 'After a decade of service moving on from the army has been a really tough decision. I consider myself incredibly lucky to have had the chance to do some very challenging jobs and have met many fantastic people in the process ... Inevitably most good things come to an end and I am at a crossroads in my military career ... I am considering the options for the future and I am really excited about the possibilities ... so while I am finishing one part of my life I am getting straight into a new chapter. I am really looking forward to it.' A royal aide recently pointed out to me he has yet to move far from those crossroads.

Just before Harry flew to New Zealand on 2 May he heard the happy news that William and Kate's second child, Charlotte Elizabeth Diana, had been born. It meant that she would now be fourth in line to the throne while Harry would drop to fifth. When I asked if he minded, his answer was firm and immediate. 'The reason I am now fifth is because of my nephew and niece and I could never wish them away. They are the most amazing things ever.' The birth of William and Kate's third child means Harry became sixth in line.

Prince Harry subsequently gave an interview to Sky TV when he was asked about baby Charlotte, his plans for the future and crucially whether he would like to settle down. Harry is, however, a master at being polite but rather vague when he doesn't want to give much away. He said: 'There comes a time when you think now is the time to settle down, or now is not, whatever way it is, but I don't think you can force these things. It will happen when it's going to happen. Of course I would love to have kids right now but there's a process that one has to go through... Hopefully I'm doing all right by myself. It would be great to have someone else next to me to share the pressure, but you know, the time will come and whatever happens, happens.'

He also neatly dodged the question of how he'd balance more royal duties with something new: 'There are a few things on the shortlist but I don't want to speculate,' he said. 'But as long as people back home know they can trust me in making the right decision and whatever it is hopefully it will be something that means I can still give something back I suppose. This is part of the job. [Royal work] is fantastic but both William and I feel we need to have a wage. We need to work with normal people to keep ourselves sane and also to keep us ticking along. I need to find something that will give me balance.' Harry has yet to earn a salary. He then added a comment that was very similar to the one Diana, Princess of Wales told him when he was nearly four, just after her separation from Prince Charles: 'I have to go along with the way my life is, and in many ways I'm very privileged.'

Harry also missed Charlotte's christening, which was held on 5 July at St Mary Magdalene Church at the Queen's Sandringham estate, as this time he was in Africa. He felt rather guilty. 'What a bad uncle I am!' he told Simson Uri-Khob, manager of Save the Rhino in Africa, with whom he was staying in Namibia, helping to track lions, elephants, rhino and leopards in the 10,000sq mile Palmwag Reserve: 'I should really be there, but today I am here, this is where I want to be.' He explained that it was a recce trip on behalf of William too, and he'd be taking 'a lot of new information back home with me for my brother and me to analyse and we're going to work out a strategy for doing more in Africa and to encourage new conservation.' It was, he said, 'something really precious to me and I'm learning a lot.'

In the autumn he attended, as he had done for several years, the WellChild Awards that recognise the courage of children and young people with exceptional health needs. Harry, who is patron of the charity, was at his most charming: 'We literally have the bravest children in the UK in this room,' he said. 'Watching these children and young people face challenges with such determination, positivity and of course good humour, never fails to take my breath away.'

A key visit occurred just before Christmas 2015 to mark the 150th anniversary of Mildmay Mission Hospital in East London and its £6 million revamp. In 1991 the Princess of Wales went to Middlesex Hospital where, by holding the hand of an HIV-positive patient, she radically changed people's attitude to Aids. Fighting the stigma became important to her. At the time, Mildmay was the first dedicated hospice for people dying of Aids-related illnesses and has remained at the forefront of specialist HIV care ever since. Harry discovered while he was there that his mother had visited the hospital seventeen times, but only three were in an official capacity.

He also met a female patient who was born HIV-positive and recalled twenty-four years earlier sitting on Diana's lap at Great Ormond Street Hospital when she was two. 'Your mother's lap was so comfortable and I cuddled into her,' she told Harry. He replied with a wistful smile: 'I remember that, too.' You could tell by his facial expressions that it was a very emotional experience for him.

Kerry Reeves-Kneip, the hospital's director of Fundraising and Communications, fulsomely praised Harry and compared him very favourably with his mother. 'You almost felt you knew him because he was so kind to everyone, and made everyone feel comfortable,' he said.

However, the year 2015 ended on an uncomfortable note when Harry was criticised for not pulling his weight within the royal family. It was reported that the Queen, who was nearly three times his age, carried out more engagements in 2015 than the Duke and Duchess of Cambridge and Prince Harry combined. There were of course extenuating circumstances – William was working part time as a helicopter pilot for the East Anglian Air Ambulance service, the duchess had a baby in May, and Harry left the army halfway through the year and then spent six weeks in the summer working on a series of conservation projects in Africa. Nonetheless, it was stated that the Queen managed 306 engagements in the UK and 35 abroad. The Duke and Duchess and Prince Harry managed

198 engagements between them in the UK and 94 abroad. If there was a cutback in Harry's appearances there was a very good reason, which he was soon to find the courage to talk about. He no doubt took the criticism to heart and in 2016 became the most travelled senior royal, clocking up approximately 61,800 miles on public engagements outside the UK.

CHAPTER 12

Heads Together

For years Harry felt he was 'very close to a complete breakdown on numerous occasions'. He knew something was wrong but, he said: 'I just couldn't put my finger on it. Instead of dealing with it I buried my head in the sand and let everything around me tear me to pieces.' He was also aware that he was becoming increasingly aggressive. In 2017 he told the *Daily Telegraph* how much it had worried him. 'I took up boxing, because everyone was saying boxing is good for you and it's a really good way of letting out aggression. That really saved me because I was on the verge of punching someone, so being able to punch someone who had pads was certainly easier.'

For years he had hidden his concerns in public. 'I was a typical twenty, twenty-five, twenty-eight-year-old running around going "life is great", "life is fine".' He could help other people, but not himself. He hadn't wanted to involve William with his internal trauma. 'You know what it is like with a big brother,' he said to me. William, with Kate's help, had worked through some of his own anxieties. Becoming a father had also given him a new perspective on the world and the chance to become the type of father and husband he wanted to be. It took a while for Harry to realise his brother would, in fact, be a good person to talk to. They didn't see too much of each other, but Harry occasionally popped into their apartment at Kensington Palace, where Kate cooked him a meal. Roast chicken is reportedly a favourite, and what he and Meghan were preparing the night he proposed.

As time passed, he felt worse rather than better and eventually began to open up a little about his problems. '[I] started to have a few conversations and actually all of a sudden all of this grief that I have never processed started to come to the forefront and I was like, there is actually a lot of stuff here that I need to deal with.'

It was one step forward but at the time he wasn't ready to take it further despite Prince William suggesting he seek help. 'For me personally, my brother, you know, bless him, he was a huge support to me. He kept saying, "This is not right, this is not normal, you need to talk to [someone] about stuff, it's OK".' Harry didn't listen: 'The timing wasn't right. You need to feel it in yourself, you need to find the right person to talk to, as well.'

Most people in such turmoil and distressed mental state would find it difficult to get out of bed in the morning, let alone sell yourself and the royal family to the public. Harry often surfaced late and many royal visits were not scheduled before noon.

His brother and close friends kept on encouraging him to get professional help. 'They said: "You really need to deal with this. It is not normal to think that nothing has affected you." I didn't want to be in the position I was in but I eventually pulled my head out of the sand, started listening to people and decided to use my role for good.' He was twenty-eight when he followed William's advice and sought the help he needed: 'I've done that [seen someone] a couple of times, more than a couple of times, but it's great.'

For someone who guards his privacy so tightly, opening up on such a sensitive personal issue took immense courage. He did so as part of a much wider campaign by Heads Together, an offshoot of the Royal Foundation that he, William and Kate put together to help remove the stigma attached to mental health issues. The proposed two-year project would, they decided, include all three of them talking about their own difficult issues. Kate admitted that motherhood 'could be lonely at times' and talked about the 'steep learning curve' of having a first baby. William admitted he hadn't talked enough about his feelings and fears, especially in relation to his mother. But it was Harry's confession that he had had mental health issues and sought professional help that made the headlines.

He hoped altruistically that if he admitted to having problems, it might encourage others to do the same. When we talked at Kensington Palace, he said he handled the public confession by ensuring he didn't reveal too much: 'I protected myself by saying just enough to make the point, but didn't give much detail. No one would know from what I said exactly what was wrong, how long it lasted and what help I was given.'

He explained that his work with the London branch of the Personnel Recovery Unit, where he listened to wounded, injured and sick servicemen and women talk about serious mental health issues, had proved a turning point in his understanding. 'I know there is huge merit in talking about your issues and the only thing about keeping it quiet is that it's only ever going to make it worse, not just for you but everybody else around you as well, because you become a problem.'

He acknowledged that it took time to get well but told me he now feels he is in 'a good place', adding: 'The experience I have had is that once you start talking about it, you realise that actually you're part of quite a big club,' and that his friends felt able to 'unravel their own issues'.

'I can't encourage people enough to just have that conversation because you will be surprised, firstly, how much support you get and, secondly, how many people literally are longing for you to come out.'

His high-profile admission has also changed public attitudes. After Harry spoke out, Mind, the mental health charity, reported a 38 per cent increase in calls on its information line, while Calm, a mental health charity specifically aimed at men, saw its website traffic double. Harry was also able to announce the important breakthrough in October 2017 that the Ministry of Defence and the Royal Foundation were joining together to put mental fitness and mental health at the heart of the training and support provided to the entire defence industry.

Harry's time in the army has taken a physical toll on him, too. 'I've actually been receiving a bit of medical care on my body, which has basically been ruined over the last ten years of army service.' Despite this, he assured me: 'I am now fired up and energised and love charity stuff, meeting people and making them laugh. [William and I] really enjoy our work and hope we are good value for money as far as the British public is concerned.

'I sometimes still feel I am living in a goldfish bowl but I now manage it better. I still have a naughty streak too, which I enjoy and is how I relate to those individuals who have got themselves into trouble.'

His own experience has made him more empathetic with individuals he meets on royal engagements, who have psychological issues or come from dysfunctional homes. Something that also helps him work on any of his own remaining demons. He continued: 'Because of the process I have been through, I've now been able to take my work seriously, been able to take my private life seriously as well, and been able to put blood, sweat and tears into the things that really make a difference and things that I think will make a difference to everybody else.'

Harry was also keen to get across to me that he gives good hugs, something he has inherited from his mother. 'Everyone needs a hug now and again and it just so happens that I'm very good with hugs,' he laughed. An attribute that would no doubt have made his mother 'smile with pride'.

He also said he is a passionate, emotional person. 'I have an incredibly large heart, which I want people to see. There is so much passion inside of me that I can also give to other people. It is how I can relate to individuals who have got themselves into trouble.' He smiled. 'Sometimes I can have too much passion fired up and I get impatient to get things done. It has got me into trouble in the past, partly because I cannot stand the idea of people mincing around the subject rather than just getting on with it.'

★ ★ ★

I saw what he meant when I spent over a year on and off accompanying him round the country. In October 2016 I joined Prince Harry in Nottingham. He feels embedded in the local community, which was one reason why he chose to take Meghan there for her introduction to royal visits shortly after they announced their engagement.

His first stop was outside Nottingham's National Ice Centre where about thirty nine-year-old boys and girls from Chetwynd Primary Academy were gathered. While they waited for him to arrive the boys practised throwing rugby balls through targets. The girls just chatted. Were they excited? I asked. 'Yes,' one of them beamed. 'Because he is a prince, a real royal person and we have never met one before.' Harry has said many times how much he longs 'to be something other than Prince Harry', but, as these children showed, being a prince is precisely what enables him to achieve things.

The royal limousine and its motorbike outriders arrived punctually and, as usual, Harry bolted out of the car like a racehorse released from its stall. It's a technique that gives the impression that he couldn't wait to get there and is delighted to see whoever it is.

Another is to totally focus on the individual – not necessarily the administrators – he talks to, and only them. He doesn't look around and instead engages them fully, listens carefully to what they say and is always sympathetic. It sounds extraordinary, but I saw time and again how a few words from him can give people, who looked scared, in pain or depressed a real boost of hope and confidence.

He initially talked to the adults involved in putting Full Effect into practice. He doesn't mind whether people curtsy or bow when meeting him and most didn't. He quickly moved on to the children, cracked lots of jokes and threw rugby balls to the boys as if he was a supercharged party entertainer. The children loved it. 'We are working with primary school children,' an organiser explained, 'because many of them aged seven and upwards are already being used as lookouts for drug dealers and it's too late once they are in secondary school.'

Harry moved on to a group of sixteen- to twenty-four-year-olds who were part of Coach Core, another Royal Foundation initiative that gives that age group a chance to train as sports coaches. Some of them were helping the nine-year-olds. Most of these teens also come from dysfunctional homes and have so far had very few life chances. They haven't fitted in with the school system and some belong to families where three or four generations have never worked. As a result the teenagers and young adults have no concept of getting up at a certain time or arriving at work promptly. Harry wants to break this cycle and he proved to be both a great motivational speaker and a good listener. 'I believe being a sports coach can change your lives,' he said to them.

Soon afterwards the teens began to tell him their own stories. One, whose parents and grandparents had never worked, had assumed he wouldn't, too. Instead, he told Harry, 'I love my job. I never knew work could be such fun.' Another said how becoming a coach had 'for the first time given structure to my life'. Harry listened intently and told them: 'It's great for you but also never underestimate the difference you are having on the kids you coach. Having a job also means you can go home knowing you have done something really important.' He then added a phrase that he admitted to me is also true for himself: 'You guys have got to believe a leopard can change its spots.'

'I love to see people excel and succeed,' he told me. 'I believe that anyone can do anything if they put their mind to it. It just depends on how passionate you are. I also believe you must be part of a team. I see a lot of myself in these guys, they want an opportunity to prove themselves and be someone.'

It was obvious that he would have liked to stay and talk to the individuals all day. He was far less interested in the bureaucracy, but at each visit time was allocated for him to be updated by the organisers. He sat politely asking questions while they eagerly filled him full of facts.

Occasionally one of his legs would tap up and down and a dark shadow would pass across his face. He would then cut through the detail to get to the core of a problem and come up with innovative practical solutions. He had obviously done his homework and got a little tetchy when others didn't think as clearly and speak as succinctly as him.

From there he was driven to the Russell Youth Centre, in a notoriously rough area, which houses the Community Recording Studio run by larger-than-life Trevor Rose, who I mentioned in connection to Meghan's first royal visit. Harry has been a regular visitor since 2013. He is drawn to those on the edge of society and uses his own experience of being an outsider to help them. More than once he sounded like a trained therapist.

On the day he visited, the centre was full of mostly black kids whose difficult lives were already engraved on their young faces. Trevor explained: 'This place is a safe haven even for kids who have been banned from school, youth clubs and sports. Many have been stabbed, thrown out of their home and have to deal with alcohol and drug issues, low confidence and self-esteem as well as normal teenage stuff. When they have been here a while they will often tell us that they have been abused and let us try to help them.

'For a long time there was no community here for them to be part of beyond getting involved in drug dealing. It was important to find them alternatives, build up their confidence so they can help the next generation. We use music and acting, and here they have the opportunity to play all sorts of instruments from drums to violas. We want them to get involved and out of gangs and crime. At first there was just this studio but now thanks to Harry we are running an increasing number of after-school clubs with a similar format.'

Harry and Trevor have a special connection and Harry regards him so highly that he has invited him to Buckingham Palace several times over the four years he has been involved, along with others who work with damaged children. As well as being introduced to Meghan, Trevor and some of the teens from the Community Recording Studio were an early item when Harry guest-edited BBC Radio 4's *Today* programme on 27 December 2017.

'It really makes a difference to the children to know they have a prince watching over them,' added Trevor. 'He is not what you would expect of a prince. He is amazing with the children and doesn't just want to shake hands, say hello and take a picture. He is focused on the long term as opposed to sprinkling royal dust and then moving on. He wants to become part of their journey.' He paused. 'I also believe it puts his own life into perspective.'

Before Harry arrived, the teenagers seemed too cool to care about an imminent royal visit, shrugging their shoulders and one or two saying, 'So what?' Trevor explained their behaviour: 'When you work with young people who are at risk they don't trust people easily, but when Harry walks in you'll see he is one of the boys.'

He was spot-on. Harry shook lots of hands, slapped the boys on the back, hugged the girls and cracked jokes. It was as if someone had turned on a switch, and within minutes he was surrounded by the same oh-so-cool teenagers who were now pleading with him to share a selfie, which he readily did. One of the girls there that day told me how coming to the studio had given her 'loads of confidence'. Another said: 'I've been helped to interact and meet new people, which I couldn't have done myself.'

I wondered if Trevor Rose had enjoyed being at Buckingham Palace. He roared with laughter and looked up at the ceiling. 'I am peculiar with food and sat down with seven or eight knives and forks in front of me and thought "Really?" What was funny, within a couple of minutes of me wondering what on earth to do with them, Harry bounced over and said: "You're not eating that food, are you? I'll get a fast car and we can go and get a Chinese takeaway." He broke the ice for me by somehow knowing exactly what I was thinking. I wanted to say: "Yes, man, let's go," but instead I replied: "next time, Harry."'

As well as engaging with young people, Harry is most at home with ex-servicemen and woman, particularly those who are going through physical or psychological problems. I joined him on a visit to the Help for Heroes recovery centre at Tedworth House in Wiltshire. It is a place for former British servicemen and women who have suffered in battle. Although their physical wounds had largely healed they had come to take advantage of the Hidden Wounds psychological and wellbeing service and the opportunity to learn new skills. Harry's experiences of life and his own instinct enables him to ask people he has never met before about their state of mind in a way that doesn't upset them.

It's something that even professional therapists might inch gradually towards. Harry is a natural. His only training has been a two-day course at the London District Personnel Recovery Unit when he left the army in 2015.

Harry was both compassionate and funny and said again how much he missed both the camaraderie and black humour. 'A lot of civilians don't get [the humour] but some in the services cannot function without it. It's certainly part of the recovery.'

It was a freezing but sunny day and a small group of men were outside making long wooden struts for a door. They stood close to a roaring fire that as well as keeping them warm would later be used to make a chilli con carne and jacket potato lunch. One of the men Harry talked to was thirty-four-year-old Mike Day, formerly a sniper section commander in 4 Rifles who was hit by a grenade in Afghanistan in 2009 and whose injuries included a broken back and shrapnel in his head and body. Harry's first question to him went right to the core: 'So what has been the biggest effect on you?' Day thought for a moment. 'I am no longer me,' he replied quietly.

It was an intensely moving moment that brought a lump to the throat, but Harry wasn't thrown. 'One of your biggest struggles must be living rather than just existing,' he continued sympathetically. Day nodded. 'Doing the woodwork and carving is so therapeutic,' he explained. 'There is no one telling us what to do, we just work as a team. I come to this place once a month for four days and it always brings out the best in me.'

Harry replied: 'Getting back your mental wellbeing is a really important thing. Rather than operating at fifty or sixty per cent you can operate at eighty or ninety per cent and be a better person.' He turned to examine the long strut Day had been working on. 'Look at what you have achieved with this. It's remarkable. I thought I was good at carpentry, but clearly I'm not.'

Another former soldier told him the centre had been a lifesaver. 'I didn't know how I would live because I was so used to being part of the military. But coming here has helped me gain land management and chainsaw qualifications to put on my CV and helped me move forwards. I tend to isolate myself but here there is camaraderie.'

Harry was in his element and it was a hard job for his support team, who kept looking at their watches, to move him on. Waiting for him in the garden area was John Geden, a former officer in the Corps of Royal Military Police. Help for Heroes encouraged him to set up his own honey business, which is doing well. Geden, in return, offers bee-keeping courses at the centre. 'I was suffering from post traumatic stress disorder,' he said, 'but it was hard to admit it. It's something no one can understand unless you have been through it. I ended up in hospital and someone there told me about Help for Heroes. I didn't think I was worthy of being here because I thought everyone would be limbless. I didn't realise it was also for people who couldn't cope. For the first three days I was so overwhelmed I didn't say a word to anyone and spent most of the time crying. But it changed my mindset.'

Harry agreed. 'These mental illnesses are just as powerful and debilitating to those who are struggling to get back on their feet from a physical injury. The stigma surrounding post traumatic stress disorder is a massive issue. I want to re-emphasise to people that it's not a ticking time bomb. Psychological illnesses can be fixed if sorted out early enough. We've got to keep the issue at the forefront of people's minds and the simplest thing is talking about it.' This was a typical example of Harry using his own experience – before he went public – to help others. 'The best thing is to help yourself and find the right people to talk to and then talking to them,' he continued. 'More and more people should have that rock to offload their emotions onto.' Geden offered Harry a jar of his honey. 'Are you sure you want to give this to me?' Harry asked. 'Thank you. I shall have it on my toast tomorrow.'

It was obvious that this particular visit was very special for him. 'We share the uniform,' he told me. 'We share the training. We share, in some cases, Afghanistan. Also I see a lot of myself in these guys. They want an opportunity to prove themselves and be someone.' Harry told me more than once that he was intent on making 'a big difference' to society. He seems to have done so with the wounded military, but an obstacle is that he often doesn't stay much longer than an hour on most of his visits. A member of his team explained that timing is often tight as senior royals usually have a full programme to get through. When we spoke at the Palace I wondered whether he feels frustrated by these strict time limitations. 'I sometimes get very impatient that things take so long to get done,' he admitted. It seems doubtful that any brief visit can be anywhere near as satisfying as his career in the army.

Speaking about trauma and depression was also Harry's focus at the Emergency Operations Centre for London Ambulance Service. It takes about 5,000 medical emergency calls a day and dispatches ambulances around London. Harry's visit was to promote another offshoot of Heads Together called Time To Talk Day. He reached back again to his own military experience as a helicopter pilot to empathise with the paramedics and drivers. He told them that he often evacuated injured servicemen and women. 'You land, hand them over, and then are radioed to do something else,' he said. 'You never find out how that guy or girl lived or died.'

It's easy to imagine that the men and women who apply to work for the Ambulance Service develop a kind of objectivity to what they see and have to deal with. But it turned out there was barely a stiff upper lip around. Shortly after he arrived Harry turned to a couple of male paramedics and said: 'It's amazing what you guys have to deal with every single day. You don't know what you are going to get, you can be attacked, abused, everything. It's not human to come away from that and not think you will be affected. Well done you.'

He then chatted at length to father-of-four Dan Farnworth, a paramedic from Blackpool, who had been suffering from PTSD after dealing with a particularly difficult case involving child abuse in which the child died. Dan told him about being in 'a really dark place' and how scared he was to admit it as it could have affected his job. Harry nodded knowingly. 'It's really important to speak out. If you keep concerns to yourself for weeks, months or years, they become a real problem. It's not weakness, it's strength to come forward, talk about it and move on. I know people don't want to come forward because they don't want to risk losing their job. But then they risk losing their job because they can't cope.'

When Harry is out and about on royal duty he stays totally alert and wary of possible trip-ups. For example, in a corner of a room in the Emergency Operations Centre a rotund male paramedic was having a massage and revealing a rather substantial amount of flesh. Harry was being led to the massage couch to speak to the physiotherapist but as soon as he saw the paramedic, his eyes opened wide, he spun round and walked in the opposite direction. 'I am not going there,' he said. 'I know too well what the photographers would make of that.'

There is no doubt Harry is expert at encouraging people to talk openly about their fears, but it's also a little sad that someone so young should hark back so often to past memories as if his life today pales by comparison. Having an 'ordinary' side to his life remains a priority. 'Thank goodness I'm not completely cut off from reality, but not everyone can understand that I can be a prince and still understand them.'

Some of Harry's highlights in 2016 included another documentary to mark his ten-year involvement with his African charity Sentebale. He appeared with the American pop singer Rihanna in Barbados to have a HIV test to raise awareness of the virus on World Aids Day.

Earlier in the year he also enlisted the help of his grandmother, President Obama and First Lady Michelle Obama to promote the 2016 Invictus Games in Orlando, Florida. It resulted in a short video of a tongue-in-cheek mock confrontation between the two countries about who would win the Games. The Queen and Harry made a great double act, with the Queen showing utter surprise that the President was determined to win. 'I didn't want to put pressure on her to take part,' Harry said. 'She's my boss as head of the armed forces. But it seemed appropriate four years after her helicopter exit to at the Olympics … And if you have the ability to up one on the Americans then why not.'

Harry later told *Hello!* magazine that his grandmother had 'great fun' filming her cameo. 'You could almost see her thinking, "Why the hell does nobody ask me to do these things more often?" She is so incredibly skilled she only needed one take. Meanwhile I was like a gibbering wreck. I was more nervous than anyone else.'

It also showed the Queen would do almost anything for her grandson. The feeling is mutual. 'I absolutely adore my grandmother,' he told me. Now in her nineties, she has cut back on her royal duties and has asked Princes Charles, William and Harry to help out. Harry said: 'The Queen has been fantastic in letting us choose what we'd like to do. She tells us to take our time and really think things through. I admire the Queen hugely and of course had no option but to agree to help relieve her load. It has, though, stopped me having a career of my own.' In the summer of 2017 Harry, a passionate rugby fan, did, for example, take over as patron of the Rugby Football Union and the Rugby Football League. He also hinted that this could involve more championing sport and that in addition he was keen on spearheading a global project aimed at reconnecting young people with nature and the environment.

In an interview to mark the opening of the Orlando Invictus Games he tried to shed his reputation as a playboy and show a more serious side. He criticised the rise of social media, saying it left some children isolated, reliant on digital 'friends' and spending less time playing or taking part in sport. 'It worries me that the majority of people now think that all their friends exist in their hand.'

He recalled how he played with toy soldiers in the garden when he was a child, adding: 'I had an imagination, now it's like, "There's an iPad, off you go." It's all created for you. All you have to do is press buttons. That worries me.' He also spoke about his fears over military budget cuts and that he and his father 'regularly talk about it'.

If anyone noticed that after the Invictus Games were over, there was an extra spring to his step and an optimistic smile on his face, the reason was he had fallen head over heels in love. Having faced and largely dealt with his demons, he was ready. Meghan Markle had arrived in his life.

CHAPTER 13

The Meghan Effect

On 31 October 2016, the *Sunday Express* reported that Prince Harry was secretly dating a beautiful mixed-race American actress, divorcée, feminist and human rights campaigner by the name of Meghan Markle. As Kensington Palace didn't deny the allegation the rest of the media quickly got on board. Within hours Meghan posted a cheeky picture of a loved-up spooning couple of bananas on her Instagram account. One, presumably female, had long inked-on eyelashes, while the other, presumably male, wore a very contented-looking smile. She added two words and a kiss: 'Sleep tight x'. Meghan had obviously been longing to shout from the highest hills that she was dating the world's most sought-after bachelor, but at the time confined herself to an original, zany hint.

What Prince Harry, then fifth in line to the throne, and a

man who 'longs for a private life' away from press intrusion, privately thought of being depicted as a banana is anyone's guess, but falling in love can change the way one looks at almost anything.

It was the first of many postings on Meghan's website – which she had named The Tig after her favourite wine, Tignanello – giving various verbal and visual clues about her life. As time went on, an increasing number of followers and a hungry press tried to guess their meaning and whether or not they related to Harry.

The woman who stole his heart was utterly unlike the long line of blondes he had been chasing since he was a teenager. Nor did she fit the prototype of a British royal consort. Meghan's bloodline is not at all regal, but has nonetheless given her strong values that may help her understand the customs and traditions of the British royal family. She also has a lot in common with Harry.

Rachel Meghan Markle was born on 4 August 1981 (she stopped using the name Rachel in her late teens). Like Harry, she has had to overcome a complex and challenging background, peppered with more money worries and rifts than would be found in several episodes of a sit-com. She has also scrupulously made her own luck, although one friend said: 'I think Meghan was calculated – very calculated – in the way she handled people and relationships. She is very strategic in the way she cultivates circles of friends.'

Meghan's forefathers on her father's side were English, Irish and Dutch, and settled in America in the eighteenth century. Her 6ft 3in tall father, Thomas Wayne Markle, is an award-winning retired movie and television lighting director now in his seventies who enjoys junk food and currently lives a secluded life in a house by the sea in Mexico. Despite a successful career, in June 2016 he filed for bankruptcy. At the time he had credit card debts of £24,181 and just £160 in savings.

He has two children from his first marriage: Samantha, who is sixteen years older than Meghan, and Thomas junior, who is two years younger. Meghan hasn't spoken to her half-sister, who has been divorced twice and has three children, for nearly a decade. She was reported as having made some spiteful comments about Meghan in November 2016 when her relationship with Prince Harry was revealed, but she later claimed she had been misquoted. Samantha and her second ex-husband, Scott Rasmussen, jointly filed for bankruptcy in 2000. Meghan's half-brother has two sons and has also been divorced twice. Early in 2017 he was, according to police records, arrested and charged with menacing, pointing a firearm at another person – allegedly his girlfriend – and unlawful use of a weapon.

Deputy Jill Elardi, of Josephine County Sheriff's Office, confirmed the arrest and charges. She said: 'He will be going to court for it.' Though, at the time of press, he has not been convicted of any criminal offence. He has also admitted to having a drink problem. Thomas, too, filed for bankruptcy in 2013, citing debts of £71,868.

Meghan's mother, Doria Ragland, in her sixties and who Meghan describes as 'a free-spirited clinical therapist', is the great-great-granddaughter of a slave who worked in the cotton plantations of the Deep South. She and Thomas met when she was twenty and he was in his mid-thirties; she was working as a temp at ABC TV. They married in Pennsylvania in 1979, separated when Meghan was two, and divorced on grounds of 'irreconcilable difference' when Meghan was nearly six.

After the divorce, Doria took various jobs to supplement her maintenance, including working as an air-stewardess, an experience she has in common with the Duchess of Cambridge's mother, Carole Middleton. In 2003, when Meghan had just started her acting career, Doria filed for bankruptcy with credit card debts of £42,900 and assets of about £12,000. She now lives in Los Angeles in a modest cottage she inherited from her father, Alvin, when he died in 2011. Meghan is her only child. She was by all accounts a sweet, positive little girl and adored by both parents.

Her father paid for Meghan to be educated privately, initially at Little Red Schoolhouse in Hollywood, which Elizabeth Taylor and Judy Garland attended, followed by Immaculate Heart, an £11,500-a-year exclusive all-girls Catholic school where she gained straight As in her graduation exams. She became school president, the American equivalent of head girl, and regularly got the lead role in school plays, not least because that way her father would always agree to do the lighting; it led to some complaints from other parents. With her mother often away working, Meghan spent much of her time in a Hollywood tenement block with her protective father and after school would pop into the TV studios where he was working. It fuelled a passion for acting.

Doria and Meghan's grandmother Jeanette, a woman born into poverty in Cleveland Ohio, had clear ideas on how to bring up Meghan, who they called 'Flower'. In common with Harry's mother, Diana, Princess of Wales, Doria wanted her to be aware of the raw realities of life. It is something that Meghan appreciates. 'My mother raised me to be a global citizen with eyes open to sometimes harsh realities. I must have been about ten years old when we visited the slums of Jamaica. I had never seen poverty at that level and it registered in my glazed brown eyes.' It is a concern she shares with Harry.

Her mother encouraged her to stay fit and healthy, and Meghan did 'mummy-and-me' yoga from the age of seven. Doria also paid for her to have regular facials from the age of thirteen.

Whenever Meghan was upset by colour prejudice she sought comfort from her father who encouraged her to take pride in her ethnic background. When she was seven she asked for a Barbie Doll family set for Christmas. Her father bought two sets – one with black figures, the other white. Meghan clearly remembers that she found 'a black mom doll, a white dad doll and a child in each colour. My dad had taken the sets apart and customised it to mirror my family.' In 2015, a year before she met Prince Harry, she wrote about what it was like to have a black mother and a white father. 'While my mixed heritage may have created a grey area surrounding my self-identification, keeping me with a foot on both sides of the fence, I have come to embrace that … To say who I am, to share where I'm from, to voice my pride in being a strong, confident mixed-race woman.' Meghan added that her mother also 'crafted the world around me to make me feel like I wasn't different but special.'

The teenage Meghan felt strongly about helping the less fortunate, something a friend believed was inspired by the Princess of Wales. 'She always admired Princess Diana's good deeds,' she recalled. 'I went with her to schools where there were less fortunate kids. [Meghan] would collect toys, gifts and clothes for them.' Meghan also developed an early interest in equality for women. When she was eleven she watched a TV programme at school and saw a commercial for soap powder that made her 'unknowingly and somehow accidentally' become an advocate for women's rights. The commercial announced that 'women all over American are fighting greasy pots and pans,' Meghan recalled. 'The boys in my classroom yelled out, "Yeah, that's where women belong. In the kitchen." My little freckled face became red with anger'. She wrote a protest letter to the soap powder manufacturers Procter & Gamble plus various prominent women, including Hillary Clinton, who was then First Lady. She got tremendous support, appeared on TV herself and within a few months the commercial changed the word 'women' to 'people'. It is something she remains proud of and often mentions.

After school she went to Northwestern University in Evanston, Illinois, the first in her family to go to university. Four years later, in 2003, she graduated with a Bachelor of Science degree from Northwestern's School of Communication with a major in theatre and a second major in international studies. Distinguished constitutional historian Dr David Starkey told me that he is impressed: 'It is an extremely respectable university, and I doubt if Harry could get in.'

Meghan then tried for nearly a decade to break her way into professional acting. She wrote of the experience: '[I] wasn't black enough for the black roles and I wasn't white enough for the white roles.' To help pay the bills she worked as a freelance calligrapher and still likes hand-written notes.

Although her career seemed stuck, her love life wasn't, and in 2004 she started dating Trevor Engelson, a promising film producer from a wealthy Jewish background who was four years her senior. After seven years together, they married on 10 September 2011 in Ocho Rios, Jamaica, a four-day celebration of dancing, drinking and playing beach games. Meghan took part in wheelbarrow races wearing a tiny yellow polka-dot bikini and baseball cap. Knowing how to party is something else she has in common with Harry.

Her tenacious pursuit of an acting career paid off shortly before she married when she landed the part of Rachel Zane, a sophisticated, sexy, mixed-race New York legal assistant in an American legal drama, *Suits*, on cable TV. Filmed in Toronto, it has been nominated for several awards. It was worth the wait as along with her professional success Meghan began to make friends with A-list celebrities and politicians. And Canadian magazines were happy to publish her views on racism, women's rights and other causes.

The one disadvantage was that her husband needed to

stay in LA for work, while she filmed in Toronto. The couple began to live separate lives and two years later their marriage was over. A friend believed that one reason it fell apart was that Meghan found flying 2,170 miles back and forth between Los Angeles and Toronto on top of her demanding work schedule just too much. However, travelling 3,547 miles between Toronto and London to see Harry was something she did enthusiastically.

The divorce in August 2013 went ahead on the grounds of 'irreconcilable differences'. There was no alimony. Her role in *Suits* also gave Meghan the idea of turning herself into a brand and she quickly built up a healthy following on Instagram and on her website, The Tig. Her mission statement was: 'I've never wanted to be a lady who lunches – I've always wanted to be a woman who works.' Her website was up and running in 2014 and rapidly became a showcase for her many interests and talents. She published her views on everything from self-empowerment and humanitarian work to recipes for spelt biscuits and 'favourite facialists' around the world. She wrote that she most liked to eat French fries, that she mainly ate a vegan diet during the week, that she loved a man in a linen shirt, especially when he was barefoot on a beach, and British men who called women 'darling', adding: 'If he makes you laugh that helps.' As for gifts, 'lingerie is always nice', she was a 'sucker for a compliment' and the best way to reach her heart was though 'kindness'. Besotted Harry perhaps looked at her website and took notes. In addition, she created her own clothing range.

The Tig also provided a platform for Meghan's self-promotion as a 'global citizen'. She embraced an increasing number of fashionable causes, carving out a career as a philanthropist and social campaigner. At a UN Women conference on International Women's Day in 2015 she said that her success on *Suits* led her to realise that 'people (especially young women) were listening to what I had to say. I knew I needed to be saying something of value ... to include think pieces about self-empowerment ... hoping to integrate social consciousness and subjects of higher value than let's say selfies.'

Meghan became involved in One Young World, a not-for-profit UK charity where young leaders round the world develop solutions to the world's pressing issues. She was also the United Nations' women's advocate for political participation and Leadership Entity for Gender Equality and the Empowerment of Women. In addition, she was global ambassador for World Vision Canada, and in 2016 she represented them in Rwanda for the Clean Water Campaign. In July 2016, Meghan shared her support for Hillary Clinton in the presidential race against Donald Trump, describing her candidacy as 'an historic moment'.

By the time the seventh series of *Suits* was being filmed Meghan had grown in confidence and refused to agree to any more steamy encounters in her underwear. She proudly told a One Women One World convention in Dublin in 2014: 'Every script seemed to begin with "Rachel enters with a towel." I said, "No, I'm not doing it anymore." She acknowledged she couldn't put her foot down earlier in her career and it remains difficult as 'lots of decision-makers are still men and you need more men to stand up for powerful women'.

On other occasions she seemed unbothered about using her feminine wiles and yoga-honed physical curves to get her point across. For example, in 2013 she appeared in a backless, sleeveless, thigh-revealing sparkly black dress ostensibly to talk about her role in *Suits* on *The Late, Late Show with Craig Ferguson* on CBS. She oozed sexuality and Ferguson, who told her she looked 'sensational', made one creepy comment after another including saying: 'What a strangely hairless body you have ... You're quite the dolphin, aren't you? You're absolutely hair-free. Are you a competitive swimmer?' When Meghan mentioned that she used to spend time at the TV studios where her father was working Ferguson commented: 'It's a very perverse place for a little girl who went to Catholic school no less to grow up. I'm there in my school uniform, right...?' Meghan looked very uncomfortable.

By 2015 so many aspects of her life were flourishing that she wrote: 'I dream pretty big but truly had no idea my life could be this awesome. I am the luckiest girl in the world without question.' Little did she anticipate that she had barely started, and that in just a year her life would be further transformed.

She was proud that her 'two worlds' of acting and humanitarian work could interact. 'Being able to keep a foot in both is a delicate balance. [Charity] work is what feeds my soul and fuels my purpose. The degree to which I can do both on and off camera is a direct perk of my job.'

Meghan also has superb networking skills and an enviable

ability to become almost instant best friends with successful women of the moment. By the time she met Harry she had her own global network. When she was a relatively unknown actress, she met tennis star Serena Williams, the seven-times Wimbledon singles winner, in 2014, and played a game of football at a charity-celebrity event. Meghan wrote on her blog: 'We hit it off immediately talking pictures, laughing and chatting not about tennis or acting but about good old-fashioned girly stuff. So began our friendship. She quickly became a confidante.' When Serena came to London for Wimbledon 2016 Meghan watched her friend play, sitting just a few rows away from Pippa Middleton, sister of the Duchess of Cambridge. She stated she was also grateful to Serena for helping her handle her relationship with Harry once it was out in the open.

Another successful friend is the Indian film actress Priyanka Chopra, whom she first met in 2015. Chopra has made more than fifty Bollywood films and is, like Meghan, a skilled networker. She is also a Unicef ambassador. Then there's Sophie Grégoire Trudeau, wife of Canada's Prime Minister Justin Trudeau, who calls herself a 'gender equality activist'. In April 2016, Sophie and Meghan went to a Canadian fashion awards ceremony together. Meghan's style advisor/girl Friday is Jessica Mulroney, the daughter-in-law of former Canadian Prime Minister Brian Mulroney. She is a social media star, and her husband Ben, a television reporter, is a friend of Justin Trudeau. Meghan and Jessica both love yoga and Pilates. Fashion designer Misha Nonoo and Meghan bonded immediately after meeting through a mutual friend and holidayed together in Europe in 2016. Her former husband, old Etonian Alexander Gilkes, is a friend of Harry's and went to William's wedding. Other best buddies include Princess Eugenie, younger daughter of Harry's uncle, the Duke of York, and *Made in Chelsea* star Millie Mackintosh.

Harry and Meghan, they revealed later, met on a blind date in July 2016 arranged by fashion PR Violet von Westenholz, the daughter of former Olympic skier Baron Piers von Westenholz, a close personal friend of the Prince of Wales. She was also a childhood friend of Harry's and had met and become friends with Meghan through her work with the fashion house Ralph Lauren. Harry and Meghan knew very little about each other. 'I didn't know much about him,' said Meghan during her engagement TV interview, 'and so the only thing that I had asked [the friend] when she said she wanted to set us up was, "Well, is he nice?" [Because] if he wasn't kind it just didn't seem like it would make sense. We met for a drink and I think very quickly we said, well what are we doing tomorrow? We should meet again.'

Harry added: 'I'd never even heard about her until this friend said "Meghan Markle". I was like, "Right, OK, give me a bit of background, what's going on here?" I'd never watched *Suits* and I'd never heard of Meghan before, and I was beautifully surprised when I walked into that room and saw her. And there she was sitting there. I was like, "OK, well I'm going to have to up my game, sit down and make sure I've got good chat."' Shortly afterwards, Meghan posted a thinly veiled hint on Instagram that she had a new boyfriend with a picture of a heart-shaped sweet with 'kiss me' printed on it.

She later explained that there were serious elements to their first date:

> One of the first things we started talking about when we met was just the different things that we wanted to do in the world and how passionate we were about seeing change. I think that was what got date two in the books probably. It was really refreshing because, given that I didn't know a lot about him, everything that I've learned about him, I learned through him as opposed to having grown up around different news stories or tabloids. Anything I've learned about him and his family was what he would share with me and vice versa, so for both of us it was just a really authentic and organic way to get to know each other.

Harry agreed. 'It was hugely refreshing to be able to get to know someone who isn't necessarily within your circle, doesn't know much about me, I don't know much about her. So to be able to start almost afresh, right from the beginning, getting to know each other, step by step, was – fantastic.'

So began their long-distance relationship. Harry inundated her with countless texts, as he usually did with potential girlfriends. 'Three, maybe four weeks later, I managed to persuade her to come and join me in Botswana. We camped out with each other under the stars. She joined me for five days out there, which was absolutely fantastic. So, then we were really by ourselves, which was crucial to me to make sure we had a chance to get to know each other.'

During the very early stages of his relationship with Meghan, Harry was thought to have also gone on dates with Burberry model Sarah Ann Macklin. They met at a private party, he took her number and bombarded her with texts, too. But it turned out to be just a fling. A friend said: 'They got on but are quite different. She is very clean-living and barely drinks, and in that respect they were on a different wavelength. Harry was a bit non-committal.' There has been some confusion too about whether or not Meghan had at the time broken up with her boyfriend of two years, celebrity chef Cory Vitiello.

Meanwhile, Harry was keen to keep his burgeoning relationship with Meghan quiet because he didn't want the publicity to scare her away before they were an established couple. They often met at Soho House in Dean Street, central London, a discreet social club with eighteen branches round the world. They also enjoyed mini-breaks at the luxury Soho Farmhouse in the Cotswolds, where regulars include George and Amal Clooney and Princesses Beatrice and Eugenie. Regular meetings between the couple were complicated to arrange as Meghan had filming obligations for *Suits* and Harry had his royal duties, but they ensured that the gap between seeing each other was never longer than two weeks. 'Five hours apart does have its challenges,' said Harry. 'But we made it work and now we're here, so we're thrilled.'

Meghan soon started staying with Harry in Nottingham Cottage, his two-up, two-down property within the grounds of Kensington Palace, directly opposite Apartments 8 and 9 where he and his brother grew up with their mother. William and Kate lived in the cottage when they were first married. It's small and cosy with no room for live-in staff, affording the couple total privacy. Harry ensured Meghan wouldn't, unlike previous girlfriends, be expected to observe the Palace's tight security. Instead, the police sentries were told she was to be allowed to come and go as she pleased without any security checks. Harry's previous girlfriends had also kept a very low profile whenever they stayed over, but Meghan didn't seem so worried. Early in November 2016 she was out shopping for flowers and food in local Kensington High Street dressed in a casual coat and boots and with Harry's brown baseball cap pulled down over her brow.

During the summer of 2016, Meghan wrote on her website a comment that, in retrospect, seems to describe her reaction to the Harry effect: 'I have to say that when I close my eyes and think of what I wish for, I come up with a blank. A big, old, happy blank. I am feeling so incredibly joyful right now, so grateful and content that all I could wish for is more of the same.' She also posted on Instagram several pictures of recent trips to London, including a view that appears to be of Kensington and another of Buckingham Palace. They were huge giveaways but guesswork at the time. It was an October photograph of her wearing a distinctive beaded friendship bracelet with blue, white and black beads identical to one Harry had been wearing for a few months that gave the game away and caused a media frenzy.

Despite being very resilient Meghan admitted: 'I did not

have any understanding of just what [the frenzy] would be like. There's a misconception that because I have worked in the entertainment industry that this would be something I would be familiar with. But even though I'd been on [*Suits*] for six years at that point, and working before that, I have never been part of tabloid culture… [I] lived a relatively quiet life even though I focused so much on my job and so that was a really stark difference out of the gate. We were just hit so hard at the beginning with a lot of mistruths that I made the choice to not read anything, positive or negative, it just didn't make sense and instead we focused all of our energies just on nurturing our relationship.'

Unusually for Harry, during the TV engagement interview he made no attempt to hide his feelings for his fiancée and believed they were meant to meet and fall in love: 'The stars were aligned, everything was just perfect. This beautiful woman just sort of literally tripped and fell into my life, I fell into her life.'

Harry was understandably keen to introduce his new love to William and Kate, but they were spending the summer at Anmer Hall, their home on the Sandringham estate. They were back at Kensington Palace in early September as Prince George was starting big school at Thomas's Battersea. Finding a gap in everyone's busy schedule for an informal get-together was not easy but all apparently went well. Meghan said Kate had been 'wonderful', and Harry added 'amazing, as has William'. They have also had several teas with his father. 'The family has been wonderful throughout the whole thing.'

Dr Starkey told me he is not surprised. 'They are so grateful that he is settling down with someone who is sensible and more than just presentable, especially when you look at what his behaviour has been like. Meghan is a handsome woman. I am sure they are all saying, "Boy done good".'

There was also the matter of introducing her to his grandmother. It's difficult to pin down when the first meeting took place, but again Meghan gave a clue in a photograph on Instagram. It was a composed picture of an elegant, old-fashioned rose-decorated cup and saucer, an elephant-shaped teapot and scattered jigsaw pieces. Looking back, it seems very likely that the cup related to those the Queen might use when a grandson brought a special girlfriend around. The elephant teapot doubtless refers to Harry, who from a toddler has been keen on elephants and their conservation. (In August 2016, around the time he met Meghan, he used his skills as a helicopter pilot to help move 500 African elephants many miles to save them from poachers. Perhaps he told her all about it.) The puzzle pieces are a reminder that the Queen loves doing large jigsaws.

Once the news broke that Harry and Meghan were an item, journalists raced to Los Angeles and Toronto to discover as much as possible about Meghan. Harry was furious at the press intrusion into her life and that of her extended family. At his insistence Kensington Palace issued an unprecedented statement on 8 November that read like something dashed off in a fury. It confirmed that Harry had been in a relationship with Meghan for several months, but attacked the 'waves of abuse and harassment' he felt his girlfriend was enduring from the press. It stated: 'Prince Harry is worried about Ms Markle's safety and is deeply disappointed that he has not been able to protect her. It is not right that a few months into a relationship with him that Ms Markle should be subjected to such a storm.'

It stated that Harry also criticised the 'racial undertones' in some of the media comments, adding, 'He knows reporters will say, "this is the price she has to pay" and that "this is all part of the game". He disagrees. 'This is not a game – it is her life and his.' One royal aide said it was 'unprecedented for a royal prince to issue such a forthright official statement naming the new love of his life'. It also revealed how worried Harry was that he might lose Meghan, as he'd previously lost Chelsy Davy and Cressida Bonas, both of whom found press intrusion intolerable. It probably brought back flashbacks of his mother being harassed by the press, too, and also showed how impulsive he could be when under stress. His unprecedented demand for press restraint knocked Prince Charles's and the Duchess of Cornwall's carefully planned tour of the Middle East off the front pages, which probably didn't go down too well. The royal hierarchy is immovable and there is an unwritten agreement and lots of cross-referencing among the royals not to double-book trips or make an important announcement that could steal the limelight away from higher-ranking royals.

Harry became so concerned about keeping Meghan safe that he volunteered to pay for a retired Scotland Yard protection officer to shield her, especially from the foreign press. Only top royals get protection paid for by the state

24/7. These are the Queen, the Duke of Edinburgh, the Prince of Wales, the Duchess of Cornwall, the Duke and Duchess of Cambridge, and Prince Harry. As Meghan was then just a girlfriend she didn't qualify. The Prince of Wales hired personal protection officers to watch over the Duchess of Cornwall before they married. The Duke of York also contributes towards the cost of protecting his daughters, Princesses Beatrice and Eugenie. It would have cost Harry, who is believed to be worth about £30 million, about £50,000 a year. He needn't have worried. Behind Meghan's soft dark eyes is an able and determined woman and she described Harry's offer of a private protection officer as 'charming' but unnecessary.

It wasn't until Meghan gave a frank and revealing interview to *Vanity Fair* magazine in 2017, before they were engaged, that it became clear how press intrusion had impacted on her. 'It has its challenges and it comes in waves – some days it can feel more challenging than others … But I still have this support system all around me and of course my boyfriend's support.' She reassured her fans that she remained strong despite the intrusion: 'Nothing about me has changed. I'm still the same person that I am and I've never defined myself by my relationship.' That's a near-impossible ambition once you become the partner of a wealthy prince at the heart of the British royal family, the most powerful royal family in the world. Certainly news of their budding relationship boosted her social media accounts and by the end of the year she had become the most Googled actress of 2016.

Sightings of the couple were rare and largely confined to

trips to the theatre. Harry also persuaded an executive to keep the Natural History Museum open at night so he and Meghan could see the dinosaurs in private.

Although they spent Christmas apart, they saw in the New Year together in London and then travelled to Norway for a romantic getaway to see the Northern Lights. The couple celebrated in a glass igloo, camping under the winter stars. Meghan had by this time shut down her website and subsequently her social media accounts. In their place she did several interviews with glossy magazines, and began to make statements through her choice of clothes and jewellery by choosing to wear designs from small, ethically aware companies.

In February 2017 *Tatler* magazine published its annual 100 Most Invited list of popular party guests. Meghan, who was described as 'smoking hot' and 'clean eating', came fourth. Harry, described as an 'all-round good-time guy' who 'likes to let his hair down', was only twenty-second.

In March, Meghan flew from Toronto to Jamaica on a private jet to be by Harry's side for the wedding of his close friend, Tom Inskip. Harry met her at the island's airport and, according to a fellow guest, the couple spent most of their week in their luxury ocean-front villa, complete with private pool and butler. In May, Harry and Meghan made their first semi-official joint appearance at a polo match – a royal rite of passage. It was also the scene of their first public embrace as they were caught on camera stealing a kiss in the car park. Meghan was Harry's guest at Pippa Middleton's wedding party later in May. She wasn't at the church, but

Harry collected her after the ceremony for the festivities. Rumours were by then flowing that their relationship was so intense she was thinking of leaving *Suits*, especially as she was only contracted until the end of 2017, and would subsequently move to London.

In the summer, Harry whisked her away from filming for a romantic celebration to mark both their first year together and her thirty-sixth birthday on 4 August. He chose Botswana again, and Zambia. It was the perfect opportunity for a proposal but it didn't happen. Proposing is always a big step, particularly for those whose parents had a bad marriage, for fear of repeating a pattern.

Little did she know that, according to ITV anchor Tom Bradby, some of Harry's friends were telling him to take the plunge, not only because they felt Meghan could cope with the unique demands of royal life but also because they were worried if he didn't she might 'get cold feet' and he would lose her. They'd also been pleased to see that whenever he was restless she had a natural way of calming him down. Harry took a small step forward in the summer when, according to courtiers, he showed the Queen YouTube videos of episodes of *Suits* on her iPad. Meghan wasn't in them to avoid any possible embarrassment. He was also believed to have told both grandparents about her charitable work and their shared interest in various causes.

Perhaps Meghan thought it was time he needed a loving push. She had agreed to do another interview with *Vanity Fair* in Toronto for more publicity for the hundredth episode of *Suits* and took advantage of the opportunity to declare her passion for Harry: 'We're a couple, we're in love,' she said. 'There will be a time when we have to come forward and present ourselves. But this is our time ... this is for us ... it's part of what makes it so special.' She added: 'I love a great love story' and denied it was a big deal to date the Queen's grandson. 'I can tell you that at the end of the day I think it's really simple. We're two people who are really happy and in love.' Her words were illustrated with photographs of her looking sexy, wistful and glamorous.

It was unprecedented for a royal girlfriend to be so outspoken and it could have been the death knell for their relationship. The general view was that she would never have given the interview without Harry's consent. I believe she was so confident of his love that she was just trying to force his hand a little, partly because at thirty-six, her biological clock was ticking rather fast. Official Palace sources dodged the question of whether Harry approved or not of her interview by merely saying said he 'was aware' of it. Perhaps Meghan took him by surprise when she confessed about the interview but shrewdly picked her time carefully and, besotted as he was, he accepted what she'd said. Many questioned whether she'd gone public before Harry had told the Queen and Prince William his intentions. In a way it doesn't matter, but it does indicate who might wear the trousers in their relationship and perhaps lends truth to what her half-brother Thomas and several friends say of her: 'What Meghan wants, she gets.'

By chance the 2017 Invictus Games was to be held in Toronto, where Meghan lived while working on *Suits*. But there was no indication of whether or not Meghan would attend until just before the opening ceremony on Saturday 23 September at the Air Canada Centre. In fact Meghan's place, in one of the stands at the end of a row by a stairwell, had been meticulously thought through. One of Harry's Scotland Yard police protection officers was stationed close by so if there was any trouble she could run down a few stairs and he could whisk her away. As they were not engaged, protocol decreed they could not sit together. Harry is not usually bothered by protocol, but if Meghan had sat next to him it could have moved the focus away from the competing athletes, which he wouldn't want. He sat with Canadian Prime Minister Justin Trudeau, Ukraine's President Poroshenko and US First Lady Melania Trump in the VIP box, four rows and eighteen seats above Meghan. She had been strategically placed so that Harry could see her easily and he was captured several times by the cameras looking longingly and occasionally anxiously at her. Perhaps he was nervous about how she was coping. Was she acting or genuinely overwhelmed by what she saw? Or perhaps he just couldn't take his eyes off her.

Meghan looked stunning in an aubergine-coloured midi dress with a pleated chiffon skirt by Aritzia, a matching Mackage leather jacket slung over her shoulders and cream Jimmy Choo heels. Sitting next to her was her friend Markus Anderson, a consultant for the Soho House Group. One row down was Rose Hall, of the Invictus Games Foundation. She provides Harry with guidance and support at Invictus events, and was there in case Meghan needed assistance.

To the casual viewer Meghan appeared completely at ease

under the spotlight and clapped enthusiastically when the British team entered the stadium. When Harry took to the stage to give the welcome speech during which he told the 550 athletes from 17 different nations 'you are all winners', she beamed and looked up at him on the large video screen with adoration in her eyes and a wondrous expression on her face. Harry's speech was rousing and powerful, and clearly showed how successful his concept had been to turn the competitors into inspirational people to look up to. His speech even included a few words of French. 'Above all, Invictus is about the example to the world that all service men and women, injured or not, provide about the importance of service and duty ... In a world where so many have reasons to feel cynical and apathetic, I wanted to find a way for veterans to be a beacon of light, and show us all that we have a role to play: that we all win when we respect our friends, neighbours, and communities. That's why we created Invictus. Not only to help veterans recover from their physical and mental wounds; but also to inspire people to follow their example of resilience, optimism, and service in their own lives.'

When Harry came to visit Meghan in Toronto he usually stayed at her home, but on this official occasion he had been booked into a suite at Fairmont Royal York, one of Canada's leading hotels, and she joined him there. On the following Monday Meghan arrived with Harry at the Games and they held hands on a mini walkabout. This time she was dressed down in a white shirt from her friend Misha Nonoo's collection. The piece was called The Husband, which was perhaps another hint. She also wore ripped, frayed jeans and flat shoes. What the Queen thought about her choice of clothing at a semi-official royal engagement was anyone's guess. Some thought it was an act of rebellion encouraged by Harry to show she wasn't going to be controlled by the Palace, others that it was badly judged. Jeans would have been fine, just not torn ones. Dickie Arbiter, former press spokesperson for the Queen, felt that it was merely a fashion statement. 'I don't see it as a problem,' he said. 'I am sure she wouldn't wear torn jeans to a garden party or anything like that. Everyone dresses down and informal. Harry himself was in a golf shirt and jeans.' This time the couple sat together while they watched a wheelchair tennis match. Harry kept whispering in Meghan's ear and laughing in full view of the general public and photographers.

Meghan appeared again for the closing ceremony the following Saturday, this time sitting at the back of a darkened VIP box to the side of the stage. Her mother had flown over from her home in Los Angeles. Harry later revealed in the BBC TV engagement interview that he used the occasion to ask her mother for her daughter's hand. He had not yet met her father. Harry could hardly restrain himself from kissing and holding Meghan in his arms before tearing himself away to go on stage to give the closing speech.

It seemed obvious that it was only a matter of time before the engagement was announced. But before Harry could formalise their union publicly he had to take into account the busy royal diary. He couldn't steal the thunder from the Invictus Games or from his royal visit to Denmark on behalf of the Queen. The beginning of November wouldn't be appropriate because of Remembrance Sunday, and it couldn't be around the Queen and Prince Philip's seventieth wedding anniversary on 20 November, the first platinum anniversary in royal history.

On 12 October, Harry and Meghan were invited to take tea with the Queen, who had just returned to Buckingham Palace from her summer break at Balmoral: teatime is believed to be her favourite time of the day. The couple arrived in a Ford Galaxy with blacked-out windows and were dropped off at the Queen's private entrance. Tea was served in the Queen's private sitting room on the first floor overlooking the palace gardens and reached by a special lift. The Queen normally lingers for half an hour eating from a selection of sandwiches, fruit or plain scones and cake, served with her own blend of Darjeeling and Assam tea, known as Queen Mary's blend. She loves it when her grandchildren are able to join her. On this occasion it was believed she spent almost an hour with her grandson and Meghan. Meghan later explained her feelings: 'It is incredible to be able to meet her through his lens, not just with his honour and respect for her as a monarch, but the love he has for her as his grandmother, so when I met her I had such a deep understanding and incredible respect for her. She is a remarkable woman.' Harry joked: 'And the corgis took to you straight away.'

From then the excitement began to mount and the word 'if' there would be an engagement was replaced by 'when'. On 16 November there were reports that Meghan's two rescue dogs, a beagle named Guy and a Labrador-shepherd mix called Bogart, were being flown to London. In fact just Guy arrived. Bogart was thought to be too old to travel and was entrusted to a friend's care. Removal vans appeared outside Meghan's Toronto home and she flew to London on 25 November, just before Thanksgiving, despite it being one of her most favourite times of the year.

The engagement was announced on 27 November, and early that afternoon Harry and Meghan gave a brief introduction to their romantic story. They held hands and Meghan gave Harry's arm a motherly rub as they posed for a photo-call in the Sunken Garden at Kensington Palace, designed to celebrate the life of Diana, Princess of Wales. They took it in turns to say how 'thrilled' and 'happy' they were, and Harry revealed he knew she was 'the one' from the first moment they met.

Meghan showed off her engagement ring, which Harry had designed. The diamond in the middle comes from Botswana, and the ones on either side are from the personal collection of his mother. A close-up of Meghan's hands also revealed that like the Duchess of Cambridge she keeps her nails very short. Or maybe she hasn't yet managed to fulfil her 2016 New Year's resolution posted on her website on 1 January to 'stop biting my nails'.

A fuller version of their love story was broadcast at 6pm that evening when they were both interviewed on BBC TV. They seemed tipsy with happiness, held hands, echoed each other's words and gazed lovingly at each other. A glowing Meghan, dressed in a sleeveless dark-green dress by the Canadian brand Parosh and vertiginous cream shoes by

Aquazzura that had seemed a little large when she walked to and from the Sunken Garden, surprised viewers who were more used to nervous, wary royal brides-to-be like Kate Middleton and Lady Diana Spencer. Meghan, on the other hand, who was well used to celebrity interviews, talked far more than Harry, who seemed happy to give her centre stage.

Harry, who wore a plain black tie, probably out of respect to his mother, revealed that he'd proposed a few weeks prior to the announcement and that: 'It happened at our home.' Calling Nottingham Cottage 'our home' rather than saying 'my home' showed that they were like any modern young couple happily living together and sharing everything. Meghan, who had previously described herself as a keen vegan, added: 'It was just a cosy night, what we were doing [was] just roasting a chicken.' She described the proposal as 'just an amazing surprise. It was so sweet and natural and very romantic. He got on one knee...' Turning to Harry and smiling, she added: 'As a matter of fact I could barely let you finish proposing, I said – "Can I say yes now?"'

It was days like this that Harry admitted he most missed his mother and longed to tell her his news. 'I think she would have been over the moon ... and so excited for me', and, like many men who marry someone who reminds them of their mother, said that he believed she and Meghan would have been 'as thick as thieves' and 'best friends'. Meghan was instantly consoling: 'She is with us,' she told him. 'Yes,' he replied looking deep into his fiancée's eyes. 'She is with us. I am sure she is somewhere else jumping up and down.'

CHAPTER 14

Harry's Vision

Prince Harry told me that he had 'three me's'. He explained: 'One in the army, one socially in my own private time, and then one with the family and royal stuff like that. So there is a switch and I flick it when necessary.' He switched between all three when we talked in 2017.

He was keen to discuss the army. This was no surprise as it was the making of him. He described his experience as 'epic' and told an army veteran that 'it can really change your life'. Despite officially leaving in 2015 after ten years' service, Harry maintains a connection through wounded veterans and those involved with the Invictus Games.

On 15 December 2017 he was also at Sandhurst representing the Queen at the Sovereign's Parade for the 162 officer cadets from the UK and 25 from 20 overseas countries who had completed the intensive year-long Commissioning

Course. He handed out awards to four of the top officer cadets. He has come a long way in the eleven years since April 2006 when he was one of the officer cadets parading in front of his grandmother, giving her a cheeky grin as she walked past inspecting the cadets. It mystified some that on this particular occasion in 2017 he had turned up in civilian clothes, especially as just the previous month he had appeared in his uniform of a senior Blues and Royals officer at the Cenotaph on Remembrance Sunday. The Ministry of Defence explained the seeming contradiction: '[He is] a member of the Royal Family and at times his duties require him to don the uniform of a tied or associated regiment.' He couldn't, however, perform a military task with a beard but could as a civilian in non-military clothes. He thought carefully about what to do and decided to keep his beard.

He referred to it as he spoke from a small platform to the officer cadets. 'It is not the first time that I have been a part of this parade,' he began, 'but it is certainly my first one facing in this direction – and with facial hair! A little over eleven years ago, I stood where you are today. Although, I confess, I don't remember any deep thoughts of duty, responsibility and leadership at that point. My head was filled with much more immediate concerns: numb feet, the buckle of my braces digging into my collarbone, a burning in my arm from the weight of the rifle.'

Later that same day it was confirmed that Harry and Meghan would marry on Saturday, 19 May 2018 at St George's Chapel, Windsor Castle. The date initially caused considerable concern as it coincided with the FA Cup Final at Wembley, and Prince William, who is President of the FA, would normally present the trophy to the winner. Perhaps, it was muttered, he couldn't attend. Shortly afterwards Kensington Palace announced that the wedding would take place at noon. A time that would enable Prince William to reach Wembley before the game started.

A few days later, two photographs were released to mark the couple's engagement. Self-made Meghan, who has far more experience of photo-shoots than Harry, looked completely relaxed. Harry, whose aim since childhood has been to avoid photographers whenever possible, less so. The black and white photograph, however, did show him smiling, with his arms wrapped around Meghan, who was wearing a cream cashmere jumper. She had her eyes closed and one of her hands gently rested on her fiancé's face. But Harry looked distinctly awkward in the more formal colour photograph where the smartly dressed couple held hands, sitting on the steps of Frogmore House, a private residence in the grounds of Windsor Castle.

An hour later another photograph was released by Kensington Palace with a comment: 'The couple are so grateful for the warm and generous messages they have received during such a happy time in their lives. As a way to say thank you, they have decided to share this candid photograph from the day of their portrait sittings directly with all of you.' It wasn't clear whether the 'candid' photograph was originally intended to be private and had been impulsively released. It showed Meghan wearing a handmade couture gown by British label Ralph & Russo that had a long black silk organza skirt, hand appliquéd with silk tulle ruffles, and an entirely sheer bodice decorated with intricate gold feather threadwork. It was reported that it cost an eye-opening £56,000. Kensington Palace confirmed the gown had been 'privately purchased'. If the purchaser was Prince Harry it would make a small, but perhaps unnecessary, dent in his estimated fortune of £30 million. (Meghan is thought to be worth about £5 million.) The photographs had been taken by fashion and celebrity photographer Alexi Lubomirski, a former assistant to the Princess of Wales's favourite photographer, Mario Testino, who took William and Kate's first official images in 2010. The three photographs looked like a celebrity fashion shoot for a glossy magazine, and it was surprising that Harry went along with them. When he invited me to Kensington Palace he'd told me forcefully that 'we [he, William and Kate] are not a bunch of celebrities and do not want to go down a celebrity route.'

Meghan, however, stayed true to what she had written on her website before she met Harry: 'My life shifts from refugee camps to red carpets. I choose them both because these worlds can, in fact, co-exist. And for me, they must.' She continued: 'I, in fact, have always had a foot in the world of entertainment as well as the world of public service. My life now is simply a more heightened version of the very reality in which I grew up. And, truth be told, it is the most beautiful gift I never knew I always had.'

It is unlikely that anyone whispered in Prince Harry's ear that such intimate, sexy photographs were perhaps not quite appropriate for a senior royal. The Duke of Edinburgh, who used to lay down the rules for his family, has stepped back since his retirement in August 2017 aged ninety-six. Prince Charles was unlikely to say anything as he felt guilty about his relationship with the Princess of Wales. He was also thrilled that Harry, who had been miserable for years, seemed to have settled down. Prince William wouldn't either, because he too delights in his brother's obvious happiness. Perhaps it doesn't matter: what is important is what Harry and Meghan would do as a team rather than what photographs they released.

However, soon after the photographs appeared in the press it was reported that the Queen, who is known for being frugal, was pushing for a prenuptial agreement to protect her grandson's wealth. If true, it didn't go down well. A source told *Life & Style* magazine that Meghan was hurt 'that it would even cross the Queen's mind that she could have an ulterior motive for marrying Harry'. Nor was Harry keen for her to sign an agreement. The source added: 'Harry loves Meghan and will do anything for her.'

December was a busy time for the newly engaged couple as Meghan was fast-tracked into the royal family. Harry took her to the Christmas parties for the royal staff at both Windsor Castle and Kensington Palace. He also secured an unprecedented invitation for her to join the royals over Christmas at Sandringham. He and Meghan were to stay overnight with Kate and William at nearby Amner Hall but would spend Christmas day with the Queen. Meghan's arrival was a significant break with tradition as, until then, not even the Duchess of Cornwall or the Duchess of

Cambridge had been invited to this intimate family occasion prior to marrying into the family.

The one issue that observant members of the public and press noticed was that Princess Michael of Kent arrived wearing a 'blackamoor' brooch. It was described as 'racist and insensitive', particularly when Meghan was present. She swiftly apologised and 'retired' it.

The royal family always go to church on Christmas morning. Meghan, wearing a light-brown coat, chestnut-coloured hat and matching boots and handbag, looked anxious when she came out of Crathie Kirk at the end of the service, and rather vulnerable as Prince William explained with gestures what happened next. She gave a rushed, rather wobbly bob when the Queen arrived and clung on tightly to Harry as they did a mini-walkabout to talk to the well-wishers, some of whom had stood in the cold since dawn to wish the family a good Christmas. For reasons unknown she suddenly stuck her tongue out at the crowd, a picture that soon appeared on social media and in the next day's papers. Some believed she was 'showing her playful side', others that it was absolutely not the right way to behave on her first royal outing with the Queen. Although she is used to being in the public eye, the scrutiny of young royals is both more intense than that of celebrities and can be fiercely critical. Another crucial difference was that before her engagement she'd merely represented herself, but afterwards she became part of the most famous royal family in the world. At present it's impossible to see how she will behave in future. David Starkey jokingly told me: 'She might wear one or two tiaras and think, "This is great", suddenly become formal and expect people to curtsy to her, and even see Harry as her way into royalty while he could see her as his way out.'

On 27 December Harry was guest editor on the BBC Radio 4 *Today* programme. He chose classic Harry topics, including an item on how the UK is leading the field in artificial intelligence. He scooped the first interview that Barack Obama has given since ceasing to be President of the United States; it was recorded in Toronto during the September 2017 Invictus Games. Harry, calling Obama 'the first media president', asked what he missed most. Obama replied: 'My team and the intensity of the work.' Harry also covered teenage gangs, the fire tragedy at Grenfell Tower, the military, a talk with boxer Anthony Joshua and women's rugby. He also interviewed his father, who called him 'darling boy'. Harry was slightly less patient with him than he had been with other guests and a couple of times deftly cut in with the words 'Moving on...'

He asked his father to 'pick one issue to focus on' in 2018. The Prince of Wales replied, 'Climate change', adding, 'You know that because I have bored you to tears.' Harry told him as someone from 'a younger generation' he felt very optimistic that people 'could work together' and 'preserve the planet'. Prince Charles went on to say, 'It makes me very proud to think that you understand.'

Harry joked: 'And that I'm listening.' A laughing Charles replied: 'That's even more amazing.' It was a touching moment when Harry, in common with many adult children who have come to realise that their parents aren't talking nonsense after all, admitted: 'I do end up picking your brains now more than I ever have done.'

Harry extended his thanks towards the programme's end: 'I am hugely grateful for this platform, ... part of my role and part of my job is to shine a spotlight on issues that need that spotlight, whether it's people, whether it's causes, issues, whatever it is. So I will continue to play my part in society and do my job to the best of my abilities so that I can wake up in the morning and feel energised.'

He then shut down somewhat when just before the end of the programme he was asked some personal questions about Christmas. The reluctant tone in his voice was audible, despite saying having Meghan with him was 'fantastic', that 'she really enjoyed it and the family loved having her there', and that he'd had an 'amazing time and great fun staying with my brother and sister-in-law running around with the kids'. He concluded that 2018 would be a 'fantastic year'.

This was a significant change of heart to how he came across when we first talked at Kensington Palace. Then it was obvious that if he had to pick one word to describe himself it would have been 'frustrated'. He was frustrated that he had no proper role or job, frustrated by routine royal visits, cutting ribbons and the rigidity of a royal timetable that meant engagements were often fleeting and he made less of an impact than he would have liked. His social life frustrated him too and he found it increasingly difficult to manage his temper, which could be triggered by the smallest thing. Anger was one of the few emotions he allowed himself to express. The rest he kept bottled up.

From his conversation it seemed to me that for years the negative side of royal life had made a greater impact on him than its privilege and status. Seething with inner resentment and deprived of being able to serve a substantial time in the army, he blamed both the media and the restrictions imposed on him by birth for much of the turmoil he was in. He often wondered how different his life might have been if his mother, Princess Diana, was still alive. He thought, for example, they could have worked together on many of the charities she had singled out for attention, particularly those that helped children with HIV.

He had also been keen to tell me about modernising the monarchy and dragging it into the twenty-first century. He said: 'We want to carry on the positive atmosphere that the Queen has achieved for over sixty years, but we won't be trying to fill her boots. It can't go on as it has done under the Queen. Things are moving so fast especially because of social media, so we are involved in modernising the British monarchy. We are not doing this for ourselves but for the greater good of the people and the monarchy we represent.'

Harry often used the royal 'we' when talking about modernising the monarchy, perhaps indicating the strength of his support for his brother once he became king. 'My job is to support my brother,' he agreed. They balance each other well. William is serious, self-conscious and awkward with people. Harry is fearless and a good communicator, and every flaw or mishap seems to make him more popular.

Now he has newfound energy, drive and enthusiasm. the *Times* revealed that in 2017 Harry had 139 domestic engagements and 70 official appearances overseas, which beat William and Kate. In July he was also involved his first state-visit duties when he accompanied King Felipe VI and Queen Letizia of Spain on a tour of Westminster Abbey and attended his first state banquet.

Harry's future vision of a slimline modern monarchy is one that uses social media to reach out to the public, rather than rely on newspapers. It has proved successful with his work on mental health issues and also means he is in charge of publicity and how and when it is released to the public. 'We are focusing on the digital platform, which we can do without being political and means the monarchy keeps up with the times ... the three of us [he, William and Kate] came together for Heads Together. It is a big cause and took a huge amount of work to successfully do a two-year campaign like that. We will soon go on to do something else, but probably not together.' He grinned. 'I think that is enough to do with your brother.'

His vision also includes the young royals' right to an 'ordinary life', where their duty to each other and their children may come before or alongside their duty to the nation. This is known to concern the Queen, who, insiders say, has quietly told both Harry and William to think first of the nation's needs rather than of their own.

It will, he hopes, also see a final farewell to the stiff upper lip that has been an ingrained part of his grandparents' and father's generation. Harry is on an emotional crusade to get people to express their feelings rather than bottle them up. 'It takes a lot to make the decision that you need help,' he said, 'but it works.'

He could lead the way within the royal family too. A former aide intimated that Prince Charles might feel rather disappointed that he was not brought up to do the same thing. Not surprisingly, some courtiers have shown concern about both Harry's and William's frankness in newspaper and television interviews, particularly around the twentieth anniversary of their mother's death in August 2017. They fear their openness will make it even harder to protect their privacy in future. One commented: 'We've had a lot of baring of souls recently. There comes a point when you feel, "Come on – time to crack on with your duties." Some worry that they are over-encouraging the media.'

The amount of charity work Harry, William and Kate will do, something that has been a huge part of the Queen's role, will be cut right back. In 2011, when the Duke of Edinburgh was ninety, he reduced the number of patronages he was involved with. The Queen, who was patron of 600 charities, followed suit after her ninetieth birthday. Prince Charles, who will be seventy in November 2018, is also making plans for a pared-down monarchy. He offered the princes the opportunity to take over as patron of some of his charities like the Royal Drawing School and the Prince's School of Traditional Arts, but it doesn't seem to have appealed to them. They are far more interested in the bigger picture – like mental health and the environment, which makes them feel more relevant.

By the time William becomes king the numbers of charities enjoying royal patronage will have plummeted, but the patronage will be stronger. A source close to Harry insists this is not due to laziness but that the princes want to be hands-on and useful rather than turn up merely to cut a ribbon. 'Prince William, Prince Harry and the Duchess of Cambridge will not sign up to support charities when it just involves one visit a year. They want instead to focus on specific charities that they research thoroughly first and then get involved in on a regular basis. The one thing they don't want is to be seen as a group of celebrities.'

'We use our time wisely,' Harry explained to me. 'We don't want to turn up, shake hands but not get involved. Nowadays because of social media and the internet you have to give so much more. We are incredibly passionate with our charities and they have been chosen because they are on the path shown to me by our mother. I love charity stuff and meeting people.'

He believes in the royal family and thinks the public does too. 'The British public and the whole world need institutions like it,' he told me. 'Our idea is to carry on going forward, keep some of its curiosity, but also prove we are completely in touch with what is going on in the world. That way we will be a force for good. There is so much negative around that we as a family try to bring something positive into this fast-changing world.'

He wants to connect with 'three to four generations' and particularly young people. 'I worry about losing touch with the younger generation. I want to give them a platform. They are going to inherit the mess society has left behind and they don't watch the BBC news.'

* * *

Meghan's arrival on the royal scene is well-timed and she will become the first bi-racial princess in the British royal family. Her background makes her a good representative for modern Britain and its young people. One in ten British couples are now from different ethnic backgrounds; Meghan marrying a senior royal moves the monarchy forwards and edges the royal family one step closer to the people. David Starkey told me he approves: 'In the 1930s the royal family was presented as the model British family and the exemplar of family virtue. But nobody could now possibly claim that Prince Philip and the Queen's children are an example of family virtue. [Prince Charles, Princess Anne and Prince Andrew have all been divorced.] So as far as the royal family is a symbol it is no longer the symbol of British virtue.

'Today a typical British family includes people with at least two marriages and lots of half-siblings. As a result, the royal family has again become an extremely effective representation of the mixed-up state of the typical British family. The Charles, Diana, Camilla relationship was the bulldozer that changed the rules and I think almost certainly he [Harry] has found someone who seems normal. Thank goodness he has decided to get married. If we are to have a royal family that is meaningful and relevant and something that new generations can relate to, it is hard to see how they can continue to look completely unlike the rest of society.'

Meghan seems to have happily jumped into the deep end of royal actuality and is learning fast how to manage a very different way of life. For her second public outing to Brixton radio station Reprezent FM, which trains hundreds of young people every year in media and employment skills, in January 2018, she ditched the handbag that had proved a nuisance during her first walkabout in Nottingham the previous month. A newly employed member of the royal staff was close by to take the endless bunches of flowers, and Meghan's long hair that had proved such a distraction in Nottingham was casually wound into a bun at the back of her head. She also wore a £45 black jumper from Marks & Spencer, albeit under a £600 coat, perhaps an economy measure after that five-figure engagement photograph dress. The tumultuous crowds screamed and shouted her name, and the press swiftly came up with the description 'Meghan Mania'. Harry again took a watchful but secondary role, trusting her to shine and joking about her wearing the trousers in their relationship. While talking to some young DJs Harry was told they had a specific question for him on gender equality. He instantly pointed to Meghan and replied: 'She answers the questions!'

Harry wanted to take Meghan to visit different areas of the UK before they were married so she could see more of the country she would live in. Wales was at the top of the list as they made their first official visit to Cardiff to celebrate the country's people, culture and heritage. Hundreds of people were waiting for them at Cardiff Castle, including some who, because the royal couple's train was delayed, had been waiting in the cold for nearly seven hours. It made no difference: the couple were greeted with huge cheers. Meghan pushed the boundaries of normal royal protocol out of the way by wearing black skinny jeans – albeit from a Welsh brand, Hiut Denim; she posed for a selfie for a schoolgirl and wrote a short note for another young ardent fan. The young couple moved on to the Star Hub community leisure centre in the economically deprived area of Tremorfa where there were lots of schoolgirls who were obviously very keen to meet Meghan. Harry mischievously excited them even further by saying loudly: 'Let's all give Meghan a group hug!' He stayed back as Meghan was overwhelmed with hugs by the shrieking children. She coped well and after a few seconds Harry jokingly gave the order: 'And release. She's mine.'

It was a typical example of what Dr Starkey described as: 'Harry doing matey.'

A group of children were scheduled to dance for them. When it was over Meghan noticed one little seven-year-old in a corner of the room who had been led away crying during the performance. She knelt down, took hold of the girl's hand and told her: 'I used to be shy, too.' Harry spotted where Meghan was, walked over and shook the girl's hand.

It's clear that Meghan, possibly unknowingly, and Harry, who knows but doesn't worry about it, are driving a steamroller through royal convention. It could be something that the rebel prince has longed to do for years, and it's proving a boost to their popularity.

David Starkey believes there will be no going back. 'She is the new kid on the royal block, she will do things her way, and I don't think there will be much attempt to stop her. I believe that Buckingham Palace is losing influence. William and Harry are now adults and running their own lives, and most human beings don't defer to their grandparents.'

Former press spokesman Dickie Arbiter explained further: 'It is a myth that any non-royal who comes into the family is automatically given instructions and assistance in how to behave. They will only be given assistance if they ask for it. Meghan is an actor and actors learn scripts. So there is no reason why she shouldn't learn very quickly. A lot of it is common sense, breeding and upbringing. For example, if they are going to meet a head of state, she needs to show a certain respect, perhaps curtsy. And also to wait until you are spoken to rather than say: "Hi. How are you?" Harry will help her and probably already has.'

Unusually for a strong feminist, she has not merely stopped working on *Suits* but will no longer be a professional actor. During her joint engagement interview on BBC TV she insisted: 'I don't see it as giving anything up. I just see it as a change.' Instead, she thinks: 'It's time to work with [Harry] as a team.' Harry would have been delighted to hear her mention a 'team' as it's how he likes to operate too.

She was baptised and confirmed as an Anglican in early March 2018 (she was previously a Catholic). She also said she plans to take up British citizenship, something that normally takes several years. David Starkey believes it is because 'she wants to play the role of princess, which means [with Kate] we are going to have two star princesses. It will be very interesting.'

Meghan has the choice of following in the path of Diana, Princess of Wales, and becoming the Queen of Broken Hearts, or Grace Kelly, the American actress who in 1956 retired from acting at the age of twenty-six to marry Prince Rainier of Monaco and devote herself to family life and philanthropic work.

Harry also talked to me about retaining his privacy. 'People would be amazed by the ordinary life William and I live,' he said. 'I do my own shopping. Sometimes when I come away from the meat counter in my local supermarket I worry someone will snap me with their phone. But I am determined to have a relatively normal life and if I am lucky enough to have children they can have one, too.' He paused. 'Even if I was king I would do my own shopping.' This sounded rather bizarre as Princes William, George and Charlotte have pushed him well down the line of succession.

Of course doing your own shopping when you feel like it is a mere drop in the ocean of an ordinary life. When Harry arrives anywhere he immediately becomes one of the people and also their friend, but his arrival and departure continue to be regal. There remains a tug in Harry's heart between wanting a private life and being a senior royal. Like his mother he is always trying to escape from the imposed limits of royal life. But he also knows that millions of people don't want him to be remotely like their next-door neighbour.

Although both Prince Harry and Prince William are in their thirties and are wealthy in their own right, they are not necessarily money savvy. Their father covers their expenses from income from the Duchy of Cornwall. In 2016 this amounted to about £3 million for Harry, William and Kate. The Foreign Office pays for all travel expenses when they are on official duty abroad. The royal family also announced that they will be paying for Harry and Meghan's wedding. Both princes still need to keep Prince Charles informed of how they spend his money and the discussion sometimes ends in an argument.

★ ★ ★

Time has proven that, whatever Charles and Diana got wrong between them in their relationship, they succeeded when it came to bringing up William and Harry. The princes are decent human beings trying their best to keep one foot on the royal carpet and another among the people. The Labour MP Frank Field spoke out shortly after their parents separated voicing his concern about the animosity between them, the resulting possible dangers for the children and how it could threaten the royal family itself. He has since reflected on his disquiet at the time.

He told me recently: 'Whatever I said then about the possible future conduct of the two princes I have changed my view about their worth and role. What I see now is Harry about to embark on a career with Meghan to reshape the monarchy. And with the Duke and Duchess of Cambridge, I see how easy they are as a couple and whenever the time is right you can see them as king and queen, wanting to carry out the role and doing it admirably.

'On the one hand there will be real safety-first from the older son and entrepreneurial talent from the younger one, and they both have partners who are really engaged with what they are trying to do. It's good that my comments then gave them all a jolt. I now think it has been a great success story. Both of them [William and Harry] have developed their own talent for what their roles will be.'

There is evidence, too, that the rebel in Harry is subsiding. This was apparent in his closing speech at the 2017 Invictus Games, where he used words he would have been most unlikely to utter a decade or so earlier. He said that what was 'lacking in the world today' was 'respect, teamwork and discipline', three virtues he learnt in the army. 'People who serve and people who continue to serve whether they be injured or not are fantastic role models that I think everyone should be looking up to and … at the same time getting young kids to look up to their parents as role models, and if their parents are in the services then even better.'

We are living in a time of generational shift and a new era for the royal family. Politicians are losing respect and trust, particularly of the younger generation, who need public role models they can look up to. It's a huge opportunity for Harry to 'give something back' and 'make the difference' he has wanted for so long.

Acknowledgements

I wish to thank Prince Harry for talking to me and to his staff at Kensington Palace for their help with the magazine interviews that led to this book.

There have been many people, some of whom want to be anonymous, who have given me fascinating information. They know who they are and I hope they are pleased with the result. I am very grateful to Dr David Starkey, Frank Field MP, Dickie Arbiter, Paul Harris and Trevor Rose for sharing their thoughts.

My husband Robert Low has been a tireless supporter and I would like to thank him and my children for their constant interest and encouragement.

I am indebted to my agent Robert Smith and much appreciate the help and support of my publisher John Blake, editor Ciara Lloyd and publicist Francesca Pearce.